NOT IN MY
WILDEST DREAMS
MEMOIRS OF A VETERAN FBI AGENT

JIM SACIA

PAGE PUBLISHING, INC.
New York, NY

First originally published by Page Publishing, Inc. 2019

ISBN 978-1-64424-212-4 (Paperback)
ISBN 978-1-64424-213-1 (Hardcover)
ISBN 978-1-64424-214-8 (Digital)

Printed in the United States of America

This book was completely written in cursive. Without the willingness and skill of Sally Huggins to read my hen scratch and transcribe it to a computer, it never would have been completed.

No words are an adequate thank you to Sally. All I can say is, thank you, Sally.

CONTENTS

INTRODUCTION

Not in My Wildest Dreams
Memoirs of a Veteran FBI Agent

My years as an FBI agent ended with my retirement in 1997.

As I write this introduction in February 2018, I am disheartened with the unbelievable attacks on the agency I hold in such high esteem. In fairness, the attacks are on some in the bureau hierarchy, and in no way are they on the rank-and-file men and women who do yeomen's work in doing what they do best "objective investigations."

The title of this book, *Not in My Wildest Dreams*, has nothing to do with the situation that the FBI finds itself in today. This is simply one agent's observation as one who was on the ground and loved every minute as a special agent in the Federal Bureau of Investigation. To this day, it was beyond my wildest dreams.

FOREWORD

I served twenty-eight years as an FBI agent commencing on September 8, 1969, and retiring in 1997. Always wanting to run a farm equipment business, with my wife, Jenny, and son Jerry, we started NITE Equipment (Northern Illinois Tractor & Equipment) in Pecatonica, Illinois. I stepped away from the business in 2002 to run for the seat of retiring state representative Ron Lawfer. I held that seat until my second retirement in October of 2013. Jenny and Jerry and several great employees kept the business growing. As I write this in the early spring of 2014, the business has grown to provide ten good jobs, does six to eight million per year in sales, and continues to provide a valuable business to the community.

This is not about NITE Equipment or my eleven years as a state representative. This book is about those twenty-eight great years as an FBI agent and the years leading up to them.

Everyone has a story to tell. Mine is about a very happy and good life. I am beginning with earnest in the eleventh month of my sixty ninth year. Four months ago I stepped down after eleven years as an Illinois state representative. Though I loved what I did, stepping down gave me my life back. That is not a complaint, rather an observation. I've always wanted to write a book "someday." Many of you who read this say the same. The reality is we are all caught up in a workaday world and that "someday" simply never comes. Stepping down from my obligation gives me that opportunity.

I'm blessed to still be in good health, have a great wife, Jenny, three great sons, and my opportunity is now. I ran for six terms that is what I promised.

Those twenty-eight years as an FBI agent are filled with memories and most bring smiles to my face. Some bring me great sorrow.

Jenny will tell you that during those most eventful years of our life, my feet never hit the ground in the morning that I didn't look forward to going to work. The privilege of being a special agent for the FBI was almost indescribable, and beyond my wildest dreams.

I certainly did not grow up with dreams of someday being an agent for the FBI. If I ever did think about it, and I doubt that I did, I would have dismissed the thought believing that FBI agents were nebulous characters from New York, Chicago or Detroit. In my wildest dreams, they certainly weren't farms kids from a rural area near La Crosse Wisconsin.

And so my story begins following a three-year stint in the Army, which I must say "grew me up" I attended college at then Wisconsin State University at River Falls. It is now the University of Wisconsin, River Falls. My desired objective, at that point in my life, was to obtain a degree and return to active duty in the US Army. Yes, the Army had become my home. I literally loved it and had achieved the rank of E-5 sergeant in a short sixteen months. My desire was to become a commissioned officer, and I certainly understood that though I could obtain a commission without a degree, long term I would need it.

College then was not expensive, and I had saved about $2,000. I recall my first quarter tuition in the fall of 1965 was about $1200 for a full-time student.

My high school grades were not good enough to enter college. In fact, though I'm not original in this statement, it does fit, "I was in that half of the class that made the upper half possible." When I share that, it usually elicits a chuckle.

River Falls had to accept me for at least one quarter as I was a veteran, and it was a state university, therefore a requirement. I rapidly proved myself as a capable student and regularly was on the honor roll.

I had no choice but to work at least part-time, and I was quickly able to obtain a position at Jerry's Citgo, a gas station and service center. Jerry Wilkens and his wife, Donna, were two of the finest people I could have been associated with. My starting pay was $1.75 per hour and at that time not considered too bad. I stayed with Jerry throughout the fall, winter and spring, pumping gas, changing oil and doing light mechanical work. I considered myself a reasonably competent mechanic at that point in my life. I had worked at several auto mechanic shops prior to and during my Army career learning to do engine overhauls, tune ups, and general auto repair under the tutelage of two great teachers Bill Barentine at Ohearn Auto Company in Melrose Wisconsin and Bob, last name forgotten, at Bob's Mobile Service in New Baltimore Michigan.

In the summer of 1966 Mike McLaughlin, another friend Jim (last name forgotten), and I traveled to the west coast in Mike's new Oldsmobile. We shared gas expenses and camped every night and truly had a great experience. Returning that fall, I certainly had my job back at Jerry's should I want it, but I had enlisted in the 1/128th Infantry Army National Guard Unit in River Falls and the AST "Bill" Junkman was in charge of the school bus transportation for River Falls Public Schools. He was able to arrange an opportunity for me to drive for the district.

By the time winter quarter rolled around, I had been accepted to US Army Ranger School and was now a staff sergeant E-6, and in November, off I went to Fort Benning.

I was able to hire a fellow college student, Dave "Tiny" Outcelt, to drive my bus while I was gone. I graduated from ranger training in February of 1967 and had only missed my winter quarter of college. Spring quarter I'm back on the bus route, and in June I'm off to Fort Benning, this time to attend Infantry OCS (Officer Candidate School). I was in Seventy-Seventh Company (RC), meaning reserve component, which, like regular OCS, was a butt kicker but more abbreviated, and we would return to our guard or reserve unit where 90 percent of those graduating from regular infantry OCS were destined for Vietnam. I graduated from OCS in time to get back to my fall quarter of college.

In the fall of 1967 I was hired by Chief of Police Perry Larson to become a police officer in River Falls. My starting pay was $2.25 per hour, and I was thrilled to be a policeman. At that time, training was mainly on-the-job-training (OJT) and after Officer Howie Miller took me to an old quarry where I fired fifty rounds from my model 10 Smith and Wesson .38 revolver. I was now a police officer.

Perry's policy for new officers was to ride along with a senior officer for six months prior to being "cut loose" to patrol as a one-man car. Perry was a firm believer that if a person possessed "common sense," they could be a great officer. He believed it trumped any degree of training. I remained a police officer throughout my remaining college years. I obtained two majors, one in psychology and one in speech, and my bachelor of science. Sadly, Perry passed away in late 2014.

In my final year at River Falls, 1968–1969, while totally immersing myself in my studies as well as my duties as a second lieutenant in the Wisconsin Army National Guard, I was the platoon leader for Second Platoon Company A First Battalion 128th Infantry Mechanized, and I could not have been prouder. I even had the privilege of swearing in my brother Tim who enlisted in our Guard Unit.

My police duties were predominately from 7:00 p.m. to 3:00 a.m. which worked quite well with my other duties.

I had the good fortune to meet the FBI agent who covered River Falls out of the Eau Claire Resident Agency, SA Gene Sather, who encouraged me to apply as a special agent. Again, I must say prior to that first encounter, I had never even considered the FBI as a career.

Now the dilemma, I am completely focused on returning to active duty; however, in my mind I'll probably have one opportunity to become an FBI agent and I'll always be able to return to the Army. Part of my dilemma is a sincere desire to serve in Vietnam. I'm an infantry man, and an officer. I'm ranger qualified and again in my mind, I can make a difference. I truly was a strong supporter of the Vietnam War, and in my heart, it was my obligation and duty to go. I even had a bumper sticker on my 1964 Chevelle "Win in Vietnam."

Jenny has always maintained that my decision to apply for the FBI kept me alive. She is convinced I would have died in Vietnam. I have said many times; it is the only regret I have in life—Jenny does not like me saying that. But it has been a great life.

Applying to become an FBI agent consisted of a ten-page application form. It was highly detailed allowing for no unanswered questions nor skips in dates. You must list every place you've lived with exact dates; every job with exact dates, names of supervisors, and coworkers; every school you've attended; references; social acquaintances—I could go on. The bottom line is, when the FBI finishes the background of you pertaining to honesty, integrity, loyalty to the United States, they know more about you than you know about you.

I thought that was somewhat hocus pocus until I answered the question which is still used today, "Is there anything in your background that could reflect unfavorably on you?" Of course I answered no.

After about three weeks a very stern-faced agent came to me with the following question, "Why didn't you tell us about the watermelon incident in Melrose?"

Well, the short answer is, I had forgotten about it. A better answer is, probably if I had remembered, I did not think it important.

Growing up in rural Melrose, Wisconsin, there wasn't a lot to do on a Saturday night. Oh, we could watch the feed truck unload or the barber cut hair, but when you're seventeen and all the juices are flowing, you are looking for entertainment.

Aaron Fisher was my high school buddy. His parents owned a 1957 Mercury four-door hardtop. At that time, I had a 1953 Chevrolet convertible. On this particular Saturday night, Aaron and I decided to go "cooning melons." He lived in rural Cataract which was sand country which is necessary for growing good watermelons.

Aaron knew that our classmate David Bullen's dad had a large melon patch. We decided that it would be fun to get a trunk load of those melons and to take them to the dance hall in either Cataract or Hatfield, which were the nearest "hopping" places on summer Saturday nights.

Of course, we took Aaron's Mercury as the trunk was huge. Well, we completed our dastardly deed only to compromise ourselves as we left and David's dad pursued us in his 1953 Oldsmobile. I was scared to death but Aaron knew every gravel road and every hill and turn, but then again, so did old man Bullen. After a lengthy chase, we did get away. Off we went nervously to Hatfield in an effort to impress the girls.

I remember it like it was yesterday. We'd walk up to a lovely young lady, of course one that we knew, with a "Here, do you want a watermelon?" Needless to say, we struck out with the ladies. Now we did the next coolest thing. It was now 1:00 a.m., and we returned to the main street of Melrose with the clever game of driving the main drag throwing the melons in the air just to watch them break when they hit the pavement. Needless to say, the Village Marshall caught up with us, and it was fair to say that law enforcement was somewhat different at that time.

After some negotiating, he agreed that he wouldn't tell our parents if we swept the street and picked up the rinds. Of course, we did it well. What he didn't tell us was that when an FBI agent inquired about my character some seven or eight years later, he might share that incident.

Well, I had some explaining to do, but apparently, I did okay. Following my testing in the Milwaukee Field Office of the FBI (which I was convinced that I failed), several weeks later my mother received an official-looking packet from the FBI addressed to me at our rural Melrose farm home.

I was walking between classes through the commons during summer school of 1969 when I was paged to call home as soon as possible. Getting mom on the phone, I asked her to read the letter, fully expecting it to be a rejection letter. It was my appointment letter signed by J. Edgar Hoover offering me a position as a special agent! Again, not in my wildest dreams.

Everyone remembers those memorable moments in life, and this was one. I can even tell you which phone I called Mom from. The appointment letter stated that the position was contingent upon proof of my successful completion of my college studies (which would be late August) and my honorable discharge from the Wisconsin Army National Guard. This was a killer to me, but of course, I did comply. The FBI is one of the only Federal Agencies requiring its agents not to have a reserve component affiliation as in a national emergency your loyalties are required by the FBI.

Fourteen weeks of intensive training at Quantico, Virginia, and Washington, DC, and I would be a special agent for the FBI. I recall I was somewhat apprehensive about the training, fearing the possibility of "washing out."

With the amount of money that the Bureau had spent ensuring our honorable backgrounds, there was a good bet each of us would hit the field running. I did just that as I prepared for my assignment to Salt Lake City. Salt Lake was one of the smaller of the fifty-nine field offices of the FBI.

At that time in the FBI, J. Edgar Hoover believed that new agents should be assigned one of the smaller of the field offices for a period of approximately one year. The theory of course was to have an opportunity to learn with close supervision. I believe that the theory was a good one and gave each of us an opportunity to "learn the ropes," gain investigative experience, and should you inadvertently "screw up," chances of you moving to your next office without issues following you were quite good.

For twenty-six of my twenty-eight as an agent, I was assigned to the Rockford Illinois Office of the FBI. I was the only agent assigned to the four North Westernmost Counties of Illinois, Jo Daviess, Stephenson, Whiteside, and Carroll. To have had that privilege is beyond description. My very livelihood was the working relationship I was able to develop with area law enforcement officials in those four counties. They looked out for me, and I did for them. Those associations are among my greatest treasures.

SA Glen McKenzie, a senior agent soon to retire, was the agent assigned those four counties prior to me. I worked with Glen for a period of time getting to know the territory and officers and other contacts in that area. Glen was a great agent and well respected so his endorsement of me made my life much easier.

And so I embark on sharing with you what truly was a grand career much is based solely on memory. At no time is there intentional deception. It is simply my recollections. Some of the more humorous situations have been told and retold many times always with my personal effort and emphasizing the humorous side. Accordingly, I'm sure I am guilty of embellishment. I loved the FBI and felt so privileged to serve in such a great organization and to receive such great assignments. Most names are changed, some are not. I remember the old Joe Friday line (from the series "Dragnet) "The names are changed to protect the innocent." Common sense just tells me I should.

SALT LAKE CITY

It was a warm July night in Salt Lake City, Utah, in 1970. The moon was bright. I was crouched in a crawl space of a deserted apartment complex with a dirt floor, musty smell, rodents, and beer cans. Why I was here is the rest of the story.

On September 8, 1969, assistant director Joe Casper swore my class of new FBI agents in as we held our badge in our right hands, promising to uphold the Constitution of the United States.

Shortly thereafter, Unit Chief Simon Tullai took over. New agent Don Weatherman and I, both Army veterans, were singled out and brought to the front of the class. The object of this exercise is to have examples of how FBI Special agents are not to dress. Both Don and I were wearing madras (which is varied designs in bright colors often run together sport coats. This was very much a "preppy" look in 1969) with loud yellow shirts. I thought we looked pretty good. By the afternoon classes, we will be wearing white shirts and dark suits, the required dress per FBI director J. Edgar Hoover.

Throughout our very thorough training in Washington, DC, and Quantico, Virginia, on any given night, you could visit the day room in Quantico Virginia where a small number of agents would be relaxing or studying. At 7:00 p.m. on Sunday evening, it was standing room only as the series *The FBI* staring Efrem Zimbalist Jr. was on TV. It was amazing, the attraction it had. Perhaps we all envisioned ourselves as Efrem.

A significant part of a new FBI agents training is informant development. I took this very seriously; as a former police officer, I understood the need to have a mind-set of the criminal element. You don't develop informants in church. You need to find the undesirables of society who know what's going on and where.

My good fortune was developing a relationship with a recently paroled bad guy we'll call William. William and I developed a good rapport thanks to both of us sharing the experience of being former Army Infantrymen.

William confided to me that he knew the whereabouts of a badly wanted fugitive, John Fitzpatrick, and for $200, he'd tell me his location. I knew that getting the $200 would be no big deal as we paid for information all the time. The hard part would be getting the SAC to okay a first office agent to take on the arrest of such a significant bad guy.

Our bad guy was certainly notorious, but adding insult to injury, he gloated in avoiding arrest and needling FBI long-time director J. Edgar Hoover. He would regularly write letters to Director Hoover, very short wording to the affect:

Dear Mr. Hoover,

Last week I was in Salt Lake City. Sorry I missed you.

Signed
John Fitzpatrick

Director Hoover was not given to levity. He would call the field office or resident agency, where Fitzpatrick said he had been, and push the issue why the FBI had not arrested him. Simple, we didn't know he was there. So here I am, brand new agent Jim Sacia with information as to the whereabouts of Fitzpatrick.

William tells me that Fitzpatrick has stashed $20,000 in negotiable bonds in the basement of a deserted apartment complex and would return for them the following morning around 2:00 a.m. Thus, my location crouched in said basement.

Obviously, the SAC did not think I had the inside track on Fitzpatrick. He allowed me to take two other first office agents with me to hope fully affect the arrest. There is little doubt that he believed our efforts would be an exercise in futility.

I placed the other two agents inconspicuously outside and I alone go into the basement crawl space. The ceiling is only about four feet off the ground. You've played in such places as a kid, beer cans, dirt floor, musty smell, mice running around.

I was in place around midnight, and for several hours, I was envisioning how cool this was. I, brand-new agent Jim Sacia, was going to arrest not only a real bad guy, but also the one who loved to get under Director Hoover's skin.

Perhaps Director Hoover would make me an assistant director; maybe I'd replace Efrem Zimbalist Jr. next Sunday.

The hours crept by, and I began to doubt my informant's information.

My mind was jolted to reality as I saw the outline of a man in the moonlight coming down the short staircase. Though I was a former infantryman and police officer, my heart was pounding, and I was sure Fitzpatrick could hear it as well as I could.

I watched him, as he proceeded, crouched to the location where he apparently had hidden the bonds. He retrieved them and started back out. It was my moment to be a hero. I drew my .38 revolver and hollered, "FBI, hold it right there," as I jumped. You guessed it, I knocked myself completely silly on the low ceiling, and Fitzpatrick bolted, not sticking around to revive me.

Fortunately for me, he was arrested by my colleagues. The stir we caused at the FBI Office afterward was amazing. Director Hoover called both of them to DC, gave them personal cash incentive awards, transferred them to their office of preference, and he sent me to Chicago.

All in all for twenty-eight years, my feet never hit the floor in the morning without being excited about my profession and duties as a special agent of the FBI.

Perhaps I was a little too hard on myself with the Chicago transfer comment.

Big offices like Chicago and New York always needed agents. At that time, FBI policy was new agents would start off in small offices. They were considered training offices. After a year, you were considered to be an "acceptable" agent and ready to conduct investigations with minimal supervision.

I was not excited about being transferred there, being west of the Mississippi. I had come to believe that I was in the "western circuit" and probably would go to Seattle, San Francisco, or Los Angeles or many of the others in the West. There just wasn't intrigue for a Midwestern boy to come back to the Midwest, although it's fair to say that Jenny and I had fallen in love with the West.

This story starts much earlier. I take you back to those days of yesteryear.

GROWING UP

Growing up on a thirty cow dairy farm gives one a unique perspective of life. Of course, what adds a little more color is being the second oldest of ten children, in the only Catholic family in a very Protestant Scandinavian community.

I didn't realize that being Catholic made us different until one day a friend and classmate, Ron Seaquist, asked me about confessions at our church. He told me that he heard that when we confessed our sins to the priest, we had to "like eat a bale of hay" or something. When you are in the third grade, comments like that are not real flattering to hear.

Unquestionably, there was some bias against Catholics, but like so many things in life, we were accepted, but perhaps with a jaundice eye cast somewhat toward us.

The town of North Bend was just two miles down Highway 54, and our grade school was right there on the outskirts of town. It consisted of two rooms; Mrs. Hilton taught grades 1 through 4 and Mrs. Pfaff taught grades 5 through 8. It sits there to this day. Following its closing as a school, it was first occupied as a lumberyard, now sits vacant.

We were a mix of farm kids and "townies." Russ Sacia, Darrell Johnson, and myself were the farm kids in my class, and Susy Lasota, Joan Schneider, and Ron Seaquist were the townies.

Moving from fourth grade to fifth grade was quite an event, and it was my first shot at graduation. The fourth- and eighth-grade graduations were on the same day as the school annual spring picnic, which was usually in the last week or two of school before summer vacation. Though my mom would protest it would always be on Friday and in the 1950s we Catholics were strong believers in no meat on Friday, so much for the picnic.

Mom had protested and she became convinced that the only reason it was on a Friday was because of her protest and that perceived belief that perhaps they were a little anti-Catholic.

Of course all the kids were eating hot dogs and maybe we thought we'd go to hell if we did so we made due with potato chips, macaroni salad and maybe a hot dog bun with mustard, ketchup, relish and pickles.

I didn't feel picked on for being Catholic but then I was moving to the big room and into the fifth grade. We had moved to the North Bend farm when I was in the second grade so this was my third year.

Half way through the picnic, enter Mrs. Katherine Sacia, my mom, straight up to and face-to-face with Mrs. Pfaff and mom's ears were smoking. I can still see her waving her arms and expressing her frustration. I intentionally moved as far away as I could as I knew a scene was brewing.

Mom made her point, got back in the car and drove seven miles to Melrose and straight to the Superintendent. Throughout my last four years in the small country school of North Bend we never again had the school picnic on a Friday.

Memories of those growing-up years on the North Bend farm are mostly quite fond. I knew we struggled financially but we were always well-fed and deeply loved.

Mom was not a huge fan of the livelihood of a dairy farm, but she certainly was supportive. When my folks bought the farm in North Bend it had two great assets and one significant shortcoming. The assets were a beautiful large country home and a well-constructed, very solid dairy barn. The shortcoming was it was a hill farm. The fields, though productive, were small and hilly. Dad had desperately wanted a large level farm, something he never got, as he and mom would stay there until their passing.

The farm Dad had really wanted to buy had a great dairy barn much like the one on the North Bend farm. The land was level and productive. The downside was the house was small and in poor condition. Dad was just fine with that. Arguably, Mom had the strongest personality. Somehow she knew that if we bought that farm, she'd never have the large nice house which was absolutely needed for a family our size. In their later years, they often joked with each other on the fact that it was a blessing that we landed where we did. Tragically, a child had been killed on the other farm following our purchase of the North Bend home. Mom kind of used that as "See, it could have been one of us."

Ah, North Bend and the many fond memories of a young lifetime.

At age fifteen Dad and Mom let me buy a Model A Ford pickup. I was in high school then riding the bus to Melrose. My new found friend, fellow farm kid and classmate Bruce Witte, sold it to me for twenty-eight dollars. He had asked me for thirty dollars, but somehow I got him down to twenty-eight, the same amount of money as its year, a 1928. I was now truly in hog heaven. Farm kids need a pickup, and I already had a tractor. When I was thirteen, I had fifty dollars saved up. Our milk man, Kenny Arneson, had an old 10–20 McCormick Deering. Though I had never seen it, I knew I had to own it.

I had saved the fifty dollars over two years with a small cucumber patch that yielded me twenty-plus dollars each year. With the money burning a hole in my pocket, Dad drove me to the Arneson farm that must have been twelve or thirteen miles away. I was sure the only reason Dad let me buy it was old 10–20s had a reputation of being excellent "belt power." At about three miles per hour, I know it took three to four hours to drive it home. The entire time I was on cloud nine, thinking "Gosh, my own tractor." To recognize the importance of belt power, dairy farms, without question in dairy country farms had silos. The silos were filled by a tractor with a belt pulley connected to a belt, attached to blower that would send the ground up corn and stalks up a large pipe and into the silo. There it fermented and in the winter made excellent dairy feed as silage. At fifteen, I felt I was on my way to a life of farming, which at that time in my life was what I hoped to do with my life.

With my Model A Ford pickup, on Saturdays I could load the truck box, with side racks, with earcorn from the crib, and haul it to Tranberg's Feed Mill in North Bend. I could get it ground with some minerals added, and I had taken care of the "grist," which the milk cows were fed during each milking. Getting the grist was always better than cleaning calf pens, a Saturday chore.

A highlight was always in stopping at Hardie's Café after the grist was finished. Alice and Bill Hardie owned the restaurant/bar and so memorable was getting a piece of Alice's warm apple pie, a huge scoop of ice cream, and a cup of coffee all for a quarter fifteen cents for the pie, a nickel for the ice cream, and another one for the coffee. For a farm kid, this was living large.

Just up the road but still in town past "Brindes" Bar and Swenson Garage was "Bump Glennys" Barbershop. Until high school, Mom had always given us kid's haircuts. By high school age, I felt I deserved a real haircut. Bump's Barbershop was little more than a large box, perhaps ten feet by twelve feet. It consisted of a barber chair, an old oil stove, a small counter and sink in the back. Maybe there were six or eight chairs and they were usually full more with those gossiping than those waiting for a haircut.

What I remember most was that a haircut was sixty cents. I never remember the price being less or more and Bump was a great storyteller. He had most of the kids my age convinced that once you got married and started having sex, that if you put a penny in a jar each time you had it during your first year and then started taking a penny out each time thereafter you would never get it empty. Naïve young teenagers believe the old "experienced" guys when it comes to sex. I didn't want to believe it but Bump's words were gospel.

With the grist in the back of the Model A, a great piece of pie, ice cream and coffee as well as a haircut I was nearly ready to fire the Model A again and get home in time to do chores. I headed diagonally across the street to DeColon's Tire Store and Root Beer Stand to talk smart for a little bit and get a fresh pack of Lucky Strike cigarettes. They were twenty-five cents a pack, and I think nearly everyone smoked. At that time, it was rather cool to smoke. The hazards to your health had not yet become an issue.

The smoking habit had been given to me by my grandpa Buytaert when I was about age six. His objective had been to break my brother Mike and me of ever wanting to smoke. He bought us each a corn cob pipe and a can of Prince Albert Tobacco. He taught us how to light up and how to inhale. Mike turned green, got very sick, and never smoked again. I talked Mike out of the rest of his Prince Albert and his pipe and I smoked until I was twenty-four years old. Quitting only because it was affecting my running, and I know I'd be a dead man today had I not.

Back to my North Bend adventure. Buying a quart of re-refined thirty weight engine oil for twenty cents I added it to the Model A, fired it and the cloud of smoke followed me home. On the occasions that I didn't have twenty cents I added used engine oil—it was free.

Sunday morning was always an adventure after milking was finished and mom had us fed. All twelve of us piled into dad's 1948 Cadillac Floral Car which he was very proud of and we headed for Church. Our nearest Catholic Church was in Galesville, the opposite way from North Bend and a distance of fifteen miles on Highway 54.

I don't know for sure where dad found the old Cadillac but I know it had been traded to the dealer from a funeral parlor and the dealer simply couldn't sell it. Back in the day, the floral car followed the hearse typically with the flowers to adorn the grave. This would be followed by the cars carrying the bereaved family.

With ten kids dad needed a big car. He traded in our 1950 Ford Station Wagon for the Cadillac and it seems that he paid $450 to boot, which Dad thought was a steal as the old Ford was on its last leg. Dad had always wanted a Cadillac and though I'm sure this wasn't his idea of the Cadillac he wanted, it was a Cadillac with very low mileage. The car was very long and the back seat was a considerable distance from the front seat. In the middle were seats that folded into the floor, thus making it a very good vehicle to transport a large family.

Mike and I being the oldest and wanting to be cool didn't really relish the idea of being seen in it. There were no excuses, we all went to church.

We usually stopped at Longwell's Drugstore after church as Mom always needed something. Dad would often buy a half gallon of ice cream, and I can still see him cutting twelve equal slabs of ice cream after lunch (we called it dinner) when we got home.

On occasion, we wouldn't stop at Longwell's but when we got on the Decorah Prairie about half way home we'd often stop at "Vira's" Store. Vira was an elderly lady who owned a tiny grocery store in the middle of nowhere. The mental image of it is deeply engrained in my mind. We were each allowed a nickel ice cream cone. I'm not sure if Vira felt sorry for us or if everyone got such a large cone for a nickel.

When her health failed and the store closed, we all knew it never would reopen. I have no idea what kind of living it yielded to her and I can't help but think that it was simply her way of keeping active and busy in her elderly years. For me she is a wonderful memory. The building stands to this day converted to a one car garage.

Earning extra money was always on my mind as I am sure it was for most kids my age. Getting away from our farm to help other farmers who always needed strapping young farm boys to help seldom happened. Dad always had plenty for each of us to keep very busy.

One day, when I was about twelve to fourteen, Hank Hilton, a neighboring farmer, drove in the yard asking my dad if any of his boys could help that day. For whatever reason, dad volunteered me. Apparently dad felt bad for Henry as he had his oat crop shocked (a process not seen any longer) and with incoming rain time was of the essence. A binder cut and bundled the oats. With manual labor the bundles were teepeed with several bundles horizontal across the top then allowed to dry for several days. Today was the day. The threshing machine was in place and young strapping boys were employed to "pitch bundles." It was hot back breaking work. It always included a great noon meal and today was no exception.

The day wrapped up around 4:30 p.m. with all of us sweating and exhausted from a long hot day. Thankfully most of us had to get back to our own farms to help with evening milking. Hank had a reputation of paying very well and at that time, for a boy my age, three to four dollars was a good wage. Hank was handing each boy a ten-dollar bill and my eyes were a big as saucers. I'll never be able to fully explain how I reacted when Hank got to me. Now keep in mind several of my classmates had already graciously accepted their ten dollars. I guarantee I worked as hard as or harder than the rest. I responded with "Oh, Mr. Hilton, I just couldn't take that much." It had to be something that had been ingrained by my parents. You know be humble. With that he said "well how much do you think," I responded with "Oh, four dollars would be fine." I swear he never said a word. He stuffed the ten dollars back into his wallet and pulled out four dollar bills and handed them to me and then moved on. I just talked myself out of six hard earned dollars. Maybe Hank was trying to teach me a lesson. Thereafter I accepted graciously what I was offered.

Writing this prompted a similar situation of helping another farmer. Our next door neighbor was John (Hunz) Huber. John came to America from Germany as a young man. He became a citizen, married and was a dairy farmer just down the road. As a neighbor and with his only son grown and gone, Hunz called on us regularly to help.

One particular day, after a long effort to get his hay baled, we finished about 3:00 p.m. As we had not stopped for a noon meal, his wife Myrtle welcomed Hunz and me to the dinner table. Under my desert plate was a used comic book left behind by the grown son, John Alan. When it was desert time I picked up the cup cake and there sat a shiny new fifty cent piece.

Smiling broadly, he said, "Jim, the comic book and money are for you." Of course, I thanked him and also Myrtle for dinner. My brother Mike had a field day laughing when I got home.

Milking our thirty-plus cow dairy herd was a ritual for the entire family in one way or another, yes, 24-7, 365. Dad, Mike, and I did most of the milking two times a day. We each were good enough at it so that if one or two of us was not there, the other one or two could easily take over.

Our farm of two hundred thirty acres was predominately dairy cows. We typically raised some hogs also and one or two occasions we had laying hens. Mike was the hog guy and Mary did the most with the chickens when we had them. Brother Tom and step brother Gene Taylor threw down the hay and silage and did most of the feeding. As

Dan and Tim became old enough, there was plenty to do, and they all pitched in with feeding and cleaning.

Those memories of the many hours in the dairy barn must be where I developed my deep love for milking cows, and throughout my growing-up years, I was quite convinced that milking cows on a farm of my own someday would be what I'd do.

We did the milking with four milker units in a stanchion barn when all three of us were there. If one or two were missing, we would cut down to three to ensure that the cows were milked being completely dry, but not to leave the units on the cows too long.

Some of my fondest memories are of dad pushing his way between two cows in stanchions with the surge unit in his left hand, the suction tube in his right to connect to the valve to activate the milker unit all the time singing at the top of his lungs. I don't know what it was about the song "Beautiful Ohio," but it stands out in my mind.

Four summers ago as Jenny and I traveled the nation to visit large dairy operations, visiting one at 3 Mile Canyon in Oregon with 22,500 milk cows, I marveled at the difference and contrast as that boy growing up, a large percentage of the population were farmers of one type or another. Farmers prided themselves with their names emboldened in huge letters on their barns invariably followed by "and son" or plural sons, such a badge of honor to keep the farms going, passing them on to the next generation. Today with the percentage of farmers in the small single digits, size can only compensate.

Technology brings us much but it also takes from a simpler time, even though the times originally were harder. The size of operations is most amazing. A new forty- to fifty-horsepower farm tractor, typical of the size used for row crop farming in the forties and fifties cost in the neighborhood of $1,600 to $2,300. The latter being for a 1952 Farmall M the most popular farm tractor ever built. Contrast that to a front line farm tractor today of two hundred fifty plus horse power with front wheel assist costing approximately ten times more or $160,000 to $230,000 farming thousands of acres. Yes, it's apples to oranges, but the point is, farming is drastically changing, and for a farm boy who grew up in the industry it's so hard to get my arms around the unbelievable contrast.

I can't talk of those growing-up years without talking of my classmate Aaron Fisher. Aaron and I were nearly inseparable in high school. Like me, he was a gear head and a farm kid. He lived on a farm in the Cataract area. We often double dated, and on Sunday afternoon, we were usually in his dad's shop on their farm.

Our dad's farming operations were similar in size, but they were in the "sand country," so they grew more beans, wheat, and melons, and we grew more corn and hay crops.

Aaron and I loved working on cars. His parents owned a 1957 Mercury four-door hardtop which was our car of choice for double dating. At that time, I owned a 1953 Chevy convertible, and Aaron and I labored to put a "split six" manifold on it. You see, to be cool, you had to have dual exhaust. Next, they had to be loud.

We decided that to do this right we needed to get a Chevrolet six-cylinder manifold from a junkyard and there were two junkyards that Aaron and I frequented. "Stumlins" was in Ettrick, Wisconsin, and "the Polish Jew" was in the Town of Independence. I don't remember his name but "The Polish Jew" was emblazoned on his wrecker doors. Stumlin wanted thirty dollars for one, which we both decided was highway robbery. The Polish Jew sold me one for ten dollars cash only.

We headed back to the shop of Aaron's dad and between the skills of his dad "Buck," his brother Brent, Aaron, and myself, over the next two Sunday afternoons, it was ready to install. Wow, a six-cylinder Chevy with dual exhaust and very noisy glass pack mufflers—life was good.

At seventeen a convertible with the top down and loud mufflers, in my world, that was as cool as it got. Life was about dreams and schemes and where do I go from here. Though I was told over and over that I was very capable studying never interested me and I had no desire to attend college.

At this age a young man's fancy also turns to love and I was no exception. I started dating Dianne who was a junior and I was a senior. I got a part-time job at Ohearn Auto Company, the Ford

Dealer in Melrose. Oliver Ohearn, known as "OL," gave me a chance and I certainly wanted to do a good job. My duties prior to graduation were general clean up, runner, and apprentice mechanic. Once I graduated I went full-time, and my salary went from $1.50 per hour to $1.75. Gradually, I was tasked with more and more responsibility.

I traded my '53 Chevy for a 1957 Ford two-door hardtop. My world was Melrose, Wisconsin. I had a job and a girlfriend and somehow I managed to graduate with my thirty classmates.

In the back of all eighteen-year-old high school graduates' minds in 1962 was the draft. I knew that not being college bound I would be drafted by age twenty-two.

Dianne's parents sat us down one Sunday and explained to us that we were never to become serious. I was Catholic and she was Lutheran. Unless I planned on becoming Lutheran I was to stop seeing their daughter. The thought of becoming Lutheran had never entered my mind and I knew it would break my parents' hearts. In fairness, at eighteen I certainly wasn't thinking of marriage. I liked Dianne a great deal and she had my class ring. We both knew she had another year of school and I would be facing the draft in a couple of years.

As I look back and compare how things are today compared to then the contrast is amazing. Several years ago, when Catholics and Protestants were killing one another in Ireland, I found a weak comparison with those growing-up years in my home area.

SCHOOL MEMORIES

The excitement of riding the school bus as a farm kid on the first day of first grade is etched in my mind.

My older brother Mike told me the driver's name was Mr. Barrentine, and Mom had warned me to be polite. She didn't need to tell me that, as it was deeply ingrained in my mind and I would never think of being any other way.

I can still see the fence posts whizzing by and watching all the conversations going on inside the bus. It was a far cry from being home with Mom, Dad, my sister Mary, and my brothers Tom and Dan. Well, now I was a "schoolkid," and it made me feel quite important.

For reasons I don't recall, after some time I developed a less than pleasant relationship with a girl named Sherri in the class. She just had a way of getting under my skin. We actually became physical, even though I knew better than to hit a girl, but, by way of rationalization, "she hit me first." This went on for some time. Apparently, I was meaner to her than she was to me, and she told me she'd tell her mom. For whatever reason, that didn't worry me.

The school year progressed and little Sherri and I still had our struggles and then it happened. Mr. Barrentine pulled up to school as classes were dismissed for the day. I boarded the bus as I always did, went back four seats and plopped myself down.

The next thing I knew, I was looking up at a lady who said, "Are you Jim Sacia?"

Of course I said yes.

With that she said, "I'm Sherri's mother," and she slapped me across the face with the promise that if I ever hit Sherri again, I'd really get walloped next time.

Yes, I was scared to death, only because she'd tell my mom and dad. It never occurred to me, as it would today, that she had no right to come on the bus and slap me. Apparently, Mr. Barrentine had no concern either. All the way home, I'd periodically see him look in the mirror, catch my eye, and smile. I was completely embarrassed. What I do remember is never hitting Sherri, again and I think we actually became friends.

From first grade to my senior year two other physical encounters come to mind. As a junior in high school, I saw myself as one of the "cool guys." One of my classmates, Melrose High School class of 1962, was David Lindberg, also known as "Jonesy." David was a bright kid. Being a "cool guy," I developed the habit of meeting him when I was with my cool friends and saying "Duh, Jonesy" in a very surely manner. We'd all laugh. With hindsight I'm sure it was a form of bullying. That was a term unknown at the time.

One day, I met David in the hallway, and I was not with my cool friends. Stupidity totally engulfed me, and I scratched my head with my clever comment "Duh, Jonesy," only to pick myself up off the floor. David completely took the "Duh, Jonesy" out of me, and I never made that mistake again.

In my sophomore year I had established myself as a capable kid with perhaps very little motivation. I have often thanked God for the United States Army as I now know that's what turned my life around, and truly grew me up.

Back to the classroom, in my sophomore year, agriculture was my favorite class as would stand to reason for a farm kid, who at that time, planned to always milk cows. Leo Mulcahey was our Ag instructor, and we farm kids all admired him as he taught us much.

Like all classes, there are the wise guys, and during class, you could see Kenny really getting under the skin of Mr. Mulcahey with his antics. When it reached the breaking point, Mr. Mulcahey grabbed Kenny by the front of the shirt with both hands, picked him off the ground, and slammed him backward through the closed door that had a glass window. I can still see the glass shattering and the door busted to smithereens.

Teaching was a little different then. If you smarted off or disrupted class, you got manhandled as Kenny did. Later that day, Roy Paff the janitor, had the door replaced. The following day Kenny was a gentleman as Mr. Mulcahey put a film on entitled "Feeds and Feeding." Why would I remember that? I have not a clue.

Thinking back on my life, I'm mystified that I wasn't a better student. I was constantly told by all my teachers, "Jim, you are very capable, just apply yourself." I would always reply that I would, but that's where it ended. I was far more concerned with just getting by. It got to be a joke when asked for my homework, my standard response was, "I forgot it at home on the top of the refrigerator."

I was so bad on homework that the teachers would often say to me while collecting homework, "Let me guess, Jim, yours is home on top of the refrigerator." Of course, there would be the snickers around the room, but that didn't bother me. I had figured out in each class just about what I could get away with.

In my entire senior class of Melrose High School, class of 1962, there were a total of thirty one students. Yes, I was very near the bottom of the class, just "getting by." It reached crisis proportion near the end of my senior year, needing a very good grade on a term paper just to pass the class. Without that good grade I simply would not graduate.

Of course, my mother was more concerned than I, so she and my sister Mary both spent long hours helping me research Henry Ford, which was my assigned paper. To my good fortune and their hard work, I received an A on my paper, and I will always believe that Mr. Newton just knew I had help. The good news is that I graduated twenty-ninth in my class.

As we lived nine miles from Melrose High School, we were picked up by a school bus driven by Pete Ostrander. Pete was always our driver throughout my high school years. I can't help but believe that each day he pulled into the Sacia Family yard, he smiled a little if Jim didn't go to school that day. I had a reputation of being somewhat of a "cut up" on the bus. Normally it would be on the long ride home. As Pete eased the bus in and out of all the gravel coulee roads, young men started goofing off. My older brother Mike and my sister

Mary tell me that I was one of the instigators. I find that hard to believe, but who am I to question?

One of the kids on the bus would wet his pants if we could get him laughing hard enough, by making animal sounds. Pete would be scanning the rear view mirror trying to figure out just which one was the "wise guy." Of course, we'd make the sound when putting our head down and then immediately sitting up with a sweet, innocent face. I got quite good at it.

Occasionally I would get caught at that, or any number of other dastardly deeds, and Pete had quite a way of dealing with it. He would literally nearly lock the brakes, putting several right on the floor, followed by "Jim, get off the bus."

As I think back, that never happened on a nasty day, perhaps on those days I acted better. I'd rather guess it was simply because he was kind. Mom and Dad were never happy when I got thrown off the bus. They certainly had no problem knowing that he only did it out of necessity. Certainly, it's not something a bus driver could get away with today. I assure you it did get my attention and I'd actually straighten out for a few days, especially after dealing with the wrath of my parents.

I guess there is some irony in my short stint as a bus driver while in college. The irony is, I really liked the job. I adopted Pete's habit of braking hard, stopping the bus and getting their attention. I never would have dared to throw anyone off, but I did get their attention.

SERIAL NUMBER **RA17635687**

Every Veteran remembers their serial number or service number, now I understand that it is your social security number. Just out of high school, I'm recognizing that the draft will be inevitable in a few short years. Loving being an apprentice auto mechanic at Ohearn Auto Company in Melrose, Wisconsin left me very conflicted. Perhaps it was only "puppy love," as the Paul Anka song of 1960 called it, but to me it was so real and only added to my confliction recalling Dianne's mom and dad warning us not to become serious that compelled me to have a serious talk with my classmate Bob Johnson who was also thinking seriously about the military.

Drinking beer at age eighteen was then legal in Wisconsin and most towns had both eighteen-year-old bars and twenty-one-year-old bars (eighteen-year-old bars were beer only). Bob's dad "Chippy" Johnson owned Chip's Bar on the main drag in Melrose. Bob and I and several others who had recently turned eighteen sat around a table at Chip's playing euchre, talking smart, and occasionally very seriously discussing what we'd do with the rest of our life.

Some guys were college bound. My friend Aaron Fisher was going to "take his chances." My cousin Russ Sacia planned to start farming which should get him a deferment. Bob and I decided that we would enlist. The next day, I went to work and asked Oliver Ohearn if I could have the next day off to take care of some business. Oliver Ohearn was a short chubby man, often with a cigar in his mouth and always adjusting his pants. He told me that the next day was impossible as a new Falcon and a new Fairlane were due in and needed to be "prepped" which was my job.

OL was inquisitive but he didn't come right out and ask me why I needed off. I dutifully prepped the new cars and the next day Bob and I headed to La Crosse to talk with the recruiters. We stopped first at the Marine Corps but the recruiting NCO had stepped out so our next stop was the Army. The recruiting NCO truly had a knack at "sucking you in." He told Bob and me of the new "Buddy Plan" that would ensure that Bob, and I stayed together through basic training. With the trepidation of leaving home and having no clue what we were getting into this sounded good.

He then told us of another new program where in we could enlist for a specific city if that city had an "Air Defense" component. Knowing that my Aunt Alice and Uncle Don lived near Detroit, Michigan, I asked if that city had such a program. I still recall the response "one of the best in the nation." I was sold. I signed on the dotted line, and Bob did the same. He was not interested in a specific city assignment so he was unassigned after Basic Training.

We scheduled our departure date several weeks down the road to get our affairs in order. We would leave July 24, 1962.

Returning to Melrose and Chip's bar that night Bob and I were the center of attention as we were congratulated for "making something of our lives." The following weekend, I visited with Dianne and her parents, Selmer and Bernice, who congratulated me with obvious relief. As long as I was leaving Dianne and I were allowed to see each other "as long as we weren't getting serious" and obviously we didn't.

Dianne and Bob's girlfriend Ginny Sawyer rode with us to La Crosse in my yellow and white '57 Ford Fairlane 500 to get the bus on July 24. I had made arrangements to sell it to Margaret Murray who would pick it up from my parents the weekend after I left for the Army. Only years later did I learn from my mom that she had wished to take us to the bus. I wasn't very perceptive at age eighteen and it hasn't improved much through the years.

We said our goodbyes to Dianne and Ginny and headed by bus to Saint Paul, Minnesota, where we were sworn into the United States Army. We boarded another bus all occupied by new "privates" in the Army and were off to Fort Leonard Wood, Missouri. Arriving at the reception center is not something one soon forgets. Sergeants in our face, all our hair shaved off, constantly being told MOVE

MOVE MOVE! Uniforms issued, stripped naked for shots and some type of cursory physical and at no time is it slowing down.

I vaguely remember that sometime around 1:00 or 2:00 a.m., we crash in our bunks only to be loudly wakened by about 0530 to 0600. (We are now on military time.) The reception center was typically a two or three day process as we go through numerous procedures to get us off to our basic training unit. Of course, in that two-day period, we have many new friends, and like it or not, we are adjusting.

Midway through the second day Bob somehow fell down the barracks stairs and is off on "sick call." Apparently, the severity of his knee injury required hospitalization. I felt bad for him, but I was ready to move on to our basic training assignment.

The entire full barracks of new enlistees is formed up and ready to move out to our basic training unit and that dreaded sound that no new private wants to hear: "Private Sacia, front and center." By now I have learned to "move with a purpose," which means at a dead run. I come to attention in front of the drill instructor shouting in his face, "Private Sacia, reporting as ordered, sir." I was now ridiculed in front of the formation for being on "the buddy plan," and I would stay in the reception center until Private Johnson was discharged from the hospital and then and only then would we move on to another new basic training unit. We would not join the guys we had been with thus far.

For the next seven days, I literally had nothing to do except pull "fireguard," which is to make sure none of the empty barracks catch fire. After seven days, Bob and I were joined up and assigned to Echo Company, Fifth Battalion, Second Training Regiment, "Saints." My depressing days in the reception center being mocked as "ole buddy plan Sacia" were finally over.

I adapted well to the regimentation and training and actually enjoyed basic training. When I do have time to think, I realize that I miss the night life of Melrose. Fast-forward, I thank God I joined the Army and got the "hell out of dodge."

My drill instructor for the Second Platoon was Sergeant Johnson. He was an African American and literally my first exposure to a person of color. Sergeant Johnson was firm but fair and I immediately liked him. He drove us hard but explained why we were doing what we were doing and the importance of it. I grew to greatly respect him He is one of those people that I will always wonder what happened to as he so positively affected my life. Midway through ranger school, five years later, I thought I saw him in a mess hall in Fort Benning, but I never knew for sure.

While still in the reception center we were each given a "flying 10." A flying ten was a ten-dollar bill, which was an advance on our private E-1 salary of seventy-eight dollars per month. Many new enlistees had no money at all and that ten dollars gave us the opportunity to purchase toilet articles and other necessities at the PX.

Some fought the regimentation, but I rather enjoyed it. Throughout basic training, I was trained on and carried the M-1 Garand, the very same weapon of WWII and Korean War fame. An eight-shot 30.06 round and a proud possession today is one that I bought in Salt Lake City as a new FBI agent. My basic training rifle serial number was 5756863. An M-1 Garand, to be exact. Though I enlisted in 1962, eight years after the end of the Korean conflict, it still was the principle infantryman's weapon.

Once the weapon was issued to us we were to memorize the serial number. The consequences for not knowing it for a new private in the US Army (and for sure, the Marine Corps) would be less than pleasant.

The following day, after it had been issued to us, Staff Sergeant Johnson, our DI, inspected his charge. Each of us was standing at attention, holding our M-1 at post arms, and as he slapped the fore stock and took the weapon from us, his first words sent a chill, "Private Sacia, state your rifle serial number."

My response was, "5756863, Sergeant."

"Good job, Private Sacia, don't you ever forget it."

Apparently, his threat held true as after all these years, I still remember as I do my service number. Private Sylvester stood next to me and knew his M-1 number as he and I had been challenging each other all morning awaiting the inspection. Simply put, the intimidating force of Sergeant Johnson in his face simply rattled him. I have no recall how many push-ups he did but Sergeant Johnson kept him in the front leaning rest position ordering him to keep banging them out until he remembered. It was a long painful afternoon for Private Sylvester.

The M-1 is an amazing weapon. Long after my days in the Army, I purchased one, somewhat sporterized that I cherish to this day. Many of you may not know this weapon due to its age, but if you saw the movie *Grand Torino*, with Clint Eastwood, it's the rifle he had in the trunk back in the corner in his garage. Those of you my age with any kind of military connection will remember the M-1 well.

The greatness of the M-1 deserves some kind of comment by someone who carried it, though only in training situations. The soldiers and marines who carried it throughout Europe, Africa, and Asia in a combat roll can attest to its reliability and accuracy.

You could drag it through the mud, the sand, the ice, the snow whatever, it would always fire. The M16 of today, though superior in many ways, certainly suffers from a reliability stand point. Sadly some of Americas finest died in Vietnam due to a jammed M16. That seldom happened to an M-1. But I get it; I'm old-school, living in the past.

I prided myself in Basic with the speed that I could disassemble and reassemble my M-1, perhaps a trivial task but when it's barked out over and over, "You better learn this well as you may die in combat." I'm sure I was as fast as Forest Gump was with his rifle in the movie of the same name. Watching that scene puts a huge smile on my face.

I took Sergeant Johnson's words to heart. "Treat your rifle like your baby. Keep it spotless and learn to use it well."

On the rifle range, I so wanted to qualify "expert" or "the best." We fired at pop-up targets that were placed from fifty to three hundred yards from the firing line. The training was extremely regimented and, as you can imagine, very safety conscious. We fired the 30.06 round from the standing, sitting, prone, and foxhole position, ten lanes with a tower behind us with NCO observing and barking the orders over a PA system. Right behind each of us was a spotter who ensured that we were looking for the right target on the right lane and of course with one thing always most important, safety. If those of us on the line screwed up it was the spotters fault. Through a well-coordinated system, part of the time we were the spotter and part of the time, the actual shooter.

"Along the firing line commence firing," a roar broke the silence as ten M-1s came to life. After the ordered number of rounds fired by each private the command "Along the firing line cease-fire, cease-fire, clear and lock all weapons, out of your foxhole, return to your numbered stump, you should have been there." Of course, none of was there yet. We were barely out of the foxhole.

Ah, that good military training, and try as I did, I missed expert by no more than two points. That made me a "sharp shooter." No not an expert, but better than "marksman" and certainly better than a "bolo" or one that did not quality. Those poor devils spent many extra hours (of which there was no such thing as extra hours in basic training) getting drilled and counseled until they could qualify as a marksman. It's not where I would have liked to have been.

Finishing basic training in October and being so close to Christmas, we were told we would be transferred straight to our next assignment as opposed to a two-week leave, which was pretty much tradition.

My orders were to report to the Twenty-Eighth Artillery Group headquartered at Selfridge Air Force Base Michigan and I was issued train tickets to get me to Detroit.

The sleeper car was a whole new experience, but then everything I had been dealing with since the day in July was a new experience. The most exciting new experience occurred after our sixth week of basic training as we were finally issued a weekend pass. Waynesville, Missouri, is the classic military town with every conceivable way of separating naïve GIs from their money.

Outside the front gate three of us got a cab and I guess our greenness was quite evident. The cabby assured us he'd take us where we "could have some fun." I should have realized that it was a whorehouse, but I was inside with my two "friends" before I realized what was going on. Perhaps it was my Christian upbringing but I had no desire to pay for sex. I excused myself to go to the bathroom. When I returned my two friends were off to their respective rooms with their girls. I tipped my hat to the madam and excused myself out the door. Back to post I went.

Other than on official business as an FBI agent later in life it's the only "cat house" I was ever in. My two friends could have had a field day humiliating me before the guys in the squad for sneaking out. That would not have been seen as "cool" and my manhood would have been challenged. Perhaps they were quietly somewhat envious as I had twenty dollars more than each of them.

From my sleeper birth to the dining car I ate breakfast alone, marveling at the silver and ornate settings. Being in uniform the waiter obviously knows I'll be paying with a military voucher. Of course, there was no place on the voucher for a tip, and even if there had been I would have no idea of "tipping"; to my knowledge, that was a big city concept and one that I knew nothing about.

Apparently, the server expected nothing as well. Arriving midday at the Detroit Rail Station, getting off the train with orders in hand, I found a pay phone and contacted the 28th Artillery Group Orderly Room, and I was told a runner would be dispatched to pick me up "in a couple of hours." Staying close to my pickup point, this small-town boy and young soldier marveled at the sights of city life.

Arriving at Selfridge, I met my new boss, Staff Sergeant Perkins, who was the Senior NCO for Alpha Crew. The good sergeant explained my duties to me and my training would consist nearly entirely of OJT or on-the-job-training.

Alpha crew is one of three crews operating as the control and nerve center for six Nike Hercules Batteries located throughout the Detroit area. The Batteries are where the surface to air missiles are maintained underground but can be surfaced and readied to fire to meet a Soviet threat in a matter of minutes.

I would be working three days, three nights and three days off. I quickly adapted, and training was always ongoing for our degrees of readiness. Our training was with the Air Force, and they were constantly trying to sneak an aircraft through our FPS 35 radar and did a simulated bombing run on Detroit. The ability to stave them off was what we literally daily and nightly trained for. Alpha Crew, which I was proudly a part of, developed a reputation as the best of the best.

If we identified a "bogey" as a bandit on radar, it was our job to notify the six Batteries and each one came to life and the impressive Nike Hercules missile came out of the bunker and pointed skyward. Our huge radar caught them miles away and as they closed to their target we would have them identified as friend or foe and convey the same information to the Batteries whose lesser-powered radar would by then be locking on.

I was trained as a "plotter," meaning I would be writing with grease pencil "backward" on clear Plexiglass walls that we plotters stood behind. Outlined on the Plexiglass was the area we were responsible for. Via headset we were given the coordinates of our "bogeys" and their trajectory and we plotted them standing at our clear wall.

Out in front of us was the "blue room" with numerous radar screens with soldiers relaying their information to us giving senior NCO's and officers in the back the ability to make their decisions by watching the "threat" of "bogeys" closing on our area.

Thinking back it was quite a sophisticated process with great coordination between those of us plotting, the radar operators giving us the locations and those in charge.

One of the soldiers on another crew, Charlie Ainsworth, was from the Detroit area. On his three days off, he would be homeward bound. All of us had to pull our share of KP on our off days but Charlie hated it. With seldom anywhere to go on my off days I would often hire out to pull KP for the guys who wanted out of it for whatever reason. The going rate was twenty dollars per day. The cooks knew who was scheduled but they didn't care as long as there was a body to do the work. There were typically three KPs; back sink man—his job was scrubbing pots and pans all day long; front sink man who was responsible for the soldiers plates, cups and silverware; and the (DRO) dining room orderly which was the best job in the mess hall simply keeping the area clean and picked up. Sometimes an "outside man" was scheduled to unload trucks as well,

Whenever I pulled KP, I tried to be the first one there and I'd have first pick. Of course, it would be DRO. The last to arrive was typically the back sink man where you sweated like a butcher all day long. Ainsworth knew I would be happy to do it but he was always broke. It got to the point, because of not having the money, he'd offer forty dollars but not until payday. The first time I accepted I was sure that on payday he would renege but he always paid as agreed.

By then I was a Private E-2 or PFC E-3 but still making less than one hundred dollars per month so nearly half of it for a day's work was to say the least, "hitting it big." I really wanted to buy a car and I was saving every dime. I had my eye on a '56 Ford two-door hardtop, and I knew by the end of the month I'd have the needed $500.

Getting to know the cooks was very worthwhile and the head chef was Sergeant "Hank," I don't think I ever knew his last name. Hank was notorious for being excessively overweight for Army standards and he would always duck back into the kitchen if ranking officer, Major or above, came into the dining hall. Hank constantly feared, and rightly so, being discharged for excessive weight.

Hank always had a cigarette hanging out of his mouth and there was little doubt that Hank would never live to be an old man. He drank like a fish and smoked like a chimney. I became well-known to the cooks as the word got around that I could be hired to pull KP if I was off shift. Hank must had had about eighteen years in and he made it clear to all who would listen that when he hit his twenty he would be gone.

Hank was a likable guy, and he knew I was making some extra money pulling KP, so one day he simply said, "Sacia, can you loan me a hundred bucks until payday?"

How could I say no? It had gotten to the point that when he knew I'd be there, even if I wasn't early enough to be DRO, he'd tell the next arriving private that "Sacia has DRO I sent him on a mission" was Hank's standard line.

I was saving money to buy that Ford, but surely I could help Hank out. It was the twelfth of the month, and only eighteen days until pay day. I carefully counted out one hundred dollars and gave it to Hank.

On the twenty-eighth I had my regularly scheduled KP day, and I arrived as the third KP. The DRO and the front sink man were in place. I was somewhat indignant. Hank always saw that I get DRO. Backup cook, Smitty, looked at me with the next line: "Hey, Sacia, did you hear Hank died of a heart attack last night?"

28ᵀᴴ ARTILLERY GROUP

W here was that motivation when I was in high school? How does one answer that? I loved being a soldier and totally immersed myself into doing the best possible job. Occasionally, I would lie in bed at night and actually ask myself where I found my motivation. The good news is, I did find it.

I think much of the credit goes to two fellow soldiers that I had befriended, Dave Goetz and John Papson. They were both friends and college graduates; perhaps it was their demeanor, perhaps simply their friendship. On the occasions that the three of us sat around talking, they somehow very subtly convinced me of the importance of "getting that sheep skin" (i.e., a college degree).

To a large degree, I think it was already there as I excelled in my MOS (Military Occupational Specialty). Never having thought of college in high school, even though I was often reminded "You have ability. Why don't you use it?" I had convinced myself prior to my Army years that my true love was dairy cows and dairy farming. My life was transitioning significantly.

I started thinking of the Army as a career, but I knew I wanted to be an officer. Staff Sergeant Perkins and Lieutenant Pendergast sat me down and encouraged me to apply to West Point. I apparently had adequately impressed them to believe I had what it took to be an Army officer. West Point had never even been dreamed of by me. Had it been, I would have been a far better high school student.

I went through the significant paperwork to apply for the "charm school," which was basically prep school for someone like myself on active duty with very little high school math and science and very poor grades. The application was never submitted as Lieutenant

Pendergast was able to determine that with the age requirements I would be too old to enter after prep school was completed.

I resigned myself to knowing I could do ROTC when I did go to college, which was more and more a reality. Of course, there was also OCS.

The day shifts were just that, day shifts. When we were on nights, we immersed ourselves in training with the Air Force and our efforts to intercept their "bandit aircraft" always preparing for the "real deal," which prayerfully would never come.

Everyone has memorable days in their life. Growing up in the hills of rural Wisconsin when television was still a very new concept, back home we could only receive one channel which was Channel 8 out of La Crosse. It was only on the air from 7:00 a.m. until 10:00 p.m., and the rest of the time was "test pattern and tone." It consisted of a pattern across your screen and an adjustable tone, so you knew your set was working. My favorite commentators were the actor Ronald Reagan who hosted the General Electric Theatre on Sunday night at 7:00 p.m. Just prior to that show was the one-hour series *You Are There*, hosted by my most favorite of all time, Walter Cronkite. I remember his introduction verbatim "What sort of day was it? A day like all days, filled with those events that alter and illuminate our times. All things are as they were then except you are there." This was followed by the explosions and machine gun fire at Normandy Beach on June 6, 1944—D-day, or perhaps the Battle of Gettysburg or whatever that particular evenings show was.

And so it was on November 22, 1963, as I was sitting in the break room at the nerve center for the Twenty-Eighth Artillery Group and Walter Cronkite appeared. "We interrupt this program as President Kennedy has been shot in Dallas, Texas." My Class A Uniform was on my lap as I was sewing on my Specialist 4 Stripe that I had been promoted to on that very day. Like everyone, I was dumbfounded.

We immediately went to the highest readiness level, Defcon 5, as a cautionary measure that immediately got each of us to the highest degree of readiness and sparred with the Air Force throughout the night.

Living and working as a soldier resumes in its own good time, and life moves on. Even the assassination of the president of the United States fails to stop the world from spinning. Safe to say, I saw firsthand history in the making, and Walter Cronkite actually teared up and cried.

A short four or five months after my promotion to specialist 4, I was promoted to sergeant E-5. I have grown to love the Army, and it loves me in return.

Prior to his assassination, President Kennedy had created the Army Special Forces. They would be twelve-man teams, cross-trained in each other's MOS, and capable of operating on their own for long periods of time. The president felt this concept would work well to assist the South Vietnamese Army in its efforts to fight the Communists of North Vietnam.

Vietnam was a word we started to hear more and more of, and about the same time, the Army was seeking young soldiers to be trained as helicopter pilots and there was a significant push to find such men. Lieutenant Doyle talked with me about it and emphasized that upon graduation, I would be a warrant officer and a certified helicopter pilot. Being the gear head that I was, I often wonder why I didn't choose that path. Simply put, I think by now I really wanted to go to college and then return to active duty, obtain my commission, and make a career of the Army.

Life has a way of not always going as planned and Garth Brooks's song "Unanswered Prayers" summed it up.

I soldiered on for three great years. Several girlfriends, several cars, several honors, many memorable experiences all came to a head in July 1965. My ETS (estimated time of separation) was rapidly approaching.

The evening news was more and more about the escalating war in Vietnam. President Johnson extended all active-duty Marines for at least thirty days. I was secretly wishing he would do the same for the Army. It would make my decision so much simpler.

I was working part-time at a Mobil Service Station right outside the front gate of Selfridge and spending most of nights at my Uncle Don and Aunt Alice's home.

July 23 arrived. I said my goodbyes, cleared post, and headed for Melrose, Wisconsin, in my '64 Chevelle. Where do I go from here?

I was registered for the fall quarter at Wisconsin State University in River Falls. My friends told me to apply for unemployment until the fall quarter. I guess I saw things differently. If I could work, I would work. I got a job with Horrell George Roofing Company, and I was learning how to hot tar flat roofs. I was making three dollars per hour, over a hundred dollars per week. I never thought I could ever make that much money. It was back-breaking work, but "unemployment" wasn't in my vocabulary, and as long as I could work, I would. The number of my friends who prided themselves on drawing "Rocking Chair" money actually puzzled me.

Mid-September rolled around. I said goodbye to my new friends at Horrell George and headed for River Falls.

College Years and
the Vietnam War

My college years were quite different from most students, especially early on. I attended Wisconsin State University at River Falls, Wisconsin. Today it is known as the University of Wisconsin at River Falls.

The difference was I was a nontraditional student. I started college at age twenty-one after serving three years active duty in the US Army. Adding to this nontraditional entry was my high school grades were horrific. I would not have been accepted at River Falls or any other institution of higher learning as a full time student right out of high school. As an eighteen-year-old high school graduate, I had zero motivation to improve my education unless it dealt with wrenches or farming.

I will always be indebted to the US Army for "growing me up" and helping me find my motivation, which was nonexistent in high school. My high school teachers to a person always encouraged me, and of course, I assured them that I would "pick up the pace" and do what I was capable of, but of course, I never did.

River Falls was "required" to accept me for at least one quarter as I was a veteran and the university was a state school obligated to give me a chance. For the record, I did very well that first quarter and every subsequent one and I was often on the honor roll.

I started school with no study habits as I had none from high school to carry over.

As a Veteran I was not required to live in the dorm as were traditional students and I believe that was a great plus, distractions were not a concern. I rented a room for a very nominal amount of money from a lady named Mrs. Tousley. She rented a room to two other students as well, Bill Currier and Al Roski, and the three of us became good friends. Neither Bill nor Al was a Veteran but they were upper classmen.

I knew I would need a part-time job and after about a month of establishing a routine and some semblance of study skills I started my search. Jerry's City Service was on the main road through River Falls and was my first attempt. Jerry hired me for $1.75 per hour. That was certainly an acceptable wage in a college town and I appreciated the opportunity to prove myself and be a productive employee for Jerry. He was more than willing to help me to schedule my hours around my class schedule which worked well for both of us.

Shortly after I stared working City Service changed its name to CITGO which is today BP (British Petroleum).

I worked as many hours as I possibly could and as Jerry's was also a full service garage, I rapidly moved from pumping gas to more and more technical skills as Jerry realized I was willing to tackle anything from oil changes to tune ups to engine changes and overhauls. My time at Ohearn Auto in Melrose and Bob's Mobil in New Baltimore, Michigan had served me well.

Of course I was a member of the Vets Club, and I also pledged and became a member of Phi Nu Chi Fraternity.

After a year of working for Jerry I drove a school bus for the River Falls Public School System and during my junior and senior years I served as a police officer with the River Falls Police Department.

My college days were full and extra time was nearly nonexistent.

To talk of my college years, I'd be very remiss not to write of my junior and senior year lodging.

I mentioned rooming with Mrs. Tousley, and later I spent a period of time rooming with my first boss, Jerry Wilkens, and his wife, Donna. From there Harry Peterson, Pat Cunningham, and I rented a mobile home.

My junior year Jack Pertz, Jim Huber, Duane (last name forgotten), and I rented a two-story, dilapidated farm home about five miles from town. Duane moved on and Harry Peterson moved in. For reasons forgotten, we named it the Chicken Farm.

We each paid seventeen dollars per month, which included heating oil and electricity. It was far from an upscale home but for four college guys with very little money and not caring about fancy it was just fine. The home was owned by a Saint Paul, Minnesota, fireman Dean Barenwald. The setting was great, high on a hill on a gravel road.

The four of us got along very well and we each came and went with friendly bantering. As I was a policeman, I might get home at about 3:30 a.m. and often Jack and Harry would be sitting around enjoying a post bar closing beer. It was great to catch up with them on recollections of the day and the latest craziness from a fellow fraternity brother. The stories at the least were legendary and at the most were scary when one reflects on some of the wildness of our youth.

One fraternity brother left his 1955 Chevrolet at the farm as he decided it was due for the junkyard. Jack and I got it running on a Sunday afternoon and decided it would be fun to wreck it. We wired the steering wheel straight, fired it up with the motor knocking and smoking. We had it in neutral, locked the foot feet to the floor and as it roared smoked and knocked one of us reached through the driver-side window, pushed the shifting lever into drive and watched the car fly across an open field headed at the woods. We found some sort of sadistic pleasure in watching it slam into the woods and the motor abruptly stop running. As the smoke and dust settled we had to run to it and check out the damage. Good fun? Then it sure was!

Ah, for the craziness of youth.

In my junior year, I was elected president of my fraternity, Ph Nu Chi, which required a degree of planning and time. As a full-time student, I had to find time to study. My duties as a new lieutenant with my National Guard unit were ever increasing. My company commander, Captain Jerry Matteson, was a PhD and professor at Wisconsin State University–River Falls, and I would meet with him nearly daily. My duties as a police officer were also ever increasing, and if I could ever work in an extra shift to earn extra money, I would sure do it. The $2.25 per hour made the difference of having extra money, and I had my eyes on buying a new Jeep Commando that had come out that year, and I had convinced myself I had to have one.

Rethinking that time frame in history as I write this some forty seven years later, I marvel at the contrast between the peaceful college town of River Falls and the world situation dominated by the Vietnam War. Carrying the contrast even further is the amazing difference of how our military is regarded today compared to the Vietnam era.

The growing discord at the time between those who supported the war effort and those who opposed it was a bubbling cauldron. The great tragedy was those in uniform were looked upon by a growing number as evil war mongers and the anger was growing predominately on college campuses. Young men were torn between serving their country and unlike previous wars that America had been involved in this one was increasingly controversial.

The draft was in full swing and young men not maintaining acceptable grades were losing that college deferment and soon drafted. Lengthy conversations, wherever and whenever soon got around to "the war." Arguably peaceful River Falls had nowhere near the issues as larger more liberal institutions of higher learning.

Demonstrations across the nation opposing the war were increasing. With each and every one more and more hatred was directed toward those in uniform. Both those in uniform and those opposing were the offspring of those who fought in WWII and Korea. Increasingly, colleges were eliminating their ROTC programs. Some draftees were fleeing to Canada rather than serve for a war they hated.

In Controversial wars in recent memory, i.e., Iraq and Afghanistan, one might oppose the war, but comments and signage was everywhere: "Support our troops." That was nonexistent in the mid and late 1960s and early seventies. Those returning from Vietnam, knowing they had done as their fathers before them were humiliated, spat upon, and called by many "baby killers."

Before Vietnam and once again since, our men and women in uniform are looked upon as the heroes that they are. For those of us who supported the Vietnam War effort have etched in our minds the ultimate insult to those serving. Widely distributed and applauded was the photo of popular Hollywood starlet and movie star Jane Fonda posing on the trigger of a North Vietnamese anti-aircraft weapon. It was the ultimate insult. People doing stupid things can usually be forgiven. I find no such ability in my heart for Ms. Fonda.

For reasons perhaps for more political than sensible, National Guard and Reserve units were not activated. Our infantry National Guard Unit Company A First Battalion, 128 Infantry Mechanized of the famed Thirty Second Red Arrow Division trained to deal with counter demonstrations against the war. America arguably was a powder keg.

Through all this, my resolve continued to return to active duty and serve in Vietnam. No, I certainly was not a warmonger. I simply believed it was my duty. I very proudly was ranger qualified, had served with pride on active duty as an enlisted man, and now was a recent graduate of Infantry OCS at Fort Benning, Georgia.

Only two issues remained, I needed to finish college and attend the Infantry basic course at Fort Benning, and I would be Vietnam-bound. Just one little caveat remained. I was growing more and more interested in Jenny Kondrasuk.

RIVER FALLS POLICE DEPARTMENT

The enjoyment of police work was solidly ingrained in me during my years as a River Falls Wisconsin Police Officer. I was the eighth officer hired on the department and from the first day I thoroughly enjoyed the work.

I was hired by Chief of Police Perry Larson, who remained a close friend until his passing in 2014. He taught me a great deal, but what he impressed on me more than any other one thing, was that "police work is 95 percent common sense." In my thirty years in law enforcement, I can assure you that I never had reason to question that.

When I was hired, it was because another officer had been "let go." I no longer remember his name. His nickname was Peaches. He apparently was released while still on probation. I related earlier that I was the eighth officer hired, but in fairness, it was because previous officer number eight had been released.

Apparently, "Peaches" lacked the common sense that was Chief Larson's major requirement. I remember two things about him that did not bode well. He was a very small man and his uniform seemed to hang on him. That type appearance would be similar to a definition from my friend Dan Ryan, "his clothes fit him like a sack of doorknobs."

Whenever you got in the squad car that "Peaches" was getting out of, coffee and cigarette ashes were everywhere. You, by now, can surmise that each of the other officers was having their issues with that very thing.

The icing on the cake was "Peaches" responding to a possible rabid animal on a lawn on Cascade Avenue in front of one of the college dorms. Apparently the animal was a mole, above ground and acting weird, not further described other than moles are typically underground. "Peaches" responds, pulls up with the squad car, red lights flashing, parks the car, grabs the twelve gauge and in front of fifty to one hundred college students, watching the stricken weird mole, with one shot of twelve gauge double 00 buckshot dispatches the mole. The students are aghast. Bad decision on the part of "Peaches" which reflected very poorly on the River Falls Police Department.

I had gotten to know Chief Larson, when I was a Lieutenant in the River Falls National Guard Unit. We had held several mutual training exercises between the Guard and the Police on how to deal with campus riots which were mounting nationwide due to the unrest over the War in Vietnam.

There was no police academy that I would be required to attend in 1967. My training was (OJT) on-the-job-training.

Officer Howie Miller took me to a gravel quarry and trained me in the fine art of using my 38 special revolver. I still remember his words "always be safe but don't be too quick to draw it."

Before an officer was released to patrol on his own, he was expected to ride with an experienced officer for about six months. Many a long night was shared with Sgt. Joe Creapo, sometimes Officer Vern Brown. Sometimes I was under the tutelage of Joe McCabe or Officer Carl Schrank.

Howie Miller was the training officer who was responsible for evaluating me. Each officer has a very different technique from the tenacity of Officer Gary Hauser, the laid back way of Joe Creapo, whose statement to me on a pouring rainy evening was "on a night like tonight you don't want to see or hear a damn thing," to Carl Schrank who had a very different approach to police work. Schrank was the inquisitive one and it was exciting to ride with him. Shrank loved making things happen. He was an outstanding officer. Working with him always had something happening. If it really got dull he'd make things happen. I like to think that I am somewhat mischievous, but I couldn't hold a candle to Schrank.

Our radio operator was retired long time Chief of Police Glen Young who became a great friend in my short two years as a River Falls Officer. Glen couldn't stand retirement and it took little, if any, coaxing for Chief Larson to hire Glen back as our radio operator. We all loved Glen but being pranksters at heart, goading him became a great pastime to Schrank and me, who formed a partnership and friendship, including the best man at my wedding, That lasted to the day of his passing.

I was the 7:00 p.m. to 3:00 a.m. shift officer, and Schrank was working 11:00 p.m. to 7:00 a.m. When the two of us were on during those hours and things got slow, "good clean fun" was our byword.

Glen would be in the office at 6:30 a.m., make coffee, and get the paper. By seven fifteen, his morning constitution kicked in, and we both knew that Glen's immediate need for the bathroom hit him five minutes before he'd fold up the newspaper and head for the men's room. Invariably if Schrank and I weren't on a call, we'd be at the top of the stairs grinning like children waiting for Glen to enter the men's room. Then, would come the, "those God damn kids again" roar as the men's room stall door was locked from the inside and Glen would have to crawl under, and more than once he didn't quite make it.

He would raise hell with Perry, "You've got to get the guys on the night shift to watch for those damn kids who keep locking the men's room stall." Somehow I think Perry knew it was us, but he never let on to Glen.

Glen was very proud of putting up the flag each morning, and winter in River Falls Wisconsin could be miserable. On sub-zero nights we would occasionally soak the area of the rope that was tightly tied to the base of the flag pole, making it extremely hard to untie, and as Glen warmed his hands back at the police department, he'd again admonish Perry to have the night guys "watch those damn kids that are pouring water on the flag pole knot."

It sure seemed funny when we did it but as I write this I feel very sheepish for being such a jerk. Sometimes humor is very different at age seventy than it was at twenty-three.

I loved listening to Glen relate police stories of days gone by. One of my all-time favorites was the police department getting its brand new 1953 Chevrolet squad car, which was a four door sedan, with the department's first automatic transmission. Back then, General Motors was new to the automatic transmission business as were most manufacturers. For whatever reason reverse was reached by pulling the column lever all the way down to the right. For all the years of the column shift for gear drive vehicles, this would be since about 1939, first gear was the very location, as it still is to this day on standard H pattern gear drive vehicles. The River Falls Police Department traded their 1950 Ford squad car their new Chevrolet.

Glen being very proud and very on the job had backed in beside Moody Chevrolet Garage on Main Street to show off the new squad to all the customers entering Moody's Showroom while also watching for speeders as well. It was approaching 3:00 p.m., and Glen would soon be relieved. It was also that time of day that folks, getting off work, could stop at Moody's to see the new arrivals.

According to Glen, the showroom had grown nearly to capacity at Moody's. Everyone had to check out the new 1953 Chevrolet in all its police regalia including spot light, red light, siren and the spiffy River Falls marque emblazoned on the door. It was parked adjacent to the showroom, occupied by then Chief of Police Glen Young watching for speeders, when fate stuck.

Traveling at what appeared to be a high rate of speed right in front of Glen was a dark colored large Buick automobile. Thinking of the safety of his citizens, he recalled to Schrank and me his thoughts, "you can't drive through my town like that." He pulled it into first the same way he had over all those years, flooring the new Chevrolet and launching it backward into the Kinikinic River. No one was hurt, save perhaps Glen's pride. Of course, it was the talk of the town for days to come. Yes, the Buick got away. Glen was the kind who could take a good ribbing and he certainly got one.

Glen swears that Moody's never charged the city for the wrecker to retrieve the squad from the river. They even gave the city their old squad as a loaner until they dried out the "new 1953 Chevrolet."

As the saying goes, "You can't make this stuff up."

Police work often has long lonely hours patrolling in a squad car. No, River Falls was not a Mayberry, but it was far from a Chicago or New York City as far as crime occurrences.

No one, no matter where you live, can truly recognize the importance of the slowly cruising marked police car. To the good citizens, it's a sense of calm and appreciation. To would be criminals, note will be taken. Perhaps we better pass on this criminal enterprise or at least try it in another city.

Though my years of police work appear to be behind me, my deep respect of the uniformed officer will always remain.

Chief Perry Larson was an exceptional officer and leader. He stood up for us when needed and never, I mean never, backed down when it came to standing up for his men and his department.

My six month "probationary assignment" was nearly complete, so I was allowed to patrol without a partner, and at about eight thirty one evening, I watched a motorist drive through a stop sign at an intersection that was notorious for accidents. I guess my ire was because he had not even attempted to slow down. Now technically, as I was still on probation, I was to stop him, politely explain the issue, and worst case write a "written warning" which literally, meant nothing. I intended only to politely explain his violation and let him go.

I guess it was the "Okay, Dick Tracy, what's up?" that turned my crank.

My response was, "Sir, you drove through that Stop sign. Could I see your driver's license please."

Of course he telegraphed his anger with every movement. He jerked the card from his wallet, shoved it through the window with "You do know who I am, right?"

I responded, "No, sir, but when I get back to the squad car, I will read it off your license."

As I seated myself back in the squad, my blood pressure was somewhat elevated, and I radio-called for a 10-27 on his name and date of birth and a 10-28 on his vehicle license. These are basic law enforcement identifier calls and to determine wants and warrants.

After 5:00 p.m., our radio calls were answered by the city water and sewer plant as there was someone on duty twenty-four hours per day. Typically the night shift operator was Roy Davis, and though I never met him, he did seem both methodical and cautious.

"PD504, you do know who he is, right?"

I, of course, responded with "Negative."

"504, he is on the City Council and Police and Fire Commission."

My response was simply "10-4." I wrote him a ticket, walked back to his car, and politely handed it to him.

His response was "You haven't heard the last of this" as he sped off.

Well, I expected Chief Perry to call me in the next day, and I wasn't let down. I came to the office at about 2:00 p.m., and both Schrank and Creapo were smiling when I knocked on Chief Perry's door. In my mind it was my last day as a River Falls Police Officer.

Chief Perry had me sit down, and he explained how this member of the Police and Fire Commission had come to his office at about 9:00 a.m. demanding I be fired. Schrank later related what happened next in far more detail that Chief Perry did, who simply told me that I had done the right thing no matter if he heard anything different on the street. I thanked the chief and left.

That evening Schrank was in grand form, explaining to me what really happened. Apparently, Schrank and Creapo were waiting to go to court and overheard the conversation that went something like, "I want the new guy fired."

Chief Perry said, "What did he do wrong, Councilman?"

"He wrote me a ticket for a Stop sign violation."

Chief Perry said, "Did you run the Stop sign?"

"Well, ya, but he hasn't been here six months yet."

Apparently at this point, Chief Perry blew up and, in no uncertain terms, ordered him out of his office with the culmination being that "if you want to press it further, you'll have my resignation before I fire him."

That was Perry, one hell of a chief.

In a college town, fair to say, at bar closing time in any town, you must be vigilant.

At 1:30 a.m., I stopped a car at the intersection of Cedar and Main, occupied by a rather large female driver. I asked for her driver's license and to step out of the car please. It was obvious she was hammered and she refused. I recognized her as a college student, or as Officer Vern Brown referred to all of us attending college as a "ra ra." Her car was blocking traffic, she wouldn't move her car and the eleven to seven officer was transporting a prisoner to Hudson and I had no choice. I had the radio operator call Chief Perry, which I hated to do, and within ten minutes he was there. By now we have some bystanders, which is never a good thing, especially if they are also just leaving the bars and are somewhat full of "joy juice."

How he got out of bed, in uniform and there so quickly, remains a puzzle. "Young lady, give me your license."

"No."

"Get out of the car."

"No."

The next happened so fast, to this day, I struggle to believe it. He had the door open, and the next thing I realized she was sitting on the pavement. Chief Perry's move at pulling her out was so quick I could hardly believe it. He handcuffed her, moved her car to the side of the road, and locked it. His next comment was, "When Schrank gets back, you guys take her to Hudson. Impound the car. I am going back to bed."

By now she was a little more cooperative and sat in my squad car to stay warm as we waited for Schrank. When Schrank arrived and I explained who I had in the squad and the charges, he was ecstatic. He had been trying to catch her leaving the bars for weeks without success.

After we booked her in St. Croix County and traveled back to River Falls, he couldn't stop grinning and carrying on about how lucky we were to get her. His attitude helped, but I was ashamed that I needed the chief to come to my aid with a drunken female.

Every community has its perverts. River Falls was no exception.

We had a window peeker, and for months, we had been trying to get him identified. Through the winter months, he had become increasingly emboldened. Schrank decided from the vague descriptions of the car that he had a pretty good idea who it was. The man was a prominent member of the community, and several of the other officers refused to believe that it could be him. Yet Schrank became more and more convinced that it was him. He and I agreed that when we were working together, we'd set him up.

Literally the next evening at about 1:00 a.m., a fearful lady notified the police that she thought someone was looking in her window. Our agreement was that I would respond to that residence and Schrank would hide himself in the area where he believed our suspect lived. His residence was a nonpretentious, modest home in a nice area of River Falls. Shortly after I arrived at the distraught lady's residence, Schrank observed our suspect come flying down the residential street where our guy lived and right into his garage.

The good news was we now knew who our bad guy was, and the following day at our officers' meeting, Schrank had no problem convincing the rest of us that he had been right all along. We really needed a plan to get this guy.

Now, do understand a window peeker is not the most heinous crime in the world. It became a news worthy event as more and more women were becoming fearful. It was being talked about at the PTO meetings, the social service organizations, and in general conversation at coffee shops. Perry was getting flack, "Why can't your guys catch that window peeker?" We never knew what area he'd hit, and with only two squads on at a time, it was a challenge.

Simultaneously to the window peeker we started getting calls about a wand waver, the police slang for someone exposing themselves. It was not the same guy. This guy was midtwenties, so Officer Vern Brown immediately decided that it was one of the "ra-ras," slang for college student, as I previously stated.

Less than a week later he was identified by a lovely young woman who worked as a checker at the local grocery store. Apparently as he came through the line with his groceries and as she grabbed each time with her left hand, and keyed the cash register with her right hand, our exposer laid his sex organ on the counter top. As she reached for the next item she panicked and screamed and out the door he ran, but fortunately, positively identified. The interview with sweet little Tammy, our checker, will remain with me always as she described the incident during our interview of her—"And I touched it"—she wailed while placing her hands over her face. Consoling her was no easy task. It shocked her to the core. And yes, he was a "ra-ra."

Back to our late night prominent citizen's escapades, by now the community seems aware of our suspicions, yet it's spoken about only in whispers. College communities are unique. The town people are very welcoming but yet their community is still their community.

We now realize we probably won't catch him in the act. Perhaps the best we can do is cause him adequate embarrassment to give up his antics or find another town. Let's face it, this guy needed some psychological help and quite honestly I think he honestly enjoyed the cat and mouse with the police.

He struck again at 2:00 a.m., and Schrank and I were ready. I responded to the complaint and this time Schrank set up radar on the lonely long street into his subdivision. Bingo, Schrank got him at seventy-eight miles per hour in a twenty-five zone. Local news did him in. The police beat reported in a local newspaper: Why were the police setting up radar on basically deserted John Street at 2:00 a.m. You don't have to be the brightest bulb in the circuit to figure that out, and the community certainly did.

To add his own insult to further injury, he decided to fight the ticket on the grounds that the police were wasting resources by running radar in a quiet residential neighborhood. I wasn't there when he appeared before Judge Bowles, who was a story in himself. The judge, very well educated and bright, was significantly crippled from his fighter-plane crashing during the Korean War.

Because he was hunched over, he looked up at those appearing before him. Our window peeker suffered the full wrath of the judge dressing him down. Of course it was all public record and reported nearly verbatim in the local paper. One has to wonder why he didn't simply pay his fine and stipulate his speeding guilt.

Over coffee, Perry was congratulated for his officers catching the window peeker. It was always with a wink and a nod. Surprisingly the window peeking ended in River falls.

Shortly thereafter, I left for the FBI and somewhere along the line I heard that Ellsworth and Hudson started having an issue with window peekers. Go figure, Hudson was nine miles away and Ellsworth was fourteen.

My experiences with the River Falls Police Department would not be complete without sharing working with Officer Joe Mcabee. Joe was a very large man, not fat in any way, simply a very big man, accordingly very intimidating. I enjoyed working with Joe as he was a very aggressive officer.

One evening, while both of us were in the same car, Joe was taking me to areas in and around River Falls where I had not previously been. Of course, these were parking spots for the young lovers and Joe loved to rout them.

We came upon a car that appeared unoccupied. As we approached the car, Joe with the largest flashlight I had ever seen, shining it down on the back seat, lay two young lovers sound asleep and naked as jaybirds. Joe banging on the window, brought them startling awake. As the young lady tried to cover herself, Joe checked their IDs. With that completed, Joe roared away straight for the local Dairy Queen, bought two ice cream cones, handed them to me and back we roared. As we arrived they were nearly dressed, Joe handed them the cones with the profound comment, "here, this will help you cool off."

I am told that several years later that young man became a River Falls Police Officer.

The year 1969 was a big one for me. In fairness, it was a big year for our nation as well.

On July 20, Carl Shrank and I were on duty and we stopped for supper at the Kinnikinic Café, a popular stop for those of us on duty. The owner Dale, never charged us for coffee and we were welcome even at 3:00 a.m. If Dale's car was there, he was, and he welcomed us. But I digress. On this night, we were watching Neil Armstrong step onto the moon's surface. This is certainly history in the making. The famous comment of Armstrong's, "One small step for man, one giant step for mankind" will live in infamy.

There has been much written about this great event. Sadly, there are those naysayers who denied that there even was a moon landing. There are also many stories told that probably can't be substantiated. My all-time favorite was a story that through the years has gained a life of its own.

Allegedly, as Armstrong and Aldrin returned to the lunar module, Armstrong said, "Good luck, Mr. Gorski." Due to everything going on, the comment wasn't questioned at the time. If it was thought about, mission control perhaps thought Gorski was a Russian Astronaut that Armstrong had befriended along the way.

Due to his famous comment about a giant step for mankind, whenever asked about the Gorski comment, Armstrong would often segue to his walk on the moon's surface. Simply put, he avoided the question for years.

Shortly before his death in 2012, when again queried about his "Good luck, Mr. Gorski" comment, Armstrong allegedly said, "Well, I guess I can share it with you as the Gorskis have long ago passed away."

While growing up in a small Ohio town, at about age twelve, he and a group of young boys were playing sand lot soft ball. It was just starting to get dark, and Armstrong was playing outfield. A long ball was hit into neighbor Gorski's backyard. As Armstrong ran to retrieve the ball, he allegedly heard Mrs. Gorski through the back window say rather loudly to Mr. Gorski, "Sex, all you talk about is sex. I'll tell you when you'll get your sex, when the kid next door walks on the moon." No, I can't document the truth, but I sure do enjoy the story.

RANGER

Throughout my first three years of college, there was little doubt that I would return to active duty in the Army as an Infantry Officer.

In the fall of 1966 (November 22, to be exact), I reported to the Harmony Church area of Fort Benning, Georgia, to begin the ranger course. It was my hope to go on to OCS shortly after ranger school and earn my commission as a second lieutenant, wearing the coveted ranger tab on my left shoulder upon graduation from Wisconsin State University at River Falls. I had just completed my fall quarter and timing was perfect to drop out of school for a quarter.

Leaving the regular Army in July of 1965, I was a sergeant E-5. I carried that rank with me when I joined the River Falls, Wisconsin National Guard Unit, Company A, First Battalion, 128th Infantry, mechanized, a part of the famed Red Arrow Division. Early in 1966 I was promoted to staff sergeant E-6, which is the rank I carried at the time of ranger school.

In my application for ranger training, I learned that I must be able to swim fifty meters in combat gear. The University had an Olympic-sized pool so I would go there in the evenings and practice swimming, wearing my fatigues and combat boots. Though I no longer remember her last name, a wonderful young woman Sharon, who was a gifted swimmer, helped me accomplish my goal.

Somewhere along the way, I learned that if, during the test, I dropped my rifle, I could still qualify for the course if I were able to complete the designated distance. A dropped rifle meant you had three pieces of luminous tape instead of two stitched to the back of your patrol cap, to designate you as a weak swimmer, meaning a strong swimmer was always to be behind you, patrolling in the swamp when you might simply disappear in water over your head especially at night.

Two hundred eighty-four soldiers fell in ranks early on that November day. Though not known at the time, only eighty-one of us would graduate in late February 1967.

Though most of us were Army, we had many allied soldiers training with us, along with several Marines and Air Force members as well.

We were assigned a "ranger buddy." Mine was Captain Bill Pendleton, a member of the Eighty-Second Airborne Division. Bill was one hell of a soldier and I've lost all contact with him over the years. We were only "buddies" for about three weeks, but in that short time I developed the deepest appreciation for this professional infantryman whose greatest concern was not having a college degree. Bill knew that as long as the Vietnam War was raging he would be fine, but what would happen to him when the War was over. It is an unanswered question as I write this.

We were all required to meet the company commander, Captain Peter Meyer. We were required, as ranger buddies, to bang on his door, were ordered to enter, we were to crash through the door and come to attention before the CO's desk.

Bill and I banged on the door, were ordered to enter, and as we crashed through the doorway side by side we locked ourselves literally in the doorway and both started laughing, big, big mistake. The amount of time we spent in the front leaning rest position, and the number of push-ups we did, I no longer remember. It was many and fair to say we slowed the process for the rest who needed to meet with the CO.

Though acting tear ass, I will always believe he and his fellow cadre laughed themselves silly over two fearful new rangers locking themselves in the CO's doorway.

The concept of ranger training specifically is to learn to operate behind enemy lines or on your own without support. The principle training vehicle is physical exhaustion. Then, being exhausted get a patrol group together consisting of other exhausted men and accomplish a mission.

Food was nearly nonexistent, sleep was even scarcer, yet we drove on. Each ranger would be required to pass four patrols being offered up to six in order to graduate with four passed. Attention to detail and physical stamina meant everything. I vividly recall several hulks of men that I felt would breeze through the course, each in their late twenties or early thirties, who washed out. Their bodies would not recover near as fast as mine as age twenty-two. Sergeant F W Brown a Marine, was an exception. He was, for two reasons: he wouldn't quit and he was so highly respected that any of us with any extra to give would fall in beside Browny and help drag him along when it really got tough. I recall he was thirty seven. The reality is that it's much like an aged football player. The reason Pendleton and I were split up after a couple of weeks was, though no rank is displayed, someone in their infinite wisdom decided that officers shouldn't be buddied with enlisted. My new ranger buddy was Freddy J. Lewis, an African American, also a staff sergeant. F J, as he was known, was also one hell of a soldier and to this day we stay in touch. He also was a member of the Eighty-Second Airborne and had been wounded in the Dominican Republic uprising several years earlier.

I distinctly recall how hard I worked to achieve the honor of attending ranger school and my dedication would never allow me to "wash out" if I could do anything about it.

All West Point graduates are required, as I understand, to attend ranger training or airborne training. Airborne, if they are to be assigned to an arborne unit, otherwise they must attend ranger school. They are not required to graduate, and this was my first taste of West Pointers. I was hugely disappointed. I had held these folks in the highest esteem. I believe that most of them deserve that. My disappointment was the number of sandbaggers who literally flunked out of ranger school rather than try to earn the Tab. The swimming test was most evident. I have little doubt that every West Pointer could swim well. Perhaps, if they had no desire to make the Army a career, they simply didn't care. It went against everything I believed in.

To this day, the training I received to win the ranger tab is the toughest thing I've ever done, and most likely ever will do. The unbelievable hunger, lack of sleep, forced marches, planning, and carrying out patrols was totally consuming.

It was not uncommon at all to see men hallucinate and try to stick a quarter into a tree to get a coke. If you didn't experience, it I don't think you can believe it. Ask any ranger, they will bear me out. The patrol would halt, the man in front of you would fall asleep standing up.

I remember being so hungry that I believed I would have given away my 1964 Chevelle in return for food at one point. Physical items mean nothing when you are starving.

We learned to live off the land. Kill and eat snakes was not uncommon but usually was done by a "lane grader" instructor. We were occasionally air dropped live chickens. We were taught how to prepare them and cook them in fifty caliber ammo boxes. Again, the training had a specific purpose. How to stay alive and outwit your enemy was constantly driven home. The lane graders most important objective, if he saw just the slightest weakening, was to get us to quit. I would have completely collapsed long before I ever would quit.

Coming out of the swamp onto high ground at approximately 0400 that late day in February 1967, I believed I could have stopped bullets with my bare hands. One of only eighty one who had successfully led four patrols and passed every milestone, I was now a ranger.

I reflected over all I had learned during those compressed nine weeks. From the demanding physical training in the Harmony Church area, to the mountain phase in Dahlonega, Georgia, where much of our survival skills were honed, other than total exhaustion, I completely ate it up. Learning to rappel off mountains, carrying your ranger buddy, learning more about knots than a twenty year Seaman, and most of all learning of the endurance of the human body was an experience that words simply cannot capture.

Leaving the beautiful yet exhausting Dahlonega for our final three weeks in the Okefenokee Swamps outside of Eglin Air Force Base Florida, encompassing 438,000 acres, would be our final test.

I never was before, nor doubt I ever will be again, so soaking wet for such prolonged periods of time. It was drilled home over and over; get your feet dried, powdered and dry socks whenever you could.

We would tie our rung out wet socks to the upper most framework of our forty-plus-pound rucksack, which was always as close as our rifle, while trying to capture whatever ray of sunlight or warmth that could possibly dry them and us.

Reflecting back, most of our injury losses occurred in the Florida phase. Between the cypress knees, a one to two foot high tree stump growing under water to crash into your knees, to the eye injuries that were constant from the foliage always slapping your face, not falling to injury was very consuming. Should you be injured and you didn't wash out, you were recycled to a class behind you, or however many classes you needed to fall behind for your injury to heal.

I would pull my field cap as close to the tops of my eyes as possible then cup the bill of it to make it very difficult for a branch to get my eyes. Somehow I made it without being injured to the point that would set me back.

Ranger training is the ultimate test of a man and it remains to this day my proudest accomplishment. Over 280 of us started on November 2, 1966, with eighty-one graduating at five in the morning on February 13, 1967. Graduation culminated a seventeen-mile force march, each of us had passed at least four graded evaluations as we were placed in leadership positions with virtually no food or sleep for days. And we were expected to prepare and patrol, order, and execute a successful mission by leading men who also had no food or sleep for days. Most of our operations were at night. From Camp Darby, seventeen miles from Fort Benning to the Mountain Ranger Camp at Dahlonega, Georgia, to Okefenokee Swamp near Elgin AFB Florida, we tested our own character as well as those around us.

It was during this that I learned what men were made of. We were a combination of enlisted men and officers, from all branches of the American military as well as allied soldiers from all over the world. No rank was worn and some of the best leaders often were junior in rank.

We came out of the swamp that cold February morning after an all-night patrol. Graduation was a ranger, pinning the coveted ranger tab on our left shoulder. We loaded the buses and headed back to the Harmony Church area of Fort Benning. I'm sure we were asleep before the buses began to move.

Once we arrived I gathered my gear, said my good-byes, drove twenty miles out the front gate of Fort Benning, checked into a motel, and slept for the next twenty hours. I had made it and I was proud. I returned to college for one quarter. I then turned around that summer and headed back to Fort Benning to attend Infantry OCS.

As we said our goodbyes, FJ asked me if I could loan him fifty dollars. My best buddy, FJ Lewis—I would have given him the shirt off my back. I loaned him the fifty, we exchanged addresses, promised to stay in touch, shook hands, and off we went on our separate ways. FJ had become very special to me as did all ranger buddies. We looked out for each other along the way.

One night, while in the mountains of Dahlonega, Georgia, the lane graders decided to go administrative due to severe cold. Water was literally freezing in canteens. When you are sweating humping hills, with heavy rucksacks, completely exhausted, fingers freezing, toes doing the same, someone on high must have feared for our safety. Going administrative only happens if it's a life-and-death issue. No matter, we accepted the opportunity to collapse as close to the fire as possible. We had been trained to put on our ponchos and sit in a fetal position with a candle burning in our lap, head and neck exposed. The lane graders nixed it, fearing that our exhaustion would cause us to fall asleep and rangers would be badly burned.

Snuggle with your ranger buddy. It was exactly what we did. FJ and I wrapped our ponchos around the two of us, and fair to say, our body heat kept us going. By morning, when the weather broke, there we were, men who had been burned, had to be evacuated. It was our only time going administrative, and there is little doubt lives would have been lost had someone on high not made the call. It kept us alive, and FJ and I kidded about sleeping together. I learned to appreciate body heat.

In 1995 four rangers in training froze to death in the swamps of Northern Florida. I'm sure some heads rolled for whoever failed to call for going administrative. There is a time for tough training and seeing what the human body is capable of, there is also a time for common sense. This was that time.

Somehow FJ and I lost touch with each other. In 2012, out of the clear blue, I got a call from him. He wondered if I remembered the fifty dollars he owed me. To express the elation of hearing from him would be difficult. Jen and I met him at Hilton Head, North Carolina, in the summer of 2015. Reminiscing with a long-lost friend leaves me at a loss. The good news is we reconnected. FJ had a remarkable military career retiring at master sergeant E-8. He shared some of his Vietnam combat experiences with Jen and me. "FJ, please write that book."

The tab and being an infantry officer meant a great deal to me. I knew that at this time in history, commissioned officers were making captain within two years of commissioning. I wanted to lead men and believed I could do it well. A war was going on and I wanted a part in it. I truly felt it was my duty and I was trained. To tear myself away and become an FBI agent was one of the most difficult decisions of my life.

Realistically, Jenny was beginning to play a big part in my life and though she was prepared to be an Army Officer's wife, we both knew that life was somewhat more stable as the wife of an FBI agent. It would be more stable on a marriage and better for kids, which we someday hoped to have.

To this day Jenny is convinced I would have died in Vietnam.

I went on to Infantry OCS in the summer of 1967 which was a cake walk after attending ranger school. By now I was there, a ranger qualified infantry officer.

Someone, years ago, told me that every day a person makes decisions but they make only five to ten really important decisions in their life, whether to go to college, who to marry, what career to follow to name but a few. Unquestionably the biggest decision of my life was to leave the Army and becomes an FBI agent. I knew either path was honorable, and I would love it; the decision came down to compatibility with married life.

I have no way of knowing what truly helps a person come to a definitive decision but in my case, I choose to believe it is divine intervention.

For reasons I don't recall I visited an old soldiers' home in Tomah, Wisconsin, a bunch of old retired guys with walls full of medals but no families to share these stories or their love with. I think it was the catalyst that pushed me to the FBI.

Somehow I was smart enough at that young age to recognize that the years would go on, with luck I'd go with them. I couldn't fathom growing older alone. As it turned out, I married up. Way up!

Part of my bucket list was to someday return to the Mountain Ranger Camp for a visit. Jen and I traveled again to Hilton Head for a weeklong stay in February 2017. One of our day activities was to travel to Atlanta, Georgia and visit an old friend of Jenny's. Well, Dahlanega was only about sixty miles northwest.

Knowing that visitors were not part of ranger training, I contacted Camp Merrill, which is now the name of the Mountain Phase Training Center. The young specialist that answered told me there was now a guest house and an apartment was available for seventy dollars a night. Needless to say, Jen and I knew where we'd spend the night. We spent the evening at the Overhang Bar/Restaurant now at the facility for the benefit of the ranger cadre. Realizing that it was fifty years to the month that I had graduated was the icing on the cake. Waitress Peggy, SFC Dan Deen, and several other rangers swapped stories of how it now is compared to "my day." Not much has changed, it's still a butt kicker. The camp maintains a museum which is one of the Quonset hut's used for housing Eight Rangers, similar to the ones from my day.

It was a lot of nostalgia but certainly a great experience to visit and numerous memories swept through my mind. Waking the next morning in our guest room to sheets of sleet and ice certainly took me back to fifty years earlier when I experienced those elements without the benefit of finding the warmth of a building or car. It kind of sent chills up my spine for those young rangers out in it all. I'm just so glad I had the opportunity to go back and once again experience the nostalgia of a fifty-year-old memory.

MEETING JENNY

My friend and roommate, Pat Cunningham, and I would often go to Mass at 5:00 p.m. on Thursdays at the Newman Center Chapel during my junior or senior years at River Falls. Often in attendance was that cute little brunette that I first saw in a one credit "social dance" class that I was taking. A certain number of "elective" courses were required and as I've been blessed with two left feet I thought social dance would be fun.

I was really trying to get acquainted with her, but try as I would in class, she was constantly paired with someone else. If I could just make eye contact maybe I could display some sort of interest. Simply put, I'm sure she knew I was staring though I was trying to be cool. I just was getting nowhere.

I'm definitely interested, and of course, I share with Pat my interest. Oh, he had to tell me that he had heard that she was dating a lieutenant in the Army who was soon to ship out for Vietnam. My prior service experience and being a new second lieutenant in the National Guard, I had very little time for "Jody."

Every active duty soldier and veteran knows of "Jody" the imaginative guy back home who steals your girlfriend while you are deployed in some far off land. Nope—I'll never be a "Jody." Most marching songs had to rub it in that "Jody" was stealing your girl. They went something like this (all sung in cadence while marching):

> Ain't no use in looking down, Jody's got your gal
> and gone
> Ain't no sense in feeling blue, Jody got your sister
> too

Hey, hey, Sergeant Hardy, Jody's home and stealing the party.

They went on and on and never helped a homesick GI.

Somewhere along the way, I learn that her name is Jenny. I really don't know that there is a guy in her life, and I really do need to find out. There is something of her indifference to me that makes me very inquisitive. I've never been a wallflower, and I've always gone the extra mile to meet someone.

No luck with Jenny. She just seems totally elusive. I see her around campus with her friend whose name I learned was Alice. That has to be my in road. Alice is also in Social Dance and I'm finally paired with her. In my effort not to be stepping on her feet, I express to her my interest in her friend Jenny. Of course, she tells me that she is seeing a soldier, Denny, but she doesn't know how serious they are.

She commented, "Why don't you ask her out?"

Why didn't I think of that? Or perhaps I had but the "Jody" thing was hindering me?

The following Thursday Pat and I went to Mass and wouldn't you know it, no Jenny. Maybe I can get a chance to ask her at class. Simply put, it just didn't happen. I just couldn't get to her, and when class was over, she was gone. Dang it!

The following Thursday I confessed to Pat that the biggest reason I was going to Mass was to meet Jenny. We both enjoyed a chuckle.

Following Mass, I was hot on her trail, and catching up with her, I blurted, "Hi, Jenny, my name is Jim."

"I know who you are" was her smiling response.

I was looking perplexed, and she pointed out my green tennis shoes. At the time an accepted collegiate shoe was colored tennis shoes. I know unequivocally that I had the only pair of olive drab ones of the three thousand students on campus.

The good news was, she stopped and talked. I was very perplexed that identifying the guy with the olive drab tennis shoes was Jim Sacia. My inquisitive mind became engrossed in that thought. A confession is in order.

Some years prior at River Falls, a group of military veterans attending the school formed a secretive group that only appeared at homecoming. Their purpose, I will defend, was solely to create good fun and much mystery. They always were pulled in the parade in a livestock manure spreader as they blew those plastic trumpets surrounding a beer keg. Their dress was gray sweatpants, sweatshirts, and a black hood completely concealing their identity. Ah, the "Dirty Dozen." One never knew where they would appear during homecoming week, and I believe even the administration recognized that they were a positive fixture to the homecoming week activities, as were the local police.

I have little doubt that they were carefully watched. One activity that could be counted on was the annual "panty raid" at Hegstead Hall, which was the girls' dorm; no men allowed except in the lounge. Of course, the abbreviated name for the dorm was "Hag" Hall. The raid was typically at about midnight, and all twelve would run through the entire dorm seeking women's underclothes to tie to the manure spreader during the parade. Good fun, oh ya, good fun! How do I know so much about them? Well, of course, I was one, never thinking my tennis shoes would give me away. Apparently, the young lady I was attempting to impress knew that this klutz was the guy who scared the h—— out of her as she was wakened from a sound sleep as "the dozen" came storming through the dorm and the guy in the olive drab tennis shoes stole a bra from her top center drawer.

She was laughing as I stuttered and stammered and turned many shades of red. I somehow mustered the courage to ask her out for Saturday night only to be refused. She offered the excuse that she was flying to San Francisco to visit her friend Cheryl as it was beginning quarter break.

Well, I guess that was a plausible excuse and not a complete blow-off. She left the door open for another opportunity. Getting to know and see Jenny was an interesting challenge.

Jenny returned from San Francisco after quarter break and seeing her at Mass I asked for a date to an upcoming Fraternity Costume

Party. She graciously accepted and as the weeks went on I found more and more excuses and reasons and time to see her.

She remained noncommittal on her friend back home who soon would leave for Vietnam. The more we dated, and the more serious we got conversations started "what if." Was there a future for us? It was becoming more and more apparent to me that this was the girl I wanted to marry. I needed to know my standing.

Jenny, by now, knew of my desire to return to active duty and her life would be that of a military wife. We all remember how the engagement goes down, and mine is almost too embarrassing to share, but here goes:

Jenny talked very little of the boy in Gilman, her home town. Yet I knew he existed. I had been talking more and more with Jenny of my future plans. Could she be an Army officer's wife? Could she deal with my going to Vietnam, which would be a given? Could she deal with a lifetime of never having deep, deep roots in a community due to constant transfers? Yes, marriage was on the table.

As our talks had gotten very serious, Jenny was going home for a weekend. She told me when she came back she would have an answer for me.

I vividly recall a warm day in River Falls, obviously a Sunday afternoon. I am lying on the grass studying. Jenny quietly snuck up on me with a big smile. Yes, I was the lucky guy. She broke it off with the guy back home.

This lady that I have fallen in love with is willing to accept a life style not at all compatible to what I'm sure had been her dreams for her life. It speaks volumes of her as it does to this day.

My mother went with me to pick out Jenny's ring. Being the klutz I was, though I must have had some input on what Jenny would like, I wanted to surprise her.

By now Jenny is realizing that my time with her is so limited, too much so for young lovers.

Jenny and her friend Patty had gotten an apartment on Charlotte Street and I can find a few moments with her by stopping by and eating with her on my shift breaks from my police duties.

How to give Jenny the ring: will she marry me? No, I didn't get down on one knee. I took her my basket of laundry which she had graciously agreed to do for me and I put the little box containing the engagement ring in the basket of laundry.

We ate dinner together, and off I went to the Police Department. I so vividly recall putting the ring in the basket of laundry but I have no recall of how she accepted. She must have, as it's forty-six years later, and we are happily married. Well, usually happily. Like all relationships, we have our moments.

There is little doubt that I married up. There has to be something very special in a woman who accepted a proposal of marriage from a basket of dirty laundry.

I bought Jenny several books obtained from the PX at Fort McCoy, where I would often be for drills and other training. The books were on becoming a military wife, protocols for an Army officer's wife—the list goes on.

REGRETS

"Regrets, I've had a few, but then again, too few to mention." Words from a famous song by "Old Blue Eyes" himself, Frank Sinatra, pretty much sum up my thoughts on life. It's fair to say, there is one that will follow me to my grave.

Those who have experienced infantry combat will shake their head in disbelief. The reality is I will never shake not going to Vietnam. From the time I finished my three year Army enlistment, July 23, 1965, a gnawing was in the back of my mind. Simply put, I really enjoyed the Army.

My total and complete intention from that day, as I drove from my final duty assignment with the Twenty-Eighth Artillery Group, a NIKE Hercules Missile Unit in Detroit, Michigan, to my home in rural Melrose, Wisconsin, was to return to active duty.

I had already been accepted for the fall quarter at Wisconsin State University in River Falls, Wisconsin. My intention was to get my degree, get a commission and make it happen. I had already contacted Bill Junkman, the AST at the Mechanized Infantry National Guard Unit in River Falls and Bill assured me I could keep my Sergeant E-5 rank and there certainly would be a spot for me.

Bill was a Chief Warrant Officer W-4 and was literally in overall charge of that National Guard Facility. Bill was one of those people who come in and go out of your life with little fanfare. He did so much for me, and I failed to appreciate it until I started writing this in earnest.

Bill had passed away in 2010 and only from his obituary did I learn of his heroics during WWII including receiving the Silver Star, our nation's third highest honor for valor in combat. He not only found me a spot in the Unit, he recognized that I needed a part-time job to help pay for college.

He questioned me, "Would you like to drive a school bus?"

I responded, "Of course."

Next question was, "How old did you say you are?"

My response was, "Twenty-one."

Bill said, "Twenty-five, that's good."

"No, Bill, twenty-one."

Bill said, "Twenty-five, remember that."

I could be licensed as a school bus driver at twenty-one, but the River Falls District had a policy of twenty-five. I'm a slow learner, but I did catch on. I passed the test, and nothing further was ever said.

Bill, along with my Company Commander, Captain Jerry Matteson, helped me weave my way through obstacles to achieve the opportunity to attend ranger school. I was flabbergasted and had no idea that a National Guardsman could attend the Army's elite ranger school. In November of 1966 I was on my way. Graduating in February 1967, I had only missed the winter quarter of college and was back in time for spring quarter.

With the coveted ranger tab on the left shoulder of my military uniform, guard drills brought me a mystique of a career bound soldier. Once again Bill and Captain Matteson were at my side helping me to arrange a spot in an upcoming Infantry OCS Class at Fort Benning, Georgia. Once again, out of college for a short while to go back to Fort Benning and receive my Commission. With the benefit of hindsight, I find it amazing that with the help of these two great officers, I was able to structure my future in the Army with all the pieces of the puzzle falling in place.

In 1966 and 1967 of course the Vietnam War was raging. Now as a highly motivated ranger qualified infantry lieutenant, I can't wait to get back on active duty.

Some will read this with, "Is this guy out of his mind?" He has his military obligation behind him, and he wants to go back? Yes. I really did. At that point in my life, it was exactly what I wanted. I knew I was still two years from obtaining that degree, and more than once I strongly considered dropping out of school and returning to active duty.

Again the advice of my two great mentors, Captain Matteson and CWO Junkman, helped keep me grounded. "Get that degree now, Jim. You can always return to active duty." I knew they were right, but there was a war raging, and I believed it was where I belonged.

No, I'm not a warmonger, but I was a highly trained junior officer something that the Army desperately needed. Simply put I fought myself to keep my focus on my college studies. There is an old saying, "Life is what happens while you're making other plans," and sure enough, that is what happened to me. Two significant events changed my ultimate decision.

For those of us who remember those Vietnam era years, we remember the unbelievable divide in this country. There were those who supported the war and truly believed that we were stopping the spread of communism throughout the world. There were also those who felt quite the opposite. There was very little middle ground, and yes, I was a strong, very strong, supporter of our being there. College campuses saw the worst of it.

Draft age young people in institutions of higher learning kept the caldron boiling. River Falls was not a liberal place. Like all college campuses, demonstrations were commonplace. One particular fall afternoon in 1967, a group was marching and carrying signs against the war. I walked into the middle of the pack, grabbed, and busted every sign. I was boiling mad. I guess with hindsight, it was good that it was a peaceful demonstration as nobody took a swing at me. Of course, I would have swung back.

The demonstrations grew in intensity around America, and the National Guard trained with local police to deal with these incidents that grew more and more like riots and less and less like demonstrations. Because of this close coordination between the Guard and local police, I became acquainted with River Falls chief of police Perry Larson, who asked if I'd like to become a policeman. He assured me he could structure my hours to fit with my college studies. Becoming a policeman was the first issue that started changing my life's path.

Because of becoming a policeman, I became acquainted with the FBI agent covering River Falls, who encouraged me to apply to the FBI.

The second issue was meeting Jenny. As our relationship matured it became apparent that Jenny would certainly stick with me through thick and thin. I bought her books on being a military officer's wife and did all I could to help her understand that there would be long periods of separation. She was accepting but there was little doubt that she so favored a more stable relationship. Realizing that "I could always return to active duty" pushed me toward the FBI.

As I write elsewhere, I could not have had a more wonderful career. "Left or right at Oak Street," I could not do both. To this day whenever we talk of it, even after forty-eight years of marriage, Jenny is convinced I would have died in Vietnam.

I am convinced that my training as an infantry leader would have not only kept me alive but those I would have been leading as well.

It's an unanswered question, but it will always be the one regret of my life.

TRANSITION—ARMY TO FBI

The transition from the life I had chosen as an Infantry Army Officer to becoming a special agent with the FBI, in retrospect, seems totally surreal. Throughout my college years there was little doubt that I would return to active duty with the US Army.

It, of course, never would have happened had I not met Special Agent Gene Sather, the resident agent from the Eau Claire Resident Agency of the FBI. Perry knew that Gene would be in River Falls and contacted me, though I was not on duty, to come to the police department and meet Gene. Perry's hope of course was that I would stay in law enforcement though I had not seriously considered it.

It did get me thinking. As I've stated previously, the thought process was that I could always return to active duty, the FBI may only come around once. So I trudged on but now my mind is working differently. Me, an FBI agent? No way, I've always thought them to be, if I had ever even thought of them, some nebulous characters from Chicago or New York. I had also heard from someone along the way that agents had to be attorneys or accountants and Gene "nipped that one in the bud" as soon as I mentioned it.

"No way, Jim, most agents are like me, a four-year college degree along with three years professional experience in a leadership role or as an investigator." Gene went on to say that only a small number of agents were accountants or lawyers, but they were always in demand.

I just couldn't get my arms around it, a small town farm kid from North Bend Wisconsin, could become an FBI agent. Still the Vietnam War was raging, and I so felt that with my training, love of the Army and desire to do my part, compelled me to return to active duty. Left or right at Oak Street. It goes back to my recognizing only about five to ten decisions in your life, among the thousands you make every day, are actually life changing. With all the cards on the table, I agreed with Gene to "at least submit an application." The large ship is starting to change course. Could I really be thinking this way?

As I pondered my decision over several days, I drove home to visit my mom and dad. They were both proud of my military accomplishments and were somewhat shocked that I was considering another path. My brother Tom was in Vietnam and I knew it bothered both mom and dad, but mom especially. I don't think she ever missed a day writing to Tom and many years later he shared with me how meaningful her letters were. Tom was in a line outfit assigned to a Duster which is a track vehicle poorly armored and having two .40 mm guns. It gave my parents great concern.

Not everyone in life is as blessed as me with having great parents, as I look back over my life, is far more meaningful now than when I was a young man. The one thing I knew for sure was they always had good advice. My dad was a great one to share anecdotes to make his point. As a storyteller and as a salesman, there were none better.

As we sat at the kitchen table and as I poured out my feelings, now involving Jenny as well as me, I could see their minds churning, wanting to give me only the very best advice.

Dad leaned back in his chair and said, "Jim, do you remember when I sold Guy Johnson a water heater?"

Well, of course, I did as every family member did, and it was lore throughout the area. I think he just wanted to tell it again.

He added, "You just have to make up your mind then, as I did, follow through."

Well, here is the story. Dad quit milking cows in 1961 and started selling gas appliances for Midwest Bottle Gas in LaCrosse. He was a road salesman and actually went into the county; for the most part selling gas furnaces, stoves, dryers, water heaters, etc. Being a farmer himself, Dad was a natural. His relating to farmers convinced many to convert their gas tractors to LP gas.

The Guy Johnson family only lived about two miles from us, winding back along "Peacock Road" I could best describe as something from the movie "Deliverance." Guy and his large family were also dairy farmers with no running water to the house or barn, only to the stock tank.

Dad convinced Guy and his wife to buy a water heater for the house and that would keep him motivated to have running water installed sooner rather than later. Of course, Guy's wife agreed with anything that might help that large family get running water in the house. For at least the next two years, every time you'd drive by the Johnson's, that new water heater was prominently displayed there on the front porch. I think Dad was somewhat disappointed when it disappeared (hopefully installed). No longer would he enter any local hang outs and hear, "Jerry, how the hell did you sell a water heater to Johnson when he doesn't have running water?"

That story, according to my dad, was his advice on helping me with my decision.

This was followed with Mom, "Jim, do you remember when you were a freshman and you had gone up the lane to bring the cows home for milking and when you came in the house for supper they had started back up the lane?"

"Of course, I remember, Mother." Well, I threw a fit. "Somebody stop the cows!" I bellowed.

Mom, who was a tiny woman, had had enough of my recent antics, caught me off guard, pushed me to the floor, and sat on my chest until I stopped my ranting and raving. Could I have thrown her off? I think so, but out of respect and fear, I lay there pouting until she let me get up. Then I started back up the lane, without supper. My feelings badly hurt but safe to say she had tempered the way I reacted to what I perceived as a difficult situation.

Did either of these anecdotes help me make up my mind? I don't think so. It did give me a chance to use my parents as a sounding board and to see the approval in their eyes regardless of the path I chose.

Arriving at my decision certainly culminated with receiving my appointment letter. By this point, I had pretty much convinced myself to go the FBI route, should I be so blessed. I had convinced myself that when I had traveled to Milwaukee for my interview and testing, I had pretty much washed myself out, so the acceptance letter was a shock and a blessing.

Devine intervention must have come into play as I think back. My company commander, Jerry Matteson, strongly encouraged me to choose the FBI, though he himself loved the Army. Though a National Guard Infantry Company Commander, he was also a PhD and the head of the Agriculture School at U W River Falls. My starting salary would be just over $9,000 per year, about the same Jerry was making with his PHD.

Jerry and I were quite close though he was the CO and I was one of his platoon leaders. He was a constant source of encouragement when I sought counsel. Conversely, the senior regular Army NCO who was assigned to our Guard Unit SFC Jackson, whom I highly regarded, would never know of my quandary. There is little doubt his encouragement would have been to return to active duty.

Did I make the right decision? A wonderful life in reflection I can only answer to the affirmative.

Dan Ryan and Entering on Duty

How could I not write of the many colorful characters that I worked with over those many years as an FBI agent? I remember some because of their amazing professionalism, some for being downright funny. Each one brought something special to my life. As I sit and reflect, I know I'll miss someone that, simply put, should be mentioned for any untold number of reasons.

The first to come to mind is Dan Ryan. We both arrived at "the Old Post Office" in Washington, DC, at the appointed time to check in on the fifth floor on September 8, 1969. Dan and I EOD'd (entered on duty) the very same day, Ryan being just before Sacia alphabetically. He was assigned credential number 8187. Alphabetically, I was next; I was assigned 8188.

Dan was a former Marine Corps captain and Vietnam War veteran, and combined with his New York City upbringing, it gave him a brashness pretty much typical of those from his neighborhood back home. "Pushing the envelope" was something Dan did well. In fact, I do believe he relished crowding it as much as he could.

Dan, Bill Stull, Dave Templeton, and I rented an apartment together, and we commuted to class via car pool each day.

In 1969, classroom training for new agents was predominately at the "Old Post Office." Fingerprinting and photography were taught at the Department of Justice building and firearms training and any other outdoor activity such as "Hogan's Alley" were conducted at the FBI Facility at the Marine Corps Base at Quantico.

While undergoing training, the new FBI Training Academy was being built at Quantico. When completed, this state of the art training academy would train all new and in service FBI agents, as well as select police officers from the entire country as well as allied forces.

Also at this time, the new FBI Facility on Pennsylvania Avenue in Washington, DC, was being built.

To say we were entering on duty (EOD) at a unique time would be an understatement. The Vietnam War was in full swing. The country, probably as much or more than any other time in history, was unbelievably divided. I don't recall much "middle of the road." You either supported the war effort, or you were very much against it.

Unlike the mentality in the 1960s as I write this in 2014, we all support our troops. In 1969, the wrath of those against the war was directed against the soldier, sailor, marine, or airman in uniform. It was not uncommon for those in uniform, simply doing their duty, to be ridiculed, have obscenities yelled at them, and to be often were pelted with eggs.

I distinctly remember the October 15 and November 15 moratorium in 1969. Many college students and other young people in major cities, in particular Washington, DC, were marching and protesting the war in Vietnam. In their "pack of wolves" mentality, it was not uncommon to see smashing windows and looting like common criminals.

The four of us became close in a unique sort of way—Dan and I were Veterans, Bill and Dave were not. Dave was married and his wife was home in Garden City, Kansas. We started referring to him as "mother," probably because he kind of "mothered" Bill, Dan, and I. Dan became well-known for his abrasive mannerisms but he certainly could make things happen.

Following his transfer, after training school, to Little Rock, Dan gained notoriety when during an interview he apparently had a cigar in his mouth that he swears was unlit. The lady being interviewed was highly indignant and wrote to J. Edgar Hoover demanding that Dan be disciplined. Well, he was—Mr. Hoover disciplined Dan with a letter of censor and disciplinary transfer to Chicago.

Apparently this "incident" occurred in West Memphis, Arkansas. Dan was doing a background investigation on a young man who was applying to become a clerical employee for the FBI at Washington, DC. In the early 1970s, there were hundreds of young men and women working for the Bureau doing such mundane tasks as classifying fingerprints, categorizing arrest record, updating files, all the tasks that today are done with computers and far less personnel.

Dan was at the credit bureau, perhaps the least invasive and controversial part of any background investigation. Because of that "contact" by Dan, to this day, an FBI mandate is that no agent will conduct any interview smoking or with smoking material visible. Dan swears that the cigar was unlit, but here's the "rest of the story."

Remember now this is a time in history and in an area where racial unrest and strong racial beliefs prevail. Dan gives the lady his name and date of birth, with which she responds (according to Dan which I believe), "Is he a white boy or a 'Nigger' boy'?"

Now remember Dan is a New Yorker and a Vietnam combat veteran. I will surmise, knowing Dan as I do, that the "Nigger boy" comment turned his crank a whole bunch, and I will further surmise that Dan's response of "He is an African American gentleman" perhaps tensed up the exchange. No matter, her letter to J. Edgar Hoover stated Dan had a cigar clenched in his teeth and blew smoke in her face.

In FBI lore the story has been repeated by many. Those of us who know Dan Ryan get great enjoyment from the exchange.

The actual best part of the story is, upon Dan's arrival to Chicago, the SAC (special agent in charge) Marlin Johnson, who was known throughout the Bureau as a disciplinarian, called him to his office.

Dan swore the exchange went something like this, "Sit down, Ryan," as he lit his cigar and offered one to Dan with a lite. "Now tell me what happened down there."

Dan never had a problem with Marlin Johnson.

I arrived some time later to Chicago from my first office in Salt Lake, on what was explained to me as a "routine transfer."

So in Chicago, Dan and I worked the streets together, both assigned to Jim Gerbelich's squad C-8 which was a unique squad dealing with military deserters and applicant matters. In 1970, there were thousands of military deserters avoiding the Vietnam War. We never did want for work as there was plenty to go around.

Dan and I prided ourselves on obtaining "hat tricks." In other words, three arrests per day. Working the south side of Chicago is exceptionally dangerous work and many of our deserters were draftees from the projects. We would often start at 6:00 a.m. with hopes of our third arrest by no later than 10:00 a.m. The projects would often sleep until 10, after that all hell could break loose.

One morning at about 8:00 a.m. we were looking for a deserter named Rice. In a nasty neighborhood, we quietly walked up to the fourth floor of his apartment complex. Dan banged on the door, no answer. He banged again and a very weak elderly sounding man said he couldn't come to the door; he had just had back surgery and was flat on his back in bed.

Dan hollered again, "Come out Rice, or we'll kick the door in." Again, the weak sounding man pleaded that he could hardly move. We gave him one more chance. As we listened, we could hear a strange clomping sound followed by sliding footsteps. Dan swears to this day that it sounded like the racking of a pump shotgun. We kept ordering him to hurry and he pleaded he was doing the best he could. We couldn't imagine what kind of ruse Rice was up to, but the sound was getting closer to the door.

At last we heard the chains and dead bolts falling aside. When he opened the door, Dan and I were dumbfounded. A very elderly black gentleman was supporting himself on the back of a kitchen chair with profuse sweat from pain, running down his face. He told us Rice was in 309, we were at 409.

As we delicately helped him back to bed, he questioned who we were with, we simply said, "Police."

We didn't stick around for him to make any calls. Rice would wait until another day. It would not be a good day to pursue him with the ruckus we had caused.

One particular morning, with two arrests under our belt and both lodged at the Pershing Street Military Lock up, it's about 9:30 a.m. Dan is set on one more as he has a good lead on one of his deserters on Root Street of Chicago's south side. We know we are "pushing the envelope," but Dan is persistent and away we go. We gain entrance to the residence and after being jerked around by the sister, we finally find our guy. Of course, he is in the attic and after a brief struggle, he agrees to go peacefully. His resistance, according to him was because he planned to turn himself in this very day. We leave the residence with our guy handcuffed and we both knew we had been inside too long.

Our car parked by the curb, is surrounded by eight to ten dudes just "sliden and gliden" and we notice the left front tire is flat. Dan and I had always had a plan.

I entered the back seat with our deserter hearing the catcalls. "Hey, man, your tire is flat."

Dan responded with his New York brashness as he got in to drive, stating, "I know, bye," and away we went with curses and catcalls behind us. We drive all the way to the Pershing lock up, shredding the tire and ruining the rim, but we avoided the obvious confrontation from a deliberately flattened front tire.

Dan Ryan left the FBI and went with ATF (Alcohol Tobacco & Tax), who promised him an assignment to Phoenix. Dan, being Dan, burned his FBI bridge when he left the FBI by admonishing them for not transferring him to Phoenix. He stayed with ATF only a short time, and when he asked to return to the FBI, it was too late, he had bruised some egos and he was persona non grata. Dan took a job in Phoenix with the Maricopa County prosecutor's office as an investigator.

The saga of Dan Ryan can best be described by quoting from an article written by Tom Fitzpatrick in the *New Times*, dated September 7–13, 1988,

> Dan Ryan, a former FBI man and investigator for the county attorney's office, testified after Mrs. Redmond.
>
> If anyone can be said to have broken the Redmond murder case, it is Ryan. Through aggressive police work, Ryan got Merrill to turn states evidence and accept a short prison term in exchange for his testimony against others.

Every defense attorney who has handled any of the cases has expressed outrage at what they refer to as Ryan's highhanded behavior. They pretend to be shocked over the fact that Ryan pursued a gang of hit men and failed to treat them with dignity.

In reality Ryan did the same things that make movie audiences stand and cheer when they watch Clint Eastwood portraying Dirty Harry Callahan.

A better description of Dan Ryan could not be written.

J. Edgar Hoover

I know there is a book out there titled *No Left Turns*, available on Amazon in used condition, for $37.53. I will order the book but only after writing my recollections of J. Edgar Hoover, the longtime director of the FBI. The book is apparently about his idiosyncrasies (of which there were apparently many).

When I was hired as a special agent for the FBI, entering duty on September 8, 1969, it was under the direction of Mr. Hoover. Of course, his name was synonymous with the FBI. In spite of his alleged shortcomings, I chose to remember him as the great man that he was. The young lawyer directed the Agency from May 10, 1924, until his passing May 2, 1972. He raised its prominence over those forty-eight years from a politically corrupt organization, when he assumed command, to what is universally agreed to be among the finest law enforcement agencies in the entire world. I am proud to say that I became an agent under J. Edgar Hoover.

Did I fear him? You bet I did, as did every new agent of my or earlier vintage. We were constantly advised by those in authority, from assistant directors on down, to avoid contact with Director Hoover unless he sent for you.

We were new agents and as such, during those years, had most of our classes in Washington, DC, either in the Old Post Office or two blocks up the street in the Department of Justice Building, which housed the office of the director. We were admonished "if Mr. Hoover is on the elevator, bypass it." This came from students over the years, who, inadvertently got on an elevator with Mr. Hoover, who was invariably accompanied by Associate Director Clyde Tolson. The conversation, according to those who were there, would go something like this (Note: new agents stand out like sore thumbs):

Mr. Hoover would say, "Mr. Tolson, I would think that the new agents would want to walk up the stairs to get themselves in the condition necessary to be FBI agents."

Mr. Tolson would reply, "I agree with you, Director, perhaps we can mention that to the class counselors so these young men recognize the importance of excellent physical conditioning."

It didn't take long for a red-faced new agent to exit the elevator, no matter what floor it stopped on, and continue to his destination via the stairway. Accordingly, very seldom did I ever use the elevator unless I had observed the director and Mr. Tolson already leave the basement cafeteria.

It was also told to us, as if it was gospel, that following lunch one afternoon, Director Hoover called the unit chief of the Training Division and told him to "get rid of the new agent that looks like a truck driver." No one knows the outcome or if anyone was let go, but like so much of FBI lore, it makes for a good story.

The numerous tales of agents attempting to stay within the weight guidelines are the best. An overweight agent shot and killed a hijacker. Director Hoover called him to his office to congratulate him. He allegedly bought a suit two sizes too big, and the director, knowing of his weight problem, congratulated him also on his weight loss.

No Left Turns' premise is apparently that Mr. Hoover's driver on an occasion had made a left turn in traffic and was involved in an accident. Allegedly, thereafter his driver was instructed to never make a left turn and he was required to plan his route accordingly. Note: I said "allegedly." I have not yet read the book.

My personal knowledge of Mr. Hoover was an opportunity to meet him while I was in training school. My recollection is that Unit Chief Simon Tulai told us that we could request, through channels, to meet the director. I followed the hoops and hurdles and in due time I was advised that I had an appointment. On that day, in my best suit and fresh haircut, I entered the office on the top floor of the Department of Justice Building. Mr. Hoover's long-time secretary, Ms. Gandy, greeted me, and shortly thereafter, I was instructed to enter the director's office.

He shook my hand, and the meeting was most cordial.

His opening comment was, "How are Katherine and Jerry [my parents]?"

Of course he had my personnel file in front of him. I was impressed. He kept the conversation light, and I was glad I had the opportunity to meet him. He made it quite clear when the meeting was over. One on one he seemed like a great guy, but the stories make up some of the best FBI lore.

All FBI cars were ordered without AM radios, as Mr. Hoover felt that agents should concentrate on their cases and not be distracted. I don't think I ever knew of an FBI car in that era that didn't have a bootleg connection for one obtained at a junkyard that was under the seat or in the glove box.

Mr. Hoover had his inspection team be alert for agents drinking coffee, which allegedly was an edict not to do, as agents do not have time to drink coffee. Yes, I continued to drink coffee, but I was cautious when the inspection team was in town.

With the six thousand to seven thousand agents that Mr. Hoover directed at the time of his passing, I doubt that he remembered my short meeting with him in his office.

In my first three years with Mr. Hoover as our director, I respected and admired the fact that the FBI had such stature and esteem. There was little doubt most of it is because of the hard work of his agents, of which I was very proud to be one. But it was Mr. Hoover who gets all the credit for ensuring his agents were the finest that America had to offer, I'm deeply humbled to think that for twenty-eight years I could be among them. I often said one of my greatest disappointments was leaving the Bureau at age fifty-three. I was eligible to retire, and in a minimum of two years to a maximum of four, I would be mandatorily retired. This was hard considering I was energetic, enthusiastic, and loved and I worked hard at this chosen profession.

I did my part to fight the age restriction. When I was hired, there was no such hindrance. Some study, maybe even after the passing of Director Hoover, convinced the powers that be, it would be a good thing. I understood the philosophy: an older agent could be chasing a bank robber and "have the big one." I will always maintain and firmly believe that at age fifty three when I retired, I was in far better condition than many who were age thirty-five. The Bureau needed a guideline, and they chose a chronological age. Go figure!

With hindsight, it gave me the opportunity to start my second career and as my favorite saying goes, "Things turn out best for people who make the best of how things turn out." Yes, it speaks volumes, and with a successful farm equipment business and eleven years as a state representative, I feel privileged and honored to have been launched from the FBI.

My used book *No Left Turns* arrived in the mail. The author sees the FBI and J. Edgar Hoover very differently than I do. In fairness, he was twenty years ahead of me, entering on duty in 1949. He was a WWII Veteran, started as a clerical employee, and went on to become an agent.

The entire book is extremely critical of J. Edgar Hoover and much of the FBI's leadership structure. I share no such animosity. I will continue to believe that though obviously somewhat eccentric, the Bureau would never have achieved its exceptional law enforcement accolades with anyone less capable than Mr. Hoover. I believe the history of the FBI, under J. Edgar Hoover, proves my point.

AL MEHEGAN AND FBI LORE AND HUMOR

Al Mehegan is a legend in the Chicago Office of the FBI. When I arrived there in 1970, I had to inquire about the elderly man I would see in the office.

Special Agent Al Mehegan came into the Bureau when the Minneapolis / Saint Paul, Minnesota, area was covered by an agent from Chicago via the railroad in the early 1930s. That agent was Al Mehegan. His exploits were legendary and there was more than one story about some blue flaming inspector who would have a problem with some of Al's cases. Al would make a discreet call to J Edgar Hoover and that ended Al's harassment, and allegedly some inspectors found themselves dead-ended in Butte, Montana, and rumor has it has happened to more than one inspector's career (that part I can't document, but it's fun to believe it anyway, given the general impression of inspectors). Al was in his early eighties when I got to Chicago. This was before the days of mandatory retirement age for FBI agents. Though he no longer carried a gun, his personal car was a Jaguar convertible and that, in itself precipitated a great deal of intrigue and speculation.

Al had liaison with all the railroads in Chicago and the CEO of each was on a first name basis with him.

Though he was greatly saddened with the passing of Mr. Hoover in May if 1972, Al made a statement no other living agent could possible make and he said with reverence, "I've seen these directors come and go" as if it had been but a fortnight.

One of the best recollections of Special Agent Al Mehegan is found in Vince Inserra's book *C-1 and the Chicago Mob.*"

"Mr. Mehegan was the longest serving agent in the history of the FBI who predated Director J. Edgar Hoover. Mr. Mehegan graduated from Purdue University and earned letters in baseball and football. He was one of the outstanding halfbacks in Purdue Football History. He joined the FBI's predecessor agency 'The Bureau of Investigation' in 1922 when Warren G. Harding was president. Special agents were not yet permitted to carry firearms. In 1924 the Agency became known as the Federal Bureau of Investigation when Mr. Hoover became director. Mr. Mehegan retired in 1975 with fifty-three years of active service. No one will ever exceed that record of service with the FBI. He began his career by tracking down bootleggers and cartage thieves, and while serving in the Chicago Office for a period of forty three years, his specialty was investigating interstate thefts from railroad and trucking lines. He was the ultimate authority in his field and served as the FBI liaison agent with trucking and railroad security police. Mr. Mehegan was a man of faith and integrity, who passed away in 1983 at the age of ninety five. He will never be forgotten by his many admirers for his unprecedented dedication and devotion to the FBI, as well as for his many contributions to the agents in the C-1 squad."

Many agents leave legacies, most like Al, for their exploits and good work, others often times simply because of some idiosyncrasies. I'm reminded of R. B. Adams, which was his official Bureau name, RB. It got to the point that agents started heckling him about "what is your real name?" his response was "R. B. Adams." In the FBI, as soon as it is perceived that someone has a "chink in the armor," the piranhas go for that jugular vein.

Each agent is required to sign in each day on what is known as a number 1 register. With RB's constant harassment, he decided to sign in "R only B only Adams." Well, you guessed it, from then on he was officially called Ronly Bonly by everyone in the office. It drove him nuts, but it would never change to the day he retired.

In the summer of 1995, John Holiman, a fellow agent from a sister division, created one of those stories that become a part of Bureau lore from that day forward. This is one of those stories that I'm sure will get better with time, but I know firsthand what happened.

It seems John had a subpoena to serve "up the road" where construction was taking place. He was stopped by a flagman who told John he could not go through. John became somewhat indignant, insisting that he be allowed to drive along the side of the road and deliver his subpoena. The flagman said no, John said that the subpoena must be served and with that he bypassed a very mad flagman.

Well things might have been okay, but as John drove the shoulder, the newly paved road looked inviting and appeared to be a hard surface. With that John put his car on the new concrete and the further he drove, the softer it got. Before long he was literally sucked down as he tried to get out of the middle of the road. There he sat, up to the hubcaps, stranded in new concrete with nothing to do but suffer the wrath of whoever would be first to get there.

The paving company was very indignant, pressed charges and John was criminally charged. The media had a field day, and John got thirty days "on the bricks" (without pay) along with a letter of censor for his activities. Also, he had to pay restitution to the paving company which was a huge amount.

John is a great guy, and it caused him much anguish. The story will be told for years to come by agents telling war stories, long after the name of the agent and the location of the incident are forgotten.

Agents of the FBI, like all law enforcement, have vehicles equipped with two way radios. Of course, strict adherence to radio protocol is a must. For reasons never identified, an agent who shall remain nameless, started identifying himself on the radio as "the green hornet." Comments like "The green hornet is 10-8 [in service]" and "The green hornet is 10-7 [out of service]" became commonplace and no one allegedly had a clue who it was. Law enforcement uses the ten codes commonplace and they typically run the gamut all the way to 10-99.

The SAC (special agent in charge) was monitoring this, and after several days, he barged into the radio room, grabbed the mic, keyed it, and stated, "Agent using call sign Green Hornet, identify yourself." After a lengthy pause, with the SAC turning red and no one keying the mic as all were waiting for the next response, and here it came, "I'm not that green," followed by utter silence other than numerous agents clicking their mics in approval. I do believe that the SAC never did determine the culprit.

Jim Thulen, the sheriff of Carroll County, and his deputies arrested a federal fugitive for me in the summer of 1977. The next day Bob Branigan went with me to Carroll County to pick up our fugitive. We had taken care of the paperwork, had a cup of coffee with Jim, and I got in the back seat with the prisoner as Bob drove the car. When he backed out of the garage, Bob hooked the front bumper on the edge of the overhead door, ripping the bumper completely off and there it lay on the ground. No one was hurt, no big deal, but as we stood in front of the car looking at the bumper on the ground, along with all the hydraulic fluid from the compression style bumper, Jim cautioned me that I'd better do an accident report. Time consuming forms swam through my head and an FBI investigation is a bummer. I took a calculated risk. I threw the bumper in the trunk, tied it in place and headed to Rockford with our prisoner.

Bob agreed to keep our secret. The passenger seemed completely indifferent to the whole situation, which made things even better. Had he decided to have a bad back or sore neck, it would have been a different story.

We delivered our prisoner, he was arraigned and then I headed to the local bus garage where my friend Merv Haskins worked. We decided it could be fixed. This is the days when Detroit "invented" the compression bumpers to absorb minor contact.

We aligned the bumper back to the front of the car and tried to get it back in place. No luck, it had been sprung too badly. We hit on an idea…get it as close as possible, put the bumper against the wall with the car against it and drive the car tightly against the bumper until it fit into place. We had the rear tires smoking as I attempted to spin my way against the bumper. Finally, Merv got behind me with the wrecker, forcing the bumper to give way slightly at the compression fittings until it went almost in place. We both agreed it was good enough and we welded it in place with the wrecker holding the car against the bumper which was against the cement wall.

The next spring during our then annual inspection, the inspector looked somewhat quizzically at the slightly tilted bumper, but never said a word. He had been around long enough to know it's sometimes best not to ask.

PROSTITUTION

Receiving orders at training school for my first office as a newly trained FBI special agent to Salt Lake City, put me on cloud nine. West of the Mississippi led me to believe that I would be in the "western circuit." Jenny and I, engaged but not yet married, had talked how we would both enjoy any of the western states.

I envisioned that after my first year in Salt Lake, perhaps I'd get Portland, Butte Montana, Seattle or—the possibilities were endless. I had no desire to go to Los Angeles or San Francisco, but I was excited about my orders.

J. Edgar Hoover's long-standing policy of a first office agent going to a smaller office to "get his feet wet" certainly was great with me. Typically, after about one year, an agent was considered fully trained and could be transferred with little concern about them performing as expected.

As I write this, long after I retired, I often reflect on the amazing changes I observed through my twenty-eight-year career. Fair to say, more than any other one thing, was the ability and actual encouragement to open cases on our own volition in my early years. That changed as the years went on.

SA Walt Anderson, my training agent, gladly loaned me to SA Jay Ferrin, who was working cases that needed two agents assigned. Jay was working predominantly on white slavery matters. The white slave traffic act, classified by the FBI as a 31 case, kept us surveilling and interviewing numerous prostitutes.

It was imperative, for what I think were obvious reasons, for two agents to do all the interviews of females. Somewhere buried in an FBI file an agent had an allegation made against him for something inappropriate, and common sense dictated that you never interviewed, transported, or were alone with a female suspect for any amount of time, which could be spun against you.

I loved working with Jay who was a highly respected senior agent and also a Bishop in the LDS Church (Mormon). Simply put, Jay was a prince of a man.

When I reflect on many of the interviews that Jay and I conducted, I can say that unequivocally I had never thought of prostitutes as anything other than girls for hire for sexual reasons. With a degree in psychology, one would think that I would have realized that often these "ladies of the night" had some unique and troubled past. I also had no concept of what "kinkiness" went on in the minds of some of the "johns," or those who paid for sex.

Juanita was a fantastic informant and we paid her well. Jay never had a problem coming up with fifty dollars or one hundred dollars for her, and sometimes more for the information provided.

Salt Lake City in 1970 was, in my opinion, very progressive in the way they dealt with prostitution. The city fathers had long ago realized that prostitution was "the oldest profession" and accordingly allowed it in an area of town where they can keep some control of it.

The area that Juanita and the other prostitutes frequented, was the area of West Second South. On any given night, after say 9 p.m., there would be cars circling the block and the ladies would do what they could to get that driver to pull up to the curb. The Ordinance required the girls (and a few guys) to stay on the curb unless they were invited into a car. If that occurred they drove away, transacted their finances, and went to the appropriate "No Tell Motel" for whatever was agreed to. All the girls were controlled by "pimps." Often a good pimp had many girls in his stable, some only two or three.

Jay and I of course were concerned with transporting the girls across state lines, always working at building our case for prosecution for those transported against their will. The "mother lode" was the ring cases, that being more than one pimp, conspiring with others, and trafficking large numbers from one state to another all for prostitution activity.

As we put those cases together, rather than work them as a white slavery case, we often worked it as a 166 case—a 166 case is ITAR

(Interstate Transportation to Aid in Racketeering—Prostitution). The bite of that charge, when proven, got the pimp and others responsible, to far more significant jail time which of course was Jay and I's objective.

I'm sure we knew we'd never stop prostitution, I guess that's job security, but we both worked hard at building our cases toward successful prosecution. Our success, in a large part, came from ladies like Juanita who was very open with Jay and me.

Reflecting back over the years, there is little doubt that I enjoyed building these cases because we were taking some significantly bad guys off the streets. It sickened me that some sweet fifteen- to seventeen-year-old runaway got caught up with some of these seedy pimps who forced them into a lifestyle that may destroy any chance of ultimately some type of a normal life. Getting them hooked on drugs and promises that never came true was the mantra of many of those who transported some sweet young thing, who soon enough had no choice but to fall in line or get beaten bloody, do whatever it took to get her back into line.

Juanita was the exception and in her midtwenties in 1970. There was little doubt her background was hard. She operated "freelance" and that was quite unique, no known pimp to protect or beat her, and maybe that is why she was such a good source.

Jay and I would have a case open as follows: 31-New UNSUB (unknown subject) driver of 1968 red Ford Thunderbird, Washington license 123456c WSTA (White Slave Traffic Act). Juanita would fill us in, that's Johnny Ringo or that's what he goes by. He's been here since Tuesday. He has two girls. He is black. They are one Mexican and one white. I'll point them out. By the end of the evening Jay and I had a good fix on who Johnny Ringo was, who Nisa and Janice were, and where they stayed.

As this was all night work, the next day at about 2:30 p.m., Jay and I would pull Nisa and Janice to the car and lean hard on them for what we could learn. If we couldn't get cooperation, we were often successful at making the pimp so uncomfortable they would leave town. That was never our objective as they would go on to another community, perhaps, in Arizona and resume their activity.

Our work was intelligence with the ultimate goal of prosecution. More than once a Janice or a Nisa would confide in us their fear and how badly they wanted to end the street life. We had limited success and those few instances gave us the sense that maybe we helped a young life get back on track. Juanita could identify them all.

Jay being such a prominent fixture, both in the Mormon Church and in the community, would shake his head in absolute disgust as Juanita would identify a prominent individual who would pay her significant money to defecate on her stomach and not engage in sex. Another prominent person would pay her for a quart of her urine. Jay would shake his head totally sickened. I would study Juanita thinking, could all this be true? So hard to believe but who knows what goes on in the minds of some men. The ones that truly saddened Jay and me alike were those looked upon as pillars of their occupation and communities, with their dirty little secrets.

To this day, and I have no doubt for years to come, it will be worked by dedicated agents. Sadly there will always be kinky folks.

Only recently, a former fellow state representative was convicted and sentenced to seven years in prison with a computer full of child pornography, including infants. Sadly, I, like so many, thought he was a great guy. There is no amount of advanced psychology training that will ever allow me to get my arms around whatever it is that makes someone think that way.

Several years after my experience in Salt Lake City and after arriving in the Rockford RA, I was assigned to work with Special Agent Bob Bales with the Illinois State Police. Bob was working a state case dealing with obscenity. The case involved several movie theatres in the Rockford area showing triple-X-rated, obscene movies. I discussed the issue with Jerry Nolan, the SSRA (supervisory senior resident agent). Jerry was fondly referred to by all of us under his command as "the big guy." The name was appropriate as he easily stood six foot, six inches and was built like a rock. If there ever would have been a perfect model of what an FBI agent should be and look like, it would be Jerry. His leadership style was somewhat unorthodox, but he always got the job done.

Jerry and I agreed that I would open an ITOM (Interstate Transportation of Obscene Material) case which was most appropriate as the films were transported interstate. The local citizens hated these theatres that showed such lewd movies, and there was outrage to close them down. Bob and I were assigned to attend each new showing and do a report being explicit about the content of the movie in question. We would then discuss the matter with the appropriate AUSA (assistant US attorney) in an effort to establish a prosecutable case.

I reflect on the hours of sitting in those sleazy movies trying to take notes and be inconspicuous. There would always be twenty to thirty men spread out in the seating and it was evident most had their coat in their lap and they were fondling themselves. Talk about making you sick. I always left feeling a little "dirty." The job needed to be done and invariably our investigations led to interviews of the theatre owners who were seldom cooperative and sent us to their lawyers. We did put the squeeze on them but I never recall one successful prosecution.

Overworked prosecutors seldom wanted to divert resources on what came to be called "social crimes," when there were so many crimes that were of a violent nature as opposed to consenting adults. I guess I can say I'm glad for the experience especially with a background in psychology, to watch how some entertain themselves. The fear I always had was the perverts watching these movies would act out their fantasies on some unsuspecting young lady.

As I write this, the Bellamy Brothers, a musical group, are singing one of their hits "It's a hard way to make an easy living." Somehow it seems appropriate sitting in those theatres. Though the whole experience is disgusting, I do agree it was necessary work. With enough pressure (Bob and I exerted much) some of these operators just went away.

More than once we'd get AUSA authority to seize some of the sleaziest films and it did some good. Not to mislead, these folks had plenty of backup films and it was no problem for them to duplicate, but squeeze we did.

The triple-X movie theatres are now gone. I like to think we helped, at least a little bit, make that happen.

FLAG BURNING UTAH

My soul-searching in deciding to leave the Army and become an FBI agent was long behind me, as I was on complaint duty in the Salt Lake City Office on a warm spring day in 1970.

The unrest over the Vietnam War was always a big subject of conversation, but somewhat tempered by five years of occupying everyone's mind. Deaths in Vietnam and the unrest the war was more like a nagging toothache than a sharp blow to the groin. Yet the war lingered on and young men continued to die.

Little had changed in my mind since I became an agent. The war was justified and I hated Jane Fonda and others who consorted in any way with North Vietnam. I had little patience with those who spoke against what we were doing there.

On this particular day, there was major unrest at the University of Utah as a group of protestors was burning their draft cards. I was on complaint duty and receiving more and more calls as concerned citizens felt duty bound to notify the FBI of what was happening.

Our ASAC was Ken McLaughlin and his face continued to show concern, as I reported to him the nature of the calls I was receiving.

Ken had been an agent for many years, and I had been told that he had started as an FBI employee in his teens while a male stenographer. Apparently in that era, women were not yet overly welcome as bureau employees and young men held those duties. I respected him as he had worked his way through the ranks to his current assignment.

Throughout the day the calls kept coming, and I was getting more and more angry, but could do nothing other than write up each call and give it to Ken. I knew he was making assignments to several agents via the radio. By midafternoon, a large crowd had apparently gathered and was burning the American Flag. This really infuriated me, but again, I was on complaint duty and my job was to write up the incidents and try to do good telephone interviews in an effort to establish probable cause for our agents to investigate those responsible.

At the time, the crime of "desecration of the flag" still was a viable violation of which prosecutors went after with vigor. I continued my telephone interviews doing everything I could to determine the person's responsibility for a crime which troubled me greatly. I have always been of a mind-set that many good men and women had died for that flag and I had little time for those who treated it with anything less than a respectful manner.

There was a percentage of young men, at that time, who openly admitted their allegiance to the FBI was little more than they had law degrees and service in the FBI made them ineligible for the draft. This was not a high percentage, but the reality did exist, and I found it despicable.

One of them, who had such an attitude commented, "I don't know why you're so upset Sacia, it's just a piece of cloth."

I saw red, one of the few times in my life when I didn't control my anger. The only other time I recall was in the fall of 1965 when the same issue set me off as a college freshman at River Falls, charging into a peaceful march against our involvement in Vietnam. I ripped the signs out of every protestor's hand and smashed them on the ground.

The "piece of cloth" thing sent me over my desk, grabbing the startled agent and attempting to knock him on his ass. When ASAC McLaughlin ordered me into his office immediately, I saw my career flash before my eyes as the door slammed behind me, and I was ordered to stand in front of his desk. My military bearing took over automatically as I stood at attention facing the ASAC as he took his seat and glared at me.

Fully expecting a complete dressing down, I was shocked as he told me, "Sacia, you can't do that. Now, I want you to walk out of here as if I really chewed your ass. I want you to know I'm glad you did what you did."

As I left with my tail between my legs, I never let on to my peers what Ken actually said. I only acknowledged their speculation that he had really chewed me out.

Over the next few weeks, individual agents got me aside, thanked me, and wished that I might have inflicted a little more pain on my "just a piece of cloth" friend. I was ashamed for losing my temper but fair to say it worked.

As I reflect on the number of years that have passed since that "incident" occurred, I marvel at the change in philosophy today. To my knowledge, though I'm sure that "desecration of the flag" is still a federal criminal violation today, it simply would not be prosecuted short of some very extenuating circumstances.

The "tempo of the times" changes many things. As I watch protestors today, I personally am amazed at the number of incidents that created protests and nearly inevitably cause the American Flag to be burned. No, I personally will never accept, it. I must accept where we are today.

Our own son John, a three tour combat veteran, tells me "Dad that's what we fight for, the right for them to burn the flag and express themselves as they see fit." I respect and admire my son's attitude. Perhaps it's because "I'm old-school." More than likely, it's remembering the importance of the "desecration of the flag" criminal violation back in the day. Add that to the stirring I feel inside every time I watch the flag while reciting the Pledge of Allegiance or standing with my hand over my heart and singing the "Star-Spangled Banner."

KAMAS, UTAH

SA Charlie Sheppard was, in my opinion, the classic poster look of what an FBI agent should be and look like. He was dedicated, hard-working, highly respected, square jawed, and well-spoken.

As a brand new agent in Salt Lake City in 1970, I was very impressed. Charlie was "the bank robbery" agent. Bank robberies occurring throughout the state would be investigated by all of us. Charlie would inevitably be the case agent and coordinate the investigation.

I don't think I was in Salt Lake City for more than three weeks when upon arrival at the office on a Monday, Charlie came into "the bull pen" and announced "Bank burglary, the State Bank of Kamas." Russ Calame, the SAC, was putting on his overcoat and going as well. That struck me, SAC's seldom go. The talk among the senior agents indicated that this was more than maybe a rock thrown through the front window.

Walt Anderson, the senior agent assigned as my training agent, said "Let's go look, Sacia," and I was right behind him. Riding with him and several other agents down the elevator to the basement of the Federal Building where the FBI cars were parked, gave a few more moments for all of us to get up to speed on just what had occurred.

"Sounds like these guys cleaned the bank out" were the words that Walt shared and he had gotten that straight from Charlie.

As a new agent, I was very excited. Walt had me grab the speed graphic camera that I convinced him I had become very proficient with in Training School. He told me it would be my responsibility to do the photographs for the crime scene. I had no idea what to expect, but at that moment, no one else did either.

Kamas is a very small town about fifty miles east of Salt Lake, and when we arrived, there were already numerous other law enforcement officers on the scene. They, of course, were all happy to see us as it was apparent in no time that this would be a major investigation.

Charlie quickly got things coordinated and we each went about our assigned tasks, me with the speed graphic. Throughout the day the facts began to unfold. It became apparent that our bad guys had to have been in the bank from late Friday night until sometime early Sunday morning.

The Utah Highway Patrol had investigated an auto accident nearly in front of the bank about midnight on Saturday. They were unquestionably inside the bank during that time and interviews with our bad guys, once they were apprehended, literally confirmed it.

The way the job went down was almost an "Amos and Andy Skit" with help from the "Three Stooges." There is one exception. They were nearly successful.

Friday night they burglarized a local gas station and stole the cutting torch. Saturday, when the gas station opened, the burglary was reported, and a police agency investigated. At that point, no one was aware of what was occurring three buildings away.

Our bad guys had to get into the building by torching the steel grates on the window in the alley. Patrolling police cars could not have seen the window unless they had exited their squad car and walked around a wall blocking the view of the rear of the bank.

The audible alarm was deactivated by simply cutting a wire. There was no other security device (hard to believe in 1970). Once through the steel grate on the window, our bad guys had to get the cutting torch inside the bank. They simply unlocked the rear door from the inside. Now they faced a significant challenge. Cutting through the door to the walk in safe, which would be visible from the street with the large front window, would be tricky.

Cutting the bottom hinge would cause no concern as the tellers' counter would block any view if anyone looked in. To their good fortune, the streets of Kamas were pretty much rolled up about 10:00 p.m., and with the exception of the car wreck, there were no other disturbances. Cutting the top hinge was no issue as one could act as a lookout. There was nothing across the street, and if a car approached, simply douse the torch.

Now it gets almost funny as they attempted to pry open the walk in safe door with the wrecking bar that they took when they took the torch. (The wrecking bars had not been noticed as missing when the gas station burglary had been discovered.) The door snapped back. Blood was all over the floor, obviously a smashed hand from trying to open the door on the hinge side. We are all looking professional yet chuckling, and leads go out to area medical facilities. With this amount of blood, someone is hurting.

We hear back soon from the hospital at Provo, Utah, Charles Riley, a well-known all-around thug was treated yesterday morning as an outpatient for a badly smashed left hand. Charlie hangs up the phone from the sheriff's office with those profound words "there surely is a god" followed with "talk about poetic justice." Charlie has previously arrested Charles, in the company of Fred Davidson who, according to the sheriff's office, matches the description of the person who came to the hospital with Riley.

The bad guys, now believed to be Riley (who is hurting) and Davidson, are now in the safe, and their work is just beginning.

Perhaps I should mention as the Bank President opened the front door of the bank at 8:00 a.m. that morning with water was running across the floor. His initial thought was a broken water pipe.

Riley and Davidson are not the brightest bulbs in the circuit but they are far from the dullest. Our President is noticing signs that send a chill through his veins. As he walks behind the teller counter, there is a running water hose on the floor. Then he notices the torched door hinges and immediately calls the police. To our good fortune, he keeps every one out of the bank until the police arrive and the crime scene is well preserved when we arrive.

Inside the walk in vault is what is commonly called a cannonball safe. This is where the significant cash and valuables are kept. It is about four feet high, three feet wide, and two feet deep.

These guys were cagy and they know what they are doing. A cannonball is about two inches of solid steel. They torch a hole through the top. This takes a good torch and a better torch artist.

These guys had learned their trade cutting up stolen cars and using a torch was second nature. Charlie had previously arrested them for ITSMV, interstate transportation of a stolen motor vehicle. Once the hole was penetrated, the cannonball was immediately filled with water. Wet money will dry out, burned money is useless. They then proceed to enlarge the hole until they can get their arm in and scoop it out.

Their proceeds were huge but we believe our bad guys are identified. Of course, an all-points bulletin was already put out and these two were well-known to most of Utah Law Enforcement.

I, of course, had been taking pictures of everything from the point of entry, to many overviews, to the garden hose that we learned had been removed from a backyard faucet nearby, to the sink basin in the back room of the bank, where the hose was now hooked.

I was intrigued with the entry to the vault but mostly by the clever way they preserved the money, by soaking it down with the initial minute hole in the top of the cannonball and the garden hose hooked to a utility basin in the back room. Had it not been for Riley smashing his hand, these clowns may have had a chance spending at least some of the loot before law enforcement closed in.

Everything had seemed to work in their favor: no further investigation Saturday a.m. of another business being burglarized and the failure to notice the missing wrecking bars, their ease in finding a garden hose, their failure to be discovered even during an auto accident investigation in front of the bank when they were inside, and the complete failure of anyone noticing anything out of the ordinary throughout the weekend.

Surely they felt by going all the way to Provo for medical assistance, it was far enough away so that law enforcement wouldn't check. This was obviously mistake number one.

The old-timers had me believing this type of bank heist was commonplace so I was sure I'd see it again. In twent-eight years, investigating numerous bank robberies, larcenies and burglaries, I never again saw anything quite like it.

Somewhere in the archives of FBI files are some great photos of the Kamas Utah Bank Job.

Jenny and I revisited Kamas in the summer of 2012. The bank is long gone and the building is now a restaurant. We ate lunch in the area I recalled as being in the walk in vault. I sure wish walls could talk as no one we spoke to could remember the bank burglary in 1970. I guess forty-two years is a long time.

THE DRUNK IN BARRINGTON

Having traveled from Salt Lake back home to Melrose in October 1970, Jen and I prepared for my assignment in Chicago.

When we had gotten to Salt Lake, the old-timers assured me we were in "the western circuit." In other words, our career would be spent west of the Mississippi River, if that is what we wanted and it really was.

The romance of the west appealed to both Jenny and I as we prepared ourselves for that lifestyle.

My orders for Chicago in late August 1970, hit me like a ton of bricks. My thoughts truly were what did I do wrong to deserve it (I think I said that elsewhere).

Our mind-set was to find a home in a northwestern suburb, preferably with some acreage.

Our first five days in Chicago, we stayed at a motel in Barrington and I commuted by train to downtown Chicago. Jenny busied herself looking for suitable permanent housing.

Jen had her horses being cared for by my parents back in North Bend, Wisconsin, and we hoped to find a place commutable to Chicago where we could keep them with us.

Agents receive overtime in a very unique way. We are not paid overtime as time and a half, as we see in so many professions; rather we receive some compensation, at that time 25 percent of a GS 10 salary, assuming we averaged a ten hour day.

Accordingly, my train ride from Chicago to Barrington didn't even start until about 7:30 p.m. On my second night in Chicago, returning to my bride by train, and as the ride progressed, I became aware of a belligerent drunk who was giving a conductor more than his share of grief.

At each stop, he became more belligerent, and when it became apparent that the conductor had more than his share, I interceded and helped the conductor keep the drunk away from the rest of the passengers. You can almost guess what happened next. As I got off at Barrington, only one other person exited—you guessed it, the drunk!

Now here I was, alone in an unfamiliar city, with an angry drunk that wants a piece of me. I had somehow come to believe if I identified myself as an FBI agent, he would immediately become docile and that would be the end of it. So I told him I was an FBI agent and he had better back off.

Well, if you had prodded him with a poker you couldn't have gotten him angrier, seems like he didn't like anyone who had anything to do with the law, so now was his chance to get me. Somehow I got into a phone booth, and by keeping both feet against the door, I held him out as I notified the Barrington police. By the time they arrived, which was only a couple short minutes, this guy was tearing at the phone booth and yelling obscenities.

The police got him in irons and escorted him to their cruiser, to the relief of a young agent. They knew him by name and agreed perhaps the mistake I made was telling him I was a law enforcement officer.

Had I not gotten in that phone booth, I choose not to think of the ramifications if I had to fight him alone on a deserted dark street in Barrington. Would he have gotten my gun? Could I have controlled him with fists alone? I'm glad these questions didn't get answered.

Transfer Chicago to Rockford

In 1970, when the Chicago Division needed someone to recruit clerical applicants in the Rockford area, to fill the many vacancies in the DC area, I couldn't get to the front office fast enough. I thought this would help me get a foot in the door for an assignment to Rockford.

Our ASAC (assistant special agent in charge), Bernie Huelscamp, assured me the only way to get to Rockford was to do an exceptional job in Chicago for "about ten years" and you will have a shot at it. I was not ready to give up and this opportunity seemed like a wise move.

Jerry Nolan was the SRA (senior resident agent) at Rockford and he welcomed me aboard. I would be in the RA territory from January 1971 until June 1971 when school dismissed for the summer.

During that tenure, I worked feverishly to "make my mark," and my results were exceptional. I was hiring young men and women, high school seniors, who would leave that summer for DC with a starting salary of approximately $4,000 per annum. I was a natural at recruiting, perhaps because my enthusiasm was contagious; more than likely, I was giving young people an opportunity with a degree of mystique and intrigue.

The FBI paid their way to DC, helped them find affordable housing and offered opportunities to go to college should they hope to one day become agents. I assured them their airline flight would be paid, if they drove we would pay them $0.20 per mile and kiddingly said if they walked, we'd buy them two pair of shoes.

From January to May, forty-six young people from Northwest Illinois agreed to employment commencing midsummer 1971. My efforts were being noticed by the powers that be and I was asked to rekindle my effort in the spring of 1972. Again, I was highly successful and Jerry Nolan agreed to do what he could to get me to Rockford.

The problem I had with Chicago was simple, I was a farm boy at heart and the two hours each morning and night riding a train, and I translated into milking a herd of forty cows night and morning while I was wasting away on the C&NW Railroad.

Under Jerry Nolan's leadership the RA consisted of six men, I would be number seven, and I was cautiously optimistic.

J. Edgar Hoover, the director of the FBI for some forty-four years, passed away May 2, 1972, sending ripples through the Bureau. L. Patrick Gray was appointed acting director.

Mr. Gray was a compassionate man and this compassion led him to grant a hardship transfer from New York City direct to Rockford, Illinois, to an agent whose father was terminally ill in the Rockford, Illinois area. I felt the sting much like I did when I got orders to Chicago from Salt Lake. I struggled with the compassion I should feel for my fellow agent's father, and the screwing I perceived in not getting to be the seventh man. Little did I know it was a blessing in disguise.

Due to the large territory Rockford covered, and the relatively few men, Mr. Nolan kept an unaddressed work file, cases that weren't crucially necessary to be worked but cases that should be handled if manpower allowed. A good example of these were local felons who had fled the state to avoid prosecution. If the FBI had the wherewithal, we could hunt them for local authorities.

Unbeknown to me, an SRA could become an SSRA (supervisor senior resident agent), if he had eight men or more. All of a sudden, Jerry had seven by mandate from the FBI; one more would give him a pay grade to GS14. He had the unaddressed work to back up his request, he had a pretty good agent (at least he could recruit applicants) waiting in the bushes, my orders were effective September 22, 1972, but only after some help from ASAC Bill Meincke.

Bill had replaced Mr. Huelscamp in the summer of 1972. When he got to Chicago, he immediately needed to find a place where he could keep his horses. We became friends, and I tried to give him what little advice I could about having experienced a similar situation.

After much discussion with him over my desire to go to Rockford and my willingness to transfer at no cost to the Bureau, Bill asked me how far my residence was from Chicago, I told him fifty five miles. He asked how far it was from Rockford; I told him sixty-five miles. He responded by saying, "You are sixty-five miles from Chicago and fifty-five miles from Rockford." I said, "No, sir, you don't under-stand." He cut me off and said, "No, you don't understand, you are sixty-five miles from Chicago and fifty-five from Rockford. You are closer to Rockford, so it seems to me you should be working there, not here." I got the drift, but he really had to kick it home. I will always be indebted to him for that act of kindness.

Once I got my no-cost transfer orders, Jenny and I immediately began looking for a rural home north or west of Rockford. I didn't want some inspector coming in two years hence, recognizing I was closer to Chicago than Rockford and coming up with an excuse to transfer me back. Furthermore, I didn't plan on driving sixty-five miles each way to work.

In December of 1972, we settled in our dream home with a house and barn on twenty-five acres near Winnebago, Illinois, on a quiet gravel road where we live to this day. My commute time is fif-teen minutes each way. I could never milk a herd of cows in that time.

Mr. Hoover was known for being very stingy with the bureau's budgeted money. I was shocked when my supervisor in Chicago, Jim Gerblick, called me into his office and presented me a letter from the director. In August of 1971, $200 was a nice piece of change. There is little doubt that my success at recruiting applicants helped signifi-cantly in my transfer to Rockford.

Each office of the FBI was mandated to send as many clerical employees to Washington as possible. Once I was officially trans-ferred, Jerry would ensure that no matter what cases I was assigned, I would find time to keep my liaison with all the high schools within the RA territory. Only after I was assigned all investigations in the four Northwestern counties of Illinois did that shrink to those high schools only.

OFFICE OF THE DIRECTOR

UNITED STATES DEPARTMENT OF JUSTICE

FEDERAL BUREAU OF INVESTIGATION

WASHINGTON, D.C. 20535

August 2, 1971

PERSONAL

Mr. James G. Sacia
Federal Bureau of Investigation
Chicago, Illinois

Dear Mr. Sacia:

  Your worthwhile contributions to the statistical accomplishments realized by the Chicago Division for the 1971 fiscal year are commendable and warrant a $200.00 incentive award which I have approved for you. Representing this award is the enclosed check.

  Your office attained an excellent record in all categories and you played a vital role in achieving such splendid results. I want you to know of my appreciation for your dedicated and loyal efforts in this regard.

     Sincerely yours,

Enclosure

OFFICE OF THE DIRECTOR
FEDERAL BUREAU OF INVESTIGATION
UNITED STATES
DEPARTMENT OF JUSTICE
WASHINGTON, D. C. 20535

OFFICIAL BUSINESS

OUR HOME

W hen Jen and I were blessed enough to find our twenty-five-acre farm home in Pecatonica, Illinois, we knew we had struck it rich.

When we got married, Jenny brought two horses and a 1966 Dodge Convertible as part of my dowry. Regretfully, the convertible is long gone and Spotty and Dutchess, Jen's two horses being mother and daughter, simply launched us into the horse business. It has brought us much happiness but very little money. I guess we never really did mean for it to, or even expected it.

Living in rural Cary Illinois prior to our transfer to Rockford gave us a chance to start increasing our horse herd, which had grown to eleven by the time we located to our Pecatonica home. I will never forget pulling into our Pecatonica farm at eleven at night, hauling eleven horses. It was minus eleven degrees Fahrenheit on the night of December 11 in 1972.

Raising horses became our avocation along with my renting some additional land to raise our own feed. As our family began to grow, and we continued to breed our horses, once again we somehow struck it rich.

We had a pretty good old black registered quarter horse stallion that became our foundation stallion. His registered name was Memphis Joe. Joe wasn't the quality we wanted to raise show horses.

More and more we set our sights on quality paint hoses. The paint horse has its foundation in the quarter horse industry and more and more we were setting our sights on constantly improving our quality of stock.

How we found "Navajo Patches" I no longer recall. "Patch" was a paint stallion, and we were very impressed with his quality. We must have purchased him at a very fair price as at that time we couldn't have afforded much. I remember the folks we bought him from, Wayne and Nancy Stading and Nancy's daughter Marie, who were successfully showing Patches. He unquestionably was show stock. Neither Jen nor I had any skills in showing horses. Our neighbor Dave Cunningham introduced us to Bob Jackalone, who asked us if he could ride him.

You hear stories where some horses and riders simply click; such was the case with Bob and Patches. Bob was ecstatic. "We just must campaign this horse, he is amazing."

As a very busy FBI agent with a large case load, I was skeptical. Many of my Saturdays were used up with work, and finding time to attend horse shows seemed like a stretch.

Jen was excited but now had two sons, Jerry two years old, and John a newborn. Oh boy, what were we in for? With our quarter horse and paint mares and now with our paint stallion Patches we were breeding our mares with Bob asking over and over to show Patches. The year was 1974. To emphasize Bob's belief in Patches, he offered to trade me "even up" his new 1974 Chevrolet four-wheel drive pickup for him.

I guess this was when two fools met, him for offering it and me for rejecting it. Jen and I couldn't believe it. We must have paid a fair price for Patches but certainly nowhere near the value of a new truck.

In August we accompanied Patches and Bob to our very first horse show. What happened next just doesn't happen to new green horns, but Bob was a very experienced showman, and he was riding what he came to call a push-button horse. By the end of the day Bob and Patches had won four trophies. Jen and I were dumbfounded, and I think many of our new found friends showing horses with us were as well.

Many friendships have stayed with us through the years, and Patches and Bob continued to click and clean house at show after show throughout the '74 and '75 season. Patches was shown widely until he obtained his "pinto championship." By now we are hooked, and throughout our children's growing-up years, showing horses was a huge part of our life.

The horses we've raised and the people we've befriended to a large part is due to the horse industry. One cannot reflect on a lifetime without recalling friends you've made throughout it. The same can be said for horses.

Two great paints that Bob competed with along the way, and that were the toughest to beat were the great paint horses "Q Ton Puddin H" and "One Man's Opinion." Bob successfully beat each of them in a "reining" class and that simple feat remains a great memory.

One Man's Opinion is the name I have chosen for my next book of my years in the Illinois General Assembly.

With our family growing, and Jerry born while we were still in Cary, in February of 1974 John came into the world. As I mentioned the summer of 1974 was also the year that Bob was extremely successful showing "Patches." I guess our kids had no choice but to become horse lovers and by 1976 Jerry was showing in "Lead Line" classes with his two-year-old brother sitting on the pony that he was leading. Horses began to consume our family life.

"Patches" being an exceptional sire, we started investing in quality brood mares. The best we ever bought was an outstanding paint mare "Do Diamond Doll." Putting more and more colts on the ground as Patch was aging, we retired him to a neighboring farm and a life of ease. We bought a young paint stallion "sky bug Sam" "Buggsy" who put many quality colts into our operation for many years. We had to have "Bugs" put down by our Veterinarian in 2012, which broke our hearts.

In the summer of John's seventh year, while we were busy baling hay, he fell from a fully loaded hay wagon that Jenny was pulling on a gravel road and his head was run over, leaving him critically injured. Our neighbor and thirteen-year-old babysitter, Lisa Calhoun, came running to me in the hay field carrying our new born Jesse to give me the scary news.

Apparently, according to Lisa, Jenny had scooped John up and raced to Rockford Memorial Hospital. Trying to remain calm, I moved the tractor and wagon off the road and cleaned up to head to the hospital. With Lisa left in charge of Jesse, I headed for the hospital, taking Jerry with me, who was in anguish for his brother.

Arriving at the emergency entrance of Rockford Memorial Hospital, Jen's car sat running with both front doors wide open. I calmly parked it out of the way and Jerry and I were escorted to where a team of doctors and professionals were doing all they could to stabilize our John. If you've never experienced a scene like that, I assure you it takes your breath away. Each and every professional was working in concert with each other to get this little boy on the mend.

John literally was bleeding from every cavity in his head which was conveyed to me by Steve Doty, a member of the Rockford Memorial Staff, whom I knew from our church. He was great at calming Jerry and I down, and expressing a positive outlook.

Jen stayed as close to John as the staff would allow. Gathering my senses, I called both my mom and dad and Jenny's as well. Both moms would link up the next day and head to Pecatonica. As both of our families are strongly faith based, they both called their home churches in Wisconsin to start prayer chains.

Once stabilized, to what extent I have no idea, John was placed in ICU, and Jen, Jerry, and I were allowed to stay with him. Dr. Mano, the specialist dealing with John, painted a "wait and see" picture. He shared that John was critical but the good news was that his swelling brain could hopefully be controlled with drugs, not available a short time ago. Of course, we silently prayed and as John was unconscious we tried to be patient waiting for him to open his eyes.

When he did open one eye, the excitement was electric. He smiled, saw his brother Jerry, and extended his right hand, saying, "Jerry shake." It's one of those moments that remain with me always.

Dr. Mano shared with us that John's youth saved his life. He noted that because his skull was not yet fully hardened, it would be like dropping a hardboiled egg—it would have cracks throughout, but it didn't shatter like a fully matured skull. John's head had taken the weight of a fully loaded hay wagon. The good doctor then reiterated his concern to keep the brain from swelling, which so far had been successful.

The neighbors at home, who seemed to have all gotten the word, picked things up and made Jen and I's life so much easier. LaRae Klinger and his family finished getting the hay in. Our moms arrived to relieve Lisa with Jesse and slowly, ever so slowly, our lives returned to normal.

For an extended period John needed to wear a patch over his eye as a nerve was damaged and that was the treatment.

Dr. Mano came to the rescue when John became a military aviator. He noted that electronic imaging, available when John was seven, could not positively say that John had had a skull fracture. Divine intervention and a great Doctor, today John is an F-16 fighter pilot.

That same divine intervention was evident when I retrieved Jen's car from the hospital. Midway between the hospital and home, the car simply quit running. A quick scan of the gauges gave no indication of the problem—plenty of gas, good oil pressure, not running hot. The car's fuel pump simply quit operating. The immediate thought was thank God that did not happen to Jenny on the way in. It's probably one of the few times I didn't grumble about the cost of the repair.

The greatest fear of every parent, I have no doubt, would be to lose a child. Living on a farm, arguably, there is always an element of danger. To this day our greatest prayer is not to outlive our children.

Our son John seems to be the one who has kept testing that. At age seventeen, John was a gifted athlete and a good student. The summer between his junior and senior year, fate struck John for a second time. It was a Saturday and somewhat ironically John was helping me bale hay. That evening as he left to do what seventeen-year-old schoolkids do, I gave him some fatherly advice. I had admonished him that when he and his buddies went somewhere he didn't always need to drive. I had been giving him too much gas money. I lived to regret that admonishment.

Jen and I had rented a movie, Memphis Belle, and along with our son Jesse and his friend/classmate Nick Bielskis we had an enjoyable evening.

Shortly after the end of the movie, very caught up in the emotion of it all, the phone rang. One of John's friends told us John had been in a bad accident and he didn't have any other details other than he was injured. He gave us the approximate location on a rural road. As I hung up the phone I realized it would be no place for Jes and Nick.

Jen and I assured them that we would go look and be back as soon as possible. The boys were both eleven and we were comfortable they would be fine for a short period of time. Unknown to Jen and me, but what will soon become more than surreal, several ambulances and a helicopter, as well as additional fire equipment had been called to the scene that was more and more sounding like a horrific accident scene.

Again, all this was before social media and cell phones, but many citizens had law enforcement had emergency organization scanners. The communities of Winnebago and Pecatonica had gone from the calm of a day coming to an end, to a day that is filled with drama.

As we arrived at the area of the accident, we were literally awe-struck at the flashing lights and large area of a significant accident scene. A helicopter was sitting south of the road with its rotor slowly turning awaiting the transport of one of the injured. My initial impression was that there were several vehicles involved based on the amount of debris scattered throughout the rural intersection.

The first thing I came upon, as we parked the car and walked toward the scene with no knowledge of the condition of our John and whoever else was involved, was a rear axle assembly and one wheel and tire attached, I was to say the least dumbfounded, then a car seat sitting in the road. Inquiring as I went, finally a fireman pointed to someone on the ground being attended by several paramedics who he believes is our son.

Staying back, but still wanting my son to know we were there I quietly said, "John, Mom and Dad are here."

The next comment I heard has haunted me to this day.

Someone near John hollered, "Get him out of here!"

I politely responded that we wanted our son to know we were there. I'll never believe that that comment was from a fireman or a paramedic. It simply was not what a concerned parent wanted to hear.

Gradually we learned that this was a single car accident and John was a passenger. My mind flashed to my admonishing my son:

"You don't have to drive every time." It became apparent that several of the boys were critically injured and the helicopter was spinning up readying to leave with the most critically injured, Garrick Harmon, a close friend and classmate of John's.

Jen and I were close to being in shock and we came upon our friends, Joe and Sally Huggins, who agreed to go to our home and stay with Jess and Nick. We began to realize that we were in for a long night at the hospital. Jenny was allowed to accompany John in the ambulance to Rockford Memorial Hospital.

We learned that the three young men who were in the car were Tom Southard, Garrick, and John. Apparently, they had been at a country party with many classmates and friends, obviously alcohol was involved. John was with his buddy Garrick who was leaving with Southard. The Mustang struck a bridge abutment at a high rate of speed literally disintegrating the car and throwing each of the young men hundreds of feet through the air.

As the night dragged on and we arrived at the hospital, we learned many more details. John had a severe foot injury and a broken leg along with many cuts and bruises. He was conscious and told us that he was in the back seat. He knows that Harmon, in the passenger seat, had his seat belt fastened. How did he fly out if he was belted? Only several days later did we learn that his seat belt was severed when the vehicle disintegrated following the impact. The days following also revealed that it took three flatbed trucks to gather up the pieces of the vehicle.

Garrick was very critical with a very severe head injury. Jen and I took it upon ourselves to try to get in touch with his mom Rita and her husband Bill. They joined us at the hospital after several hours. Tom and John were both stabilized and in surgery. The long wait and prayers continued for Garrick.

The "horrificness" of the crash became a significant news story. Investigators determined the Mustang was in excess of one hundred miles per hour when it struck the concrete abutment. The only conclusion they could make, was that due to the excessively high rate of speed and the car disintegrating on impact, was probably why the young men lived. They were each thrown clear of the impact area.

Though the least critically injured, John spent the longest time in the hospital due to the severity of his foot injury.

The car was placed in front of the Winnebago High School for all to see the results of alcohol and driving.

There is no logical explanation on how these three young men lived and went on to live productive lives. Excellent doctors, no doubt. Divine intervention, just had to be.

To this day we continue to reside in our Pecatonica farm home. Though my FBI years are now but a fond memory, as are my eleven years as an Illinois state representative, the farm and the horses take a considerable amount of time, or perhaps I'm just slower completing tasks for the nine head that remain.

We no longer show our horses as they continue to age with grace and excellent care. With the amount of acreage that we have, they have plenty of pasture and I'm able to raise all their hay to get us through those cold winter months. The enjoyment of caring for them certainly goes back to my "up fetching" on a Wisconsin dairy farm. Jen had horses as long as she can remember, and her love for them, I'm sure, outweighs mine.

To say that they are a joy and add so much happiness to our lives, even if now it's simply looking over the fence at them and remembering all the joy that they brought us for so many years, would be an understatement.

FBI Agents and 9-11-2001

To say that I was beyond proud to be a special agent with the FBI would be an understatement. Having the privilege of being a "resident agent," one assigned to a RA (resident agency), in my opinion, was the icing on the cake.

J. Edgar Hoover, who served as director of the FBI for some forty-four years looked at resident agencies as a necessary evil. Long gone were the days that agents would leave a major field office, such as Chicago, and travel by train to Saint Louis or Saint Paul to cover leads.

Agents assigned to headquarter cities became specialized in certain crimes: the "bank robbery squad," the "theft from interstate shipment squad," "organized crime squad," "foreign counter intelligence," to name just a few.

Resident agents became a jack-of-all-trades. At that time, the FBI was specifically responsible for 286 violations, all falling into three categories: (1) a crime of an interstate nature—an example would be ITSMV (interstate transportation of stolen motor vehicle); (2) a crime where the United States government was a party of interest—an example would be a bank robbery (all banks are insured by the Federal government; therefore, any crime against that institution would be investigated by the FBI); (3) fair to say the biggest reason for the FBI being in existence at all, that being wherever the security of the United States is involved. At this writing, the most obvious example would be the horrific acts of September 11, 2001.

I would be remiss if I didn't opine my sadness in what I feel was a great failure of the agency I love as much as life itself, for the failure to prevent it from happening. Ever since that horrific crime, I have often stated that the world had been lulled into a complete false sense of security, save some of the horrific crimes around the world—the bombing of the Marine Corp Barracks in Beirut in 1983, the bombing of the USS *Cole* in 2000, and of course, the Oklahoma bombing of the Murrah Federal Building in 1995.

But I digress. My point is, if someone had said on September 10, 2001, that someone would fly commercial airliners into the World Trade Center and the Pentagon, we would probably take that someone to a mental institution.

RA assignments were highly sought after and competitive. I previously shared that my significant success at operating by myself recruiting applicants in Northwest Illinois, had a significant impact on my assignment. The down side could be the long hours and the untold number of cases you would be assigned and expected to complete.

I caught on quickly to regularly discussing my case load with my supervisor and seeking help when I needed it as opposed to muddling through.

A resident agent was expected to be somewhat of an expert in all investigations, which of course was impossible, but with help of fellow agents and in return helping them, made it roll rather smoothly.

It was not uncommon at all to hope to be home say 6:00 p.m. only to get a call from a fellow agent with the need for assistance in an apprehension, or to work a stakeout with that agent. Conversely each was ready at any time to help me as well. Local, county, and state police were regularly called upon to assist as well and the good working relationships between the RA and the locals were the most important job of a resident agent.

One did have to sacrifice however. If you cemented yourself into an RA, it probably meant the end to advancement to the position of supervisor, inspector, to ASAC (assistant special agent in charge), to SAC (special agent in charge of a division). Of course, also assistant director positions were out there somewhere.

I readily accepted my obligation to remain a "brick agent." We still would be promoted, assuming we performed adequately to become a senior GS-13, which is the journeyman grade for an FBI agent. In the overall scheme of things I was well paid compared to my fellow law enforcement officers.

I also believed I possessed "the best kept secret in the FBI" being assigned to the Rockford RA. For my money it didn't get any better than that. Outstanding work with new challenges, everything came my way from bank robberies to applicant matters. Once I was assigned the four northwestern counties of Illinois—Jo Daviess, Stephenson, Carroll, and Whiteside—any of the federal issues occurring in those counties was automatically assigned to me.

Jenny and I could not have been happier. We had the honor and privilege to raise our children in a rural environment. An outstanding school district in Winnebago for our children to attend. We could raise and enjoy our horses away from the hustle and bustle of Chicago and I could be a gentleman farmer. I don't know how life could be any better, and of course the highlight was the honor to work with the finest police officers anywhere.

Perhaps I could have been an ASAC or SAC had I chosen the path to promotions. Had I stayed in the Army, there is little doubt that I would have done all I could to become a General Officer, or at least advance as far as I could. As an FBI agent, specifically a resident agent, that requirement to climb was never there. I give great credit to J. Edgar Hoover for establishing that opportunity for me and like-minded agents. It was a career well loved.

On April 22, 2004, I wrote my weekly column as an Illinois state representative about the events of 9/11/01, the World Trade Center and Pentagon attackss. Seventeen area newspapers across the eighty ninth Representative District published what I wrote.

The following article appeared in those newspapers, and was sent to my contact list as well.

From the Desk of
State Representative Jim Sacia

For Immediate Release: Contact: Rep. Jim Sacia

April 22, 2004 (815) 232-0774

Guest Column

The FBI and CIA are not to blame for 9-11. The terrible tragedy that occurred on September 11, 2001, could not have happened 15 to 20 years ago. As a 28-year veteran FBI agent, and with my 30 years of law enforcement experience, the 9-11 Commission has compelled me to write this.

For those of you who look forward to my weekly article as your state representative on state issues, please forgive me. This issue is simply too important not to address. Having had the privilege of being a resident FBI agent (the only agent in the northwestern counties in Illinois' Jo Daviess, Carroll, Stephenson, and Whiteside counties) for nearly 27 years, I speak with a certain degree of knowledge.

As the only agent in those counties, I was a "jack of all trades." In other words, each of the violations investigated by the FBI occurring in those areas at that time was automatically assigned to me. Accordingly, much of my specialized "in service" training at Quantico, Virginia had to deal with keeping me up-to-speed on all issues investigated by the Bureau.

I was trained not only as a criminal investigator, but also in Foreign Counter-Intelligence (FCI). Not many agents get that privilege, as the vast majority of them are assigned to specialized squads. Unfortunately, from my early days in Salt Lake City in 1969 until my retirement in 1997, I watched as the FBI, CIA, and other intelligence agencies were systematically gutted by our own US Congress, who now takes the FBI and CIA to task for their *alleged* ineptness.

Should someone have come to me in the mid-1980s and allege that for example, a particular person or group was building bombs, I would have in a matter of hours, days, or weeks at the most, conducted a thorough investigation and either verified or proven false the allegation. And if it was in fact false…"case closed." Each agent *at that time* had the authority to open a case on their own initiative.

How soon we forget the tempo of the times prior to 9-11…it was far different. This nation was living with a false sense of peace and tranquility. I want you to know that there is not a person alive that believes in individual rights more than I. But this was the guise used by Congress to begin restricting our intelligence agencies and disallowing agent-initiated FBI investigations starting sometime in the late 1980s and early '90s.

I want to believe that the American people understand that Congress sets the parameters, that our intelligence agencies must follow. And I want to respond with the way our young people respond to a tremendous grasp of the obvious with, "Hello?"

Congress is solely to blame for the tragedies that occurred on September 11, 2001, although they will never admit that responsibility. At any one time, there are over 50,000 young people on file applying for the position of an FBI agent, and the FBI does yeoman's work in hiring good citizens and the most loyal Americans. Then Congress ties their hands and tells them to do a good job.

There is no doubt in my mind, that the FBI and CIA could have prevented 9-11…but how could they with their hands tied behind their backs?

There is little doubt that Congress' perceived misconduct of the FBI led them to restrict the intelligence agencies' jurisdiction. But as an agent in the trenches, throughout those many years, I write with authority when I say that I saw it happen.

To have watched the likes of Ms. Jamie Gorrilic and Mr. Richard Ben-Veniste of the

9-11 Commission chastise the FBI and CIA with their grandstanding has saddened me greatly. In my heart I know that the agents will continue to do the best they can as allowed by our Congress.

Following my article, I did expect some feedback. From who, I'm not sure, maybe other agents who felt as strongly as I did.

I so vividly recall the kidnapping of Patty Hearst by the Symbionese Liberation Army (SLA) in 1974. She was the granddaughter of William Randolph Hearst, founder of Hearst Media Empire. Shortly thereafter she publically announced she had joined the SLA. The SLA was notorious at the time and soon thereafter she was caught on camera toting a weapon during a bank robbery that she participated in, with the SLA. During her captivity she released many tapes extoling the greatness of the SLA. She actively participated in many crimes with them. After her capture she was sentenced to thirty five years for bank robbery. That sentence was commuted by President Clinton after she had served two years in prison.

In my opinion Patty suffered from classic Stockholm syndrome which I write about at length in the chapter on bank robberies. I mention the Patty Hearst case here as during the two years that she was with the SLA many would ask my opinion, "Why haven't you FBI guys captured Patty Hearst?" The answer is simple: This is America, that's why. Across the nation including across northwest Illinois where I worked and lived calls constantly, and I do mean constantly, came in telling us that Patty Hearst was sighted at such a place. We would methodically follow up on each sighting that seemed to have merit.

American law enforcement is not the "Gestapo." We couldn't go kicking in doors where she was believed to be. Had we such authority, we would have had her much sooner than the two years it took us. Thankfully our laws are such that a person's home is their castle. Individual rights are sacred and they are to be honored by law enforcement. Many that I would speak with simply could not get their arms around that. "Well, you guys should get her caught" was a common response.

So I do get it. At least I try to. I will always believe that our intelligence agencies need a free hand. Yes, they need oversight. They do not need knee jerk reactions. There is an old saying, "You can never go back." I will go to my grave believing that the authority stripped from individual agents to open cases on their own initiative if they felt it merited, was a significant mistake. The time taken to get through a cumbersome process of requesting permission from an agent turned predominately bureaucrat back at WDC, when time is of the essence, those on the ground and directly involved can make the best decision. Perhaps it's because most of my career I was a resident agent. Quick decisions were required. Going through old notes from "back in the day," I came across the following:

"The love of this job cannot be expressed in words. The prestige, the camaraderie, the mutual respect among law enforcement officers is something seldom seen in other professions. The humor is something so often overlooked but it is there every day. Perhaps sometimes we laugh at the morbid, I'm reminded of the Waylon Jennings song, 'I may be crazy but it keeps me from going insane.' How many days started off with the usual bantering and kidding with one another only to receive an urgent call—be it a bank robbery, extortion, kidnapping, a possible fugitive located, or any number of untold cases. We all know what to do and we all respond. Resident agency life is quite different from being assigned a specific squad in a "headquarters city." There you respond only to the cases assigned to your squad except in major situations. As a "road trip agent" I was responsible for the entire litany of FBI cases in those four northwestern counties in Illinois."

A man I respected greatly from our mutual working together as fellow investigators in the early '70s, was State Trooper Dave Reed. Dave and I worked many cases together and I had profound respect for his investigative abilities and his leadership in sharing matters of mutual concern.

Such was the case of extortion in Sterling, Illinois. As I was responding to a frantic call from a young mother whose little boy had been grabbed by his father and her ex-husband, there was little doubt the boy would be hard to find. Are you ready for this chronic twist? The father called the mother to say that for $50,000 he would surrender the boy at a designated drop site. Ah, a father's love for his son. Sterling is sixty miles from Rockford, and I was maintaining contact through our office with then Lieutenant Jack Rhinehart of the Sterling Police Department.

Dave who was at the Sterling Police Department at the time, in a manner so typical of him offered the services of the Illinois State Police, on his radio. He advised me his agency had a plane in the air running radar close to the designated drop site for the extortion loot. Dave made it happen and in no time the plane had the car, occupied by the boy and his dad, in sight. The plane coordinated the ground units and the loving father was arrested as he stopped the car at the drop site and tried to retrieve his money. Mom had just received a settlement from a job-related accident and dear old dad decided to cash in on the proceeds.

A law enforcement officer gets to see far too many cases of the scummy side of life and I can understand a loving father kidnapping his son from an ex-wife, but extorting her for money leaves that hollow feeling in your stomach. Had it not been for Dave, the cooperation of the Sterling Police Department, Illinois State Police, Whiteside County, and the Rock Falls Police Department, I never could have put it together. In his warm humorous way, Dave noted that once again the Illinois State Police bails out the FBI. It's closer to the truth than I care to believe, but our mutual respect for one another is something I'll take to my grave.

Dave went on to become the Commander of District 1, Illinois State Police Sterling, Illinois. A position he got the old fashioned way, he earned it. Sadly, shortly after he retired in his early fifties he passed away of a heart attack.

A Day in the Life of
an FBI Agent

Often, whether at a speaking engagement or with a group of folks other than FBI agents, I would be asked, "What is a typical day for an FBI agent?"

Most importantly, I was far from a typical agent. That would be a person assigned to a headquarters city and being on a specific squad working specific cases. The squad could be say the "theft from interstate shipment squad" perhaps the "organized crime squad," "foreign country intelligence" squad. These would be examples in a larger field office such as New York City, Los Angeles, or Chicago.

Smaller offices would have several violations assigned to one squad. In my case, being the only agent in the four Northwest counties of Illinois if a federal violation occurred in any of those counties, it would be assigned to me. With over two hundred specific violations that are the responsibility of the FBI, I never knew what would come to me.

I typically carried a caseload of forty to sixty investigative matters at a time. On any given day, I might work on six or seven different issues. Of course I tried to organize my time and cases, depending on their location, in my large geographical area. Another day, depending on the complexity I could spend all day or several days on one issue. Citing a bank robbery in my area, I'm on it, typically working with one or more detectives and we dog it together, interviewing victims and developing subjects and if the leads take us in the area to our subject or subjects we would coordinate an arrest if at all possible.

In my life, diversity was everything and I enjoyed that. On any given day, I could be dealing with an issue that took me to interview the most influential person in the county. He may have knowledge of a major embezzlement or scam being perpetrated. On occasion that interview to gain insight into a case, turned into a subject interview, and experience as an investigator allowed me to switch gears, advise him of his Miranda rights to counsel and not to incriminate himself, and occasionally they would then simply clam up. More often than not, if it started off as a witness interview and the discrepancies in his answers turned to advising him or her of their rights, he felt even more compelled to help me understand. These were the interviews that I loved, "Give them enough rope and they hang themselves."

Whenever I even remotely suspected that an interview could become a subject interview, I would have a detective with me. I can't begin to adequately express the close working relationships among local, county, and state law enforcement agencies with the FBI. I never could have been successful without them.

On that very day where I may have been interviewing that highly influential official, I may have found myself that very afternoon in a salvage yard talking with some rather rough individuals about a lead I had from Portland, Oregon, about a load of catalytic convertors being transported in interstate shipment to the Detroit, Michigan, area. It was believed to be being "fenced" in small lots at junkyards across Illinois, "fencing" being a slang term for stolen items being sold on the "black market."

Junkyard guys, loosely speaking, aren't always happy to see law enforcement guys. Again, I prided myself on being able to "speak their language." As a gear head, the truth be known, I felt very at home.

A junkyard in Freeport could have easily blown me off, but one of the guys was actually an informant of mine, and like clockwork I would stop to see him at least once every thirty days. He played it well, not tipping his hat that in the past he had helped me, he took me to his boss.

His boss was somewhat suspicious of what I knew or didn't know, and playing dumb confessed when I specifically asked, "Have you purchased any new catalytic convertors?"

His response was, "Well, ya, but he told me that these convertors were flawed and couldn't be installed on new cars."

I was about ready to treat this as a subject interview when he produced paperwork which was believable. He had purchased two pallets which were positively identified coming from the stolen shipment. With that one interview, we positively identified our thieves, since the salvage yard owner had purchased from him before. With that information we were able to notify the Assistant United States Attorney in Rockford, as well as Stephenson County's States Attorney, to seek a complaint and warrant against our identified bad guys who actually stole the load.

The tractor, trailer, and the load were all missing but we were gaining ground having located these two pallets of valuable convertors from the load. These have been mandated on all automobile exhaust systems since the 1970s. A new one is valued between 300 and 600 dollars each. We also believe we now knew the identities of the two who stole the load, and we were attempting to get a warrant for their arrest. One of the detectives at the Freeport Police Department ran our two bad guys through the computer system and it took little time to realize that "this is not their first rodeo." Both have lengthy "wrap sheets" for arrest records. The good news is neither had a history of violence so our approach will be different than if they were to be the violent type. They appear to be opportunists. Also, both were "career criminals," not the type that a little jail time will bother. They have both been there and as the pace quickened, I believed it wouldn't be long until we'd have a grip on them.

When I left home that morning and coordinated my day's work, I believed that "if" I got the lead from Portland regarding the stolen convertors I would maybe have an interview or two, sending out a teletype or air tel regarding my results and then moved on. As it then looked, we may have had our bad guys in our backyard, and we could be closing in quickly.

With the close cooperation of Freeport City Police, Stephenson County Sheriff's Office, and the State Police we determined that our bad guys and the load we're now at a junkyard in the Milwaukee Wisconsin area. I sent a teletype, and telephoned the Milwaukee FBI

NOT IN MY WILDEST DREAMS

office in their agents arrested our thieves and recovered the tractor trailer and what remained of the load. Total value of both the rig in the load was $150,000.

No day, at least very few days in the life of an FBI agent goes as planned. The number of times that I left home in the morning telling Jen that I should be able to be home for dinner reached a point of humorous. Jen had gotten to the point where she would simply say, "I'll see you when I see you," and that really was the deal.

Now in my early seventies, reflecting on those days gives me a sense of great warmth and comfort of knowing it was a job well done. Also a day in the life of an agent includes identifying the perpetrators, conducting the necessary investigation to locate and convict those responsible.

Did I stop crime in Northwest Illinois? Not even close. Did I enjoy the close working relationship with the finest law enforcement officers in the nation? Absolutely. We'd jokingly call it job security. A law enforcement officer will always have the satisfaction of knowing with a deep sense of gratitude that he or she is keeping America safe and arguably great.

There are those among us in this great society who have little, if any, respect for those who wear the badge. From where I sit I can only say "thank you." To those still on the front lines both in uniform and in soft clothes, their contribution cannot be adequately measured.

In my opportunities to speak to groups, clubs, and organizations, I seldom miss the chance to comment that society will never know the number of crimes prevented by the presence of the uniformed officer and the marked squad car.

I've gotten somewhat away from the start of "A day in the life of an FBI agent." I just can't write about it without giving significant credit to all law enforcement. Simply put, I could not have had a day at all without the backup and assistance of great city officers, sheriff's deputies, and state troopers.

Nowhere in this memoir have I addressed the old comment that rears its head periodically that the FBI is a glory stealing organization. I always played it off. In my case with humor often told by me on our agency.

I taught numerous police schools on the various expertise I had learned attending specialized schools at Quantico, Virginia and FBI Headquarters in Washington, DC. The story that always got the biggest laugh was a competition was held between law enforcement agencies to tout their expertise. It was determined that each agency would train a dog and the dogs would compete to show off their respective agency.

After several months it was determined that each agency's dog was ready to extol the virtues of that agency. A large event was planned. The NYPD (New York City Police Department) dog came onstage, a large German shepherd, sniffed around, found some cookies, pushed them around and spelled out "stop crime." There was thunderous applause.

The Chicago Police Department was next, and their canine was a large female pit bull. The dog sniffed around and found the cookies. She pushed them around to spell out "no more drugs." Again there was thunderous applause.

Next was the FBI dog, a bulldog in the likeness of J. Edgar Hoover. The dog sniffed around, found the cookies and ate them, seduced each of the other two dogs, made a press release and took the afternoon off.

The cops invariable loved it. There was always friendly banter. Have there been occasions when the FBI was pushy? I have no doubt. By and large there are excellent working relationships between the FBI and other law enforcement agencies.

In my twenty-eight years, I could not have existed without the close working relationships with local, county, state, and other Federal agencies. They truly were my "bread and butter." And hopefully, I contributed back to them.

WHERE'S MY GUN

I dare say everyone who has carried a gun as a part of their profession has had something similar happen.

My morning started very early in Galena, Illinois, a hard hour from home when the roads were good. This was the dead of winter. The roads were icy and drifting snow. I left home early and was on time for my early start to the day.

As I finished my interview I stopped at the McDonald's for a cup of coffee and use the facilities. Typically, when I would be that far from the R.A. I would spend the day in the area covering leads on other cases. The weather was deteriorating and good judgement had me with coffee in hand heading east on Highway 20 to the Rockford RA. It was becoming increasingly apparent that this was becoming a significant weather issue.

After about an hour, arriving in the Freeport area, that automatic right elbow into the butt of my gun gave me a startling revelation. No gun! I had left it on the tank of the toilet in the Galena McDonald's. This was before the days of cell phones and of course my immediate reaction was to call the Jo Daviess Sheriff's office and have them dispatch a deputy to retrieve it. My fear—many folks had scanners. If they dispatched someone, the call might be heard and some ne'er-do-well would beat the deputy to it.

I had to chance it, I did a U-turn placed my red light on the dash and drove as fast as I felt I could while keeping the car out of the ditch. I said numerous Hail Marys, praying that my gun would be there. I know I got back in half the time it took me to get to Freeport; but still, at least an hour and a half had transpired since I had used the facilities.

The weather was continuing to deteriorate, which worked to my good fortune as McDonald's was far less busy than normal. I briskly walked into the restroom, and there it lay, right where I left it. Relief, jubilation, I'm sure there are many other adjectives as well. What I remember most was wait a minute; two hours ago I had my gun and was not near as happy as I now was.

An FBI agent's credentials (ID) and gun are his two most guarded items. When not in our possession, that cold rush of blood to the heart is nearly overwhelming.

I drove on up to the sheriff's office to share my scare and story with my friend Detective LaDon Trost. We both enjoyed my good fortune but both agreed I needed to head out. The weather was really getting bad. It probably was the most relaxed drive I ever made to Rockford.

MY LOVE AFFAIR WITH OLD IRON

From my growing up days on our thirty cow dairy farm near North Bend, Wisconsin, I have always had a love affair with the internal combustion engine. Dad, allowing me to buy a 1020 Farmall Tractor from our milkman, Kenny Arneson, truly was the catalyst starting my "gear head" mentality.

At the point I'm at now in my life, I'm not nearly as interested in "wrenching" as simply buying and selling. Throughout my FBI years, my principle hobby was always working on an old tractor when time would allow. It truly was and is my principle hobby. Try as I would, I could never get interested in golf, fishing, hunting, or any other sport activities. My excitement, particularly on weekends when the farm or Jenny had nothing specific for me to do, was to either attend a farm auction or work in my garage or shed on some old tractor that I didn't have too much money in.

Shortly after we moved from our three acre farmette in Cary, Illinois, to our existing farm in Pecatonica, I nearly gave Jenny a cardiac arrest. On a bitter cold January day, I attended a farm equipment auction put on by machinery dealer Harold Nelson and George Ils. Standing in the biting wind, I found myself the successful bidder on five farm tractors. Because farm tractors were "in my blood" I knew values quite well. My total investment for all five was $3,300. In the early 1970s raising a family on an FBI agent's salary truly had me in over my head.

I was convinced I had purchased the tractors for pennies on the dollar, and it would now be my challenge first to convince Jenny that I wouldn't lose the farm, and secondly borrow all $3,300. I had written the check but had no money to cover it. Don Pratt, the president of North Towne Bank listened as I assured him that I could double my money and he loaned me the $3,300.

The tractors were the collateral, and I agreed to pay each one off as I sold it. Don knew farm equipment values and we knew each other from professional law enforcement dealings. He had the confidence in me knowing I was a good risk. My recollection is that Jenny cried herself to sleep for several nights but she gradually came to believe as Don Pratt did that I could "make it work."

The FBI frowns on outside employment or any outside business for its agents, so I was very circumspect at the office about how excited I was with my purchases. I didn't even have a way of getting these tractors home and they were thirty five miles away. I was able to hire George Ils, one of the previous owners of the tractors, to haul them home with his truck and gooseneck trailer.

I very successfully marketed them which had a positive effect. I proved to Jenny that I could successfully do this and make a little extra money, while I proved to Don Pratt that I was a good risk. That was the start of NITE (Northern Illinois Tractor and Equipment), which has grown to a reasonably successful farm equipment truck and trailer business. Two of our three sons, Jerry and Jesse, along with ten other fine people keep the business running today.

I still have "old iron in my blood" and the Bureau was and still is very gracious with its agents at the time they take their vacation (annual leave). Criteria permitting, we could take anything from an hour at a time to a more significant amount as long as it had been earned. I would occasionally take the first Monday of the month off, leave on Sunday, and travel the 450 miles to Sikeston, Missouri to attend, on Monday, one of the largest farm equipment auctions in the nation. The sale was often over by 6:00 p.m. I'd pay for my purchases and beat feet back to Pecatonica, often being able to get a couple of hours of sleep before heading to the FBI Office. If I were really beat, I'd take Tuesday morning off to get some rest. I would often travel by pickup or car, but occasionally, I'd pull a gooseneck trailer. I quit the trailer routine as I would often have a semi load and needed to hire it hauled anyway.

One memorable late night as I fought to stay awake, I gave it up and pulled into a parking area in a truck stop. I quickly fell asleep on the seat and after an unknown period of time there was a rap on the passenger window. We've all had those wake up occasions where, as you are coming to, you have no idea where you are; such was this memory. As I pulled myself together and attempted to shake the fog from my brain, I saw a rather scantily clad young lady with a big smile, and as I rolled down the window, she seductively asked, "Would you like to have a party?" I'm slow, but I was getting the drift. First, I was angry that she woke me up; second, no I didn't want a party; and third, though I've heard all the stories of "lot lizards" who made a pretty fair buck, peddling their wares of the world's oldest profession, I was an FBI agent, and I simply didn't need this.

My credentials were on the dash. I displayed them to the young woman, identified myself, and told her in no uncertain terms she needed to get the hell out of the truck stop or I would have her arrested. (I doubt I could have, but she didn't know that.)

Her eyes got as big as saucers as she stated, "Yes, sir. Mr. Super Smoky, can I get my friend?"

I responded with "Where is your friend?

She stated, "In one of them trucks."

I told her, "Get your friend and get out of this truck stop."

In a flash (no pun) she was gone.

I, of course, was now wide awake, and I was off to the comfort of my Pecatonica home. I think I laughed most of the way home, as this was the one and only time I was propositioned in my travels. As this was in the days before cell phones, I waited until I got home to tell Jenny. She, like myself, enjoyed the humor.

Of course I got a little of well, "What if she had been real pretty?"

I said, "Jenny, let's move on," and of course, we did.

Occasionally, Jenny and the boys would go with me. We'd get a room in a motel with an indoor pool and my family would spend much of the day swimming and relaxing. A favorite memory often re-enjoyed at family gatherings, was a trip to Sikeston with Jerry and John when Jen was pregnant with Jess so she couldn't go. The sale ran late, and I really needed to be back to work on Tuesday. Sikeston is 150 miles south of Saint Louis. I'm north bound about 60 miles north of Sikeston when John wakes up on the bed in the back of our van crying, "Dad, I can't find my blanky." He of course tells me he had it at the motel last night. I'm using my negotiating skills to convince him I'll get him a new one. I'll get him a new toy. I think I tried it all when Jerry says, "Dad, he really needs it." Well, that melted my heart, and back to Sikeston we traveled but to no avail. The lady at the motel checked lost and found to no avail. John was heartbroken but gradually got over it. It was a very long night, but finally, with the sun coming up, I pulled into our Pecatonica farmyard. The location of "John's blanky" remains a mystery.

Someone once told me that a good hot shower was worth four hours of sleep. I guess I tested that theory. Jen fixed us a great breakfast. I hugged my family goodbye, and off I was to my "other world."

SHERIFF JIM THULEN

J immy Thulen was the classic county sheriff for rural America. Jim, a democrat, served for many years from the late 1960s to the mid-1980s as the Sheriff of Carroll County in Northwest Illinois.

As the only FBI agent in the four Northwest Counties of Illinois, of which Carroll was one, my time with Jim was quite often. I'd often arrive (intentionally) at about 11:30 a.m. just in time for the feeding of the prisoners. Jim's wife, Dorothy, was the cook and according to accepted policy, law enforcement officers could pay fifty cents and enjoy a Carroll County special cooked meal by Dorothy. It might be a hamburger and French fries, or it could be anything from country fried steak to baked chicken. The prisoners and those of us who paid our fifty cents were very well-fed.

Like all law enforcement agencies, the coffee pot was always on and the stories shared were legendary. Many came from Jim Thulen. Many happened before I started covering the counties, the unsolved homicides were among my favorite.

Jim was an "Andy Griffith and Mayberry" kind of sheriff. Everyone loved Jim. He came across as "just a good ole boy," which was exactly what he was. Don't ever sell Jim short—he was one hell of an investigator.

Among his many tales was a body found in a rural cabin in the hills of Carroll County. David Johansen, the owner, was found lying on his back in his living room, shot in the chest, and it was treated as a homicide.

In rural counties where law enforcement officers are few and far between, neighboring agencies and the Illinois State Police offer all the services necessary. The FBI is available for out of state leads.

For weeks, the leads took all investigators nowhere. It remained an unsolved murder for months.

Jim was troubled. He knew Johansen well, and something, though he can't identify it, wasn't setting well with Jim. It was a fall afternoon, and Jim drove back to the crime scene. He went alone for no particular reason, other than to see what possibly he could have missed.

Jim chose to sit in the long deserted home in the exact spot where Johansen's body had been found. The more he studied the situation, and as he had been thinking for months, it looked like a suicide. All indications were that Johansen had been shot at close range. Jim's recollections of Johansen were of a very unhappy man. But Jim thought the obvious. No gun equals no suicide. He remained unsettled. He told us that he sat there for hours just analyzing. One might compare Jim to Columbo. He simply wasn't satisfied. The home was scheduled for demolition the following week and Jim wanted to ensure that no stone had been left unturned.

Jim sat, then lay in the exact spot where Johansen had been located and on a whim looked over at and then into the fireplace and up the chimney. There it was, the weapon that had killed Johansen, a .38 caliber revolver. It was attached to a strong elastic band that pulled it up the chimney once Johansen relaxed his grip.

Ever the astute investigator and knowing the importance of preserving evidence, Jim got Dave Reed of the Illinois State Police to respond to his location and had him take charge of the evidence. Also responding to Jim's call was Chief Deputy Jack Thulen and Chief Investigator Harlan Carbaugh. It remains in my memory as an amazing piece of police work.

In less than a week the building would've been destroyed, with all the evidence lost forever and the "homicide of Dave Johansen" would still be unsolved to this day.

Death by suicide—no note left behind—case closed.

An entire book could be devoted to Sheriff Thulen and it would certainly include Jim and the prostitution activity that was becoming near epidemic in Carroll County.

Becoming an FBI agent after serving two years as a police officer gave me a perspective different than many other agents. My training, in many cases, had been rough and tumble police work, along with my Army infantry and ranger training.

Yes, I enjoyed methodical investigations, but there wasn't much I enjoyed more than responding to crimes in progress. Unless you were on a bank robbery squad, most agents were deeply involved in investigations.

Jim Thulen, Jack, and I were enjoying one of Dorothy's fifty-cent lunches one day and over a cup of coffee, and Jim confided that they really needed a cop to do some undercover work on a prostitution case that wasn't known in the County.

The good old farm boy in me surfaced and I asked Jim if I could do it. He and Jack looked at each other, both smiled, and said at the same time "Hell yeah."

This would be totally verboten to the FBI, so I got them to assure me that they tell none of the other agents. I knew I'd have to take annual leave and do this totally "under the table" with no one in the FBI being aware.

I already knew most of the scenario. A motel just west of Lanark with an attached bar was unquestionably running hookers and the locals were all over Jim and Jack to close it down. Simply put, try as they would, they could never quite catch anyone in the act and they needed evidence of actual prostitution.

It was agreed that the following Thursday evening I would get a room under an alias and spend the night at the bar. I'd see if I could get something going with the dancer who had been identified by Jim and Jack as an established prostitute from the Chicago area.

The preliminary work had been well cemented by Jim and Jack. She was well identified, as was her pimp; who did not hang out in the bar while she was dancing. Lanark was pretty much all white folks and though our dancer was black, a black man in that bar would have been cause for some concern. Rest assured, he would be nearby to protect her should he be needed.

This, of course, added concern, but due to there not being issues while she was dancing, he had established a pattern of leaving once she started and he was satisfied that all would by okay. Jack and Jim had determined that he would go to Clinton, Iowa to a gambling establishment.

It was agreed I'd check in about 9:00 p.m., go to the bar, have several drinks, keep giving her the eye and buying her drinks with money supplied to me by the Carroll County taxpayers and hope-fully build a case.

I invited her to my table during her break and she agreed to join me for a drink when she was through dancing. I continued to play the role and as 1 a.m. rolled around she agreed to accompany me to my room.

She kept asking me if I had "some shit," of course I assured her I did. She wanted to get high and made no bones about it. She was already on something more than booze and once in my room she immediately disrobed and insinuated she needed some money. I supplied the fifty-dollar bill offered by the good citizens of Carroll County. After a few minutes, I knew Jim and Jack were at the door and on our prearranged signal they failed to come in.

I was slowly disrobing, and she kept saying, "What's wrong with you? Why are you rolling your socks up?"

Jim and Jack, I later learn, were outside the door laughing their asses off and stalling as long as they possibly could. It was well beyond the time that the money was exchanged but they were doing all they could to build not only evidence but to create a very tellable story for days to come. When it got to the point where she started saying "Are you a cop or something?" they finally came in and placed her under arrest.

I followed them to the sheriff's office, did my report for them, and with their profuse thank-you and smiles, got on my way.

The story grew in humor with each telling to all the cops in Carroll County. "Jim Sacia—he's the guy who rolls his socks up when he takes them off, right?"

SHOTS FIRED, OFFICER DOWN

Bacino—Mayborne

Bank robbery is a Federal crime. Accordingly, the Federal government, namely the FBI, has jurisdiction. Most are also armed robberies, thereby local jurisdiction. The reality is that whenever a bank "goes down," all of law enforcement responds.

As with any violent felony, catching the bad guys is of the utmost importance. We'll sort out who does the prosecuting later. Sometimes, an interesting twist to the particular crime determines who will prosecute.

Such was the case in October 1974 when the Poplar Grove Illinois bank was robbed. It was a "heavy hit," with two bandits coming through the front door displaying weapons and announcing a holdup.

Theodore "Ted" Bacino had conspired to rob the bank with Glenn Loy and at some point decided to take the president hostage. They fled the bank, Loy in Bacino's car and Bacino with the bank president in the president's car.

They had obtained over $12,000, and in very short order, the Boone County Sheriff's Police and the Illinois State Police were in pursuit of Loy, forcing him off the road and following a foot chase, apprehended him in a farmer's field.

Bacino and the president were still on the run, and law enforcement throughout Northern Illinois was on the lookout for the well-described car.

155

Astute Loves Park Illinois officers and Winnebago County Deputies flocked to an area on North Second Street in Loves Park where the car was spotted.

Trying to keep up with the radio chatter on both my FBI frequency as well as ISPERN (Illinois State Police Emergency Radio Network), I was en route 10-39 (lights and siren) from Freeport to Poplar Grove with an approximate distance of some forty miles.

Eastbound and approaching Loves Park on Highway 173, I learned that the crime in progress was moving my way. I turned south on North Second St. where reports indicate the president has been dumped from the car.

Radio traffic was highly conflicted as I heard "Shots fired, officer down," simultaneously seeing numerous squad cars converge on what I recall as Jack's Barber Shop, only to learn the tragic reality. Bacino is gut shot, handcuffed, and the ambulance is en route.

Detective Mike Mayborne, a seasoned and well-liked deputy with the Winnebago Sheriff's Police, husband and father of two, lies dead in the alley having been hit three times from a volley of five rounds fired by Bacino at near point blank range.

My two most vivid memories of the entire incident are: the investigation revealed that Mike held up his hand as he fell badly wounded. In my opinion and to those doing the investigation, he was signaling to Bacino to stop firing, but he continued, shooting Mike through the hand and striking Mike's head, immediately killing him. My second vivid recollection is standing, shivering in the cold and seeing Mike's lovely wife holding his beautiful daughters at the funeral several days later.

At that moment I wished I'd have remained a farm kid in Wisconsin. These are the moments that simply tear your heart out.

Our senior resident agent, Jerry Nolan, was the case agent, and all the RA was involved in the investigation. Certainly Boone County authorities and Winnebago County authorities all had a significant interest in the case. It was determined that Winnebago County would prosecute the case.

At this writing, Bacino is seventy-nine years old and scheduled to be released by the Illinois Department of Corrections on March 4, 2015.

It was summed up best by Winnebago County Retired Sheriff Dick Meyers and former partner of Mayborne, "Bacino deserves to stay in prison. The forty years he spent in prison doesn't make up for the life he took." He went on to say, "He's seventy-nine now, and Mike's been dead all these years."

In my eleven years as a state representative, I'd meet with the Mayborne family regularly as the hearings came up year after year. This one is close and personal to me, and I ache so for Mike's survivors.

Another interesting twist is the little community where my children went to school and I served on the school board, Jay Bacino, Ted's youngest son, attended school and was a classmate with my oldest son, Jerry. Jay is a fine young man who spent his growing-up years under an unspoken cloud. His mom, LaVonne, worked hard and was a good provider. She raised four other children as well, who were older than Jay.

LaVonne passed away in June of 2013. Jay has gotten on with his life.

Criminal activity has more tentacles than an octopus. There is always more than just one victim.

SCALES MOUND BANK

Scales Mound in northwest Illinois could best be described as Sleepy Hollow. The community is nestled in the rolling hills of JoDaviess County. The school mascot is the Hornet. Like so many small rural communities, the school is the anchor for the community. The two churches provide balance to the two taverns. The lumberyard, appliance store, two service stations, and the general store make up the entire footprint for the community, including the Scales Mound Bank.

Lieutenant Raleigh Schleicher of the JoDaviess County Sheriff's Police waited for a passing train at the tracks which cuts through the peaceful little burg on the chilly November day of 1974. The train passed and Raleigh drove by the bank where he learns twenty minutes later that about the time he passed the bank, the employees were ordered into the vault of the bank. All four were fearful to come out. They had been ordered in there at gun point and told not to come out for a half hour. After about twenty minutes, Bank President Ida Travis hears nothing outside the vault and decides to bravely step out.

Ida ran to the nearest phone and dials the sheriff's office. The recording at the sheriff's office reveals the recorded transcript from Ida, "My god, the bank's been robbed," and then she hung up. This was before the days of 911, and the bank also had no alarm system tied to the sheriff's office.

At that time there were nine total banks in the little county of JoDaviess with a total population of twenty-three thousand souls. The dispatcher on duty begins frantically calling each bank, one after the other, starting with the two in Galena. We are all familiar with Murphy's law: "What can go wrong will." Such was the case as the ninth bank called is the bank of Scales Mound.

Lieutenant Schleicher, the only marked squad on duty, swore under his breath when he got the call, makes a u turn on Stage Coach Trail, engages his emergency equipment, and responds as fast as Stage Coach Trail allows as the turns and curves are similar to the road up to Pikes Peak.

SA Glen McKenzie and I were the first arriving FBI agents. Numerous other law enforcement officers from surrounding agencies, also Sheriff Marlo Specht and the Illinois State Police were already on site. We quickly learned that a lone white male wearing a hat and mask, displaying a black revolver, had gotten away with a significant amount of money.

As always our friends in the State Police and local officers have set up road blocks, all realizing that too much time has elapsed and our bad guy is more than likely gone.

How we arrived at our prime suspect has long since slipped from my mind, but we determine he is a village official in a small town just north of the Wisconsin State Line. The line is only just over a mile from Scales Mound. For several days our efforts begin to center on him.

In law enforcement, I can say with some authority "dumb luck" trumps good investigation many times. Our suspect has not been at work, so no chance yet to interview him. His coworkers all agree that he has become rather strange.

Two elderly sisters in their eighties live alone in a house on the family farm along Stage Coach Trail. They have been traveling during the past month and it is believed that they are not home. Several nights after the robbery, at approximately 10:00 p.m., our suspect decides to burglarize the old gals' house, not realizing they have returned home. If you told me what happened next, I would be waiting for the punch line as it's too good to be true.

The old gals are lying in bed upstairs and they hear him rummaging around downstairs. One of our sisters quietly grabs the twelve-gauge shotgun loaded with double 00 buckshot. As our suspect quietly starts up the stair, she pulls the trigger while standing in the doorway of her bedroom, and one pellet of the buckshot literally parted his scalp, not only his hair, his skin and all. Needless to say, he flees, grabbing a towel from the hallway and our gal gets the sheriff's department on the phone. She knows she has hit him with the buckshot due to the large amount of blood on the stairs and at the front door.

One of the responding officers is State Trooper Leo Haefle, who goes on, in later years, to become the sheriff of JoDaviess County. Leo can't believe his eyes as he sees a man running down the road with a blood-soaked white towel wrapped on his head and he is hitchhiking. Leo had not yet engaged his red lights as he was hopeful he might come upon someone.

Our suspect was dumbfounded to realize he was being given a ride by a state trooper, in handcuffs, of course. Too good to be true? For once, Murphy's law backfired. Thank you, Trooper Haefle.

History cannot record the number of times we, in law enforcement in Northwest Illinois, have been told this story and retold it. The mental image I have of that scared but brave old lady pulling the trigger just makes me feel warm all over.

ROCHELLE BRIBERY

Rochelle, Illinois, is located just south of Rockford about twenty-five miles. In the past twenty years, it has grown to a major rail transportation hub with trucks and railcars dominating much of the traffic.

In 1975, one could have described it as a peaceful farming community and perhaps somewhat of a bedroom community commutable to the City of Rockford. The chief of Police, Winston Brass, was among the finest men I've ever known. Winston was a native of India coming to this country in 1959 and joining the Rochelle Police Department in 1968. He attended both the Southern Police Institute and the FBI National Academy. He was appointed chief in 1974 and served in that capacity until his retirement in 1993.

Winston was a cop's cop. Many emulated him, but in fairness, he would have been hard to duplicate. He taught law enforcement techniques at area colleges and traveled often back to India as a guest lecturer at their National Police Institute. A more likable and capable person would be hard to find.

Though Rochelle was not in my territory, the Ogle County agent coordinated with Winston and me, as an over the road trucker who was on the Rochelle City Council had come to me very concerned about a possible bribery matter. The trucker/city councilman GB Davis and I were well acquainted from having worked together on a previous theft from interstate shipment case that had been assigned to me.

As GB laid out what was happening to Winston, the Ogle County agent, and I and the wheels of justice slowly started turning. Rochelle was attempting to annex a large parcel of property and GB was one of the holdouts on the council. In fact, he was the one that was adamantly against it.

Harlan Askvig was a realtor with much to gain should the annexation take place. GB was a steel hauler, and he was gone a great deal. Harlan was relentless in his efforts to win GB over to his way of thinking. Well before the days of cell phones, Harlan would leave messages at Trucking Terminals where GB was known to be heading. Yes, you could call it classic white-collar crime; I would add "stupid" white-collar crime.

GB shared with us that in his excitement to win him over, Harlan had offered him a new Cadillac or $10,000 cash. The offer was made, according to GB both personally and telephonically. In FBI vernacular this classification is a 166 matter (ITAR) Interstate Transportation to aid in Racketeering—Bribery. All the necessary elements are present, now we just have to prove it. Actually even before proving, I need the Assistant United States Attorney for the Northern District of Illinois, Western Division, to agree to authorize me to record a conversation between GB and Harlan. AUSA Tom Durkin authorized the monitor, and I instructed GB in the fine art of affixing the suction cup to the earpiece on the phone when he next had a conversation with Mr. Askvig.

GB did a masterful job and returned from his run out west with the recording. During the conversation, Harlan outlined that whatever Cadillac he wanted or the $10,000 cash would be his for his yes vote. Winston and I interviewed Mr. Askvig and to this day, what is most perplexing was that he just couldn't understand what he had done wrong.

Throughout the several months of the investigation, Winston was able to keep the Ogle County agent and I updated on the tempo of the annexation in Rochelle. His relationship with all the city councilmen was superb, and the dynamics of the investigation, had they been known along the way, would have blown the efforts out of the water.

FBI director Clarence Kelly saw fit to send me an incentive award for resolving the issue and successful prosecution of Mr. Askvig. The credit should have gone to Winston. Sadly, he passed away in 1993 just shortly after he retired.

In life's reflections getting to know and respect a man like Chief of Police Winston Brass was a highlight.

OFFICE OF THE DIRECTOR

UNITED STATES DEPARTMENT OF JUSTICE

FEDERAL BUREAU OF INVESTIGATION

WASHINGTON, D.C. 20535

January 29, 1976

PERSONAL

Mr. James G. Sacia
Federal Bureau of Investigation
Chicago, Illinois

Dear Mr. Sacia:

You certainly *merit commendation* for the superlative services you rendered incident to the investigation of the Interstate Transportation in Aid of Racketeering - Bribery case involving Bob Meadow and Harlan J. Askvig. Additionally, I have approved a $150.00 incentive award for you and you will find a check enclosed which represents this award.

As the result of your determination and high degree of skill, you successfully overcame obstacles in this difficult and involved investigation. The successful prosecution of Askvig is attributable to your professionalism and I want you to be aware of my gratitude.

Sincerely yours,

C. m. Kelley

Clarence M. Kelley
Director

Enclosure

JOSEPH "JOEY" DIDIER

It was March 4, 1975, just the day before my thirty-first birthday. The early morning discussion in the Rockford Office of the FBI was the edict from the Chicago front office that due to a fuel crisis, vehicles in the FBI fleet would curtail operating by 25 percent. "The big guy," our slang term for SSRA Jerry Nolan, was certainly meant as a term of endearment, the reality was when he said how something was going to be that was how it would be, no sense arguing, he had spoken.

Jerry was insistent that we in Rockford would comply. Suddenly it all seemed unimportant as Detective Sgt. Bill Francis called to share that they had a missing juvenile believed to be kidnapped. Initial reports indicated that fifteen-year-old Joey Didier, the son of Rockford Alderman George Didier had disappeared while delivering the Rockford Morning Star Newspaper earlier that day.

At the early hour there is much speculating. Maybe the boy ran away. Nothing is making sense. One neighbor on the boy's paper route swore she heard a struggle and heard a car speed away. Detective Roland "Rollie" Donelli calls our office and expresses hope that the FBI can help.

As the newest agent to be assigned to the Rockford RA, I was shocked when I heard the big guy state, "We stay out of it unless it proves to be interstate."

I was shocked. I had always believed we get involved from the get-go as police cooperation, but Nolan decided that because of fuel cutbacks, we would only get involved if, in fact, an interstate crime is established or a demand for ransom is received.

It was not my place to be, but I am angry. The relationship between the Rockford Police and the FBI to this point in time, I believe, were exceptional. Senior agents Brad Riggs, Jack Sheridan, and Glen McKenzie all pushed Jerry a little to get us involved, but the big guy had spoken; I couldn't believe it. Seldom am I ashamed to be an agent, but I am embarrassed, what the hell?

We all monitored the case daily and continued with our workloads as Rockford City, the Winnebago Count Sheriff's Department, and the state police work the disappearance of young Didier. More and more there was little doubt that he had been abducted. I just couldn't believe that we couldn't simply throw caution to the wind and help Rockford City. This fuel shortage crap had me mad as hell. On March 15, all hell broke loose. The nude frozen body of Joey was found hanging from a rafter at a scout camp cabin in rural Jo Daviess County.

Investigators rapidly closed in on Robert Lower, a truck driver who traveled daily from Rockford to the Stockton, Illinois, area. He had been a suspect in two previous newspaper delivery boys abduction. One occurred in Rockford in 1973 to a twelve-year-old boy and a fourteen-year-old in 1974. In both cases, the boys had been sexually molested and their genitals painted with spray paint. Lower had been arrested in both Reno, Nevada, and Freeport, Illinois, previously for sex-related crimes.

As always, in cases of this magnitude, it's good police work that solves the crime.

Rollie Donelli was the classic old-school detective. He and Detective Jes Otwell sat with Lower explaining to him that they had airtight case against him on March 20, 1975. Donelli explained as only an excellent investigator could that he understood liking young boys and how he himself fantasized about having sex with young boys. Donelli explained how Lower lit up and literally laid out how he grabbed the boy and drove him to the scout camp, beat him, and molested him. The hardest part to tolerate, according to Donelli, was Joey pleading with him not to kill him. Lower told the boy that he could identify him and he had no choice. He tied his hands, put a rope around his neck, and threw it over a rafter, pulling the rope tight, forced young Didier to step up on a stool. He was crying and pleading for Lower to "please don't hang me." He told Lower he had a bad memory and would never be a witness against him. Lower calmly tied the rope off, kicked the stool away, and Joey Didier died by hanging. Lower simply walked out the door with no remorse. He was sentenced to one hundred to 150 years in prison.

Throughout my eleven years as a state representative the Didier family repeatedly came to Springfield to plead to keep Lower in prison. During my first four years in Springfield, from 2003 to 2007, the family came yearly. In 2007 we changed the law where appeals of this magnitude could only occur every three years. I always did what I could for them.

The most difficult part of the Didier abduction was the failure of my agency, the FBI, to get involved. Technically, Jerry Nolan was right. I always felt it was wrong.

DAN GRAY

The Rockford Illinois Police Department in the 1970s had an intelligence division consisting of Sgt. Gene Watson, Detective Joe Davis, and Detective Dan Gray. Dan was a minority because he had a bachelor degree, not all that common at that time. Fair to say, Dan was a rising star, and as far as a likable person, simply put, he was awesome.

I spent a considerable amount of time working with Dan; I enjoyed his sense of humor and certainly his work ethic. We spent considerable time discussing cases of mutual interest. Dan was sought after, not only by his fellow officers, but law enforcement throughout Northern Illinois as he was a trained polygraph operator, commonly known as a lie detector.

Polygraph, as an investigative tool, was tremendous. As years rolled on, it became more and more difficult to get a polygraph confession admissible and to some extent they aren't used to the degree that they were in the seventies. I continue to believe in them, as an investigative tool to be used in conjunction with other investigative techniques.

Dan possessed a wit that was extremely unique. Throughout my lifetime, I've known others to have the mischievous humor and wit, but it is truly rare. In police work it is often a great asset. Combine his wit with his polygraph skills and interview skills and you had one hell of an investigator.

I often encouraged Dan to apply for the FBI but there is little doubt Rockford was home, and that's where he'd stay.

Dan's skills were personified with a case that reeked with heartbreak. How the young woman was located I no longer recall. Uniformed officers found her nude and beaten beyond recognition.

The two things I will never forget as Dan described them to me was that along with the beating, a soda bottle was smashed inside her vagina and her eyelids were cut off with scissors. No she did not survive and perhaps that's a blessing.

The evil side of humanity is one of those issues that creates a lifetime struggle trying to understand.

Dan shared that the two responsible for the despicable act admitted their involvement after considerable investigation, and there is little to requite someone following such an unbelievable atrocity. How they tracked them down I no longer recall. The good news is that they did. My hope is that they spend their natural life behind bars. This is among the reasons I do strongly believe in the death penalty,

As Dan shared the details with me, we're en route to lunch and we happened to be directly in front of the Colonial Village Mall. A call went out on the city channel that an "exposer" was in front of the mall. The police vernacular, of course, is a "wand waver" and Dan and I literally see a man matching the description not fifty yards away.

As we were in Dan's unmarked squad, we rolled up to the guy with him, showing no concern. Dan exited the vehicle, grabbed the guy before he knew what was happening and turned the guy to face me while pulling his trench coat away, commenting, "Hey, Jimmy, do you think we've got our guy?" He was still fully erected with the front cut out of his pants.

Trying to be professional at that moment in time totally failed me, and I'm sure I laughed out loud. Dan had him "cuffed and stuffed" in a matter of thirty seconds, and we radioed en route to the Public Safety Building with the subject in custody.

To go from near depression to hysterical laughter in such a short time makes police work what it is. Sadly, times can make it go exactly opposite. Dan Gray could smooth the transition.

At the time the Detective Bureau was commanded by Captain Anderson.

Coming into the Detective Bureau one evening, as we were all eating pizza, Dan reached for the good captain's suit lapel, commenting on such a beautiful, well-made suit, all the while cleaning his greasy pizza hands on the captain's suit. The captain was humbled and thanked Detective Gray for the compliment. Only Dan could have gotten away with that.

FRANK DEBOER

Sometimes we learn too late that someone is developing serious mental issues.

Frank DeBoer was a troubled man. Friends and relatives related that he was becoming more difficult to talk with. "He just seemed mad all the time" related a disbelieving uncle learning that his nephew Frank, age forty-two, had just been in a shootout with police.

The entire situation began slightly before noon on March 22, 1977. Apparently Frank was mad at a local lumber company in Freeport after learning that he would only receive a small amount of Worker's Compensation from an injury he had received years earlier while working there. He apparently "lost it" according to his wife.

Frank left home with several guns telling her that he was going to "get things right" at the lumber company. Mrs. DeBoer contacted the sheriff's department fearing the worst and an "all-points bulletin" was put out to area police. Somehow, while in route to the job site, Frank's car broke down, and he made contact with his aunt, Mrs. Bunnell, who picked him up and they agree that she will take him home.

While traveling to Frank's Florence Station Home, they were intercepted by police, and a shootout ensued. Frank shot and wounded Officer Lyle Kuhlemeyer. Mrs. Bunnell suffered a stress attack, and Lt. Jack Munda, who knew Frank well, dropped his gun belt and accompanied Frank back to Frank's home. Great, now we had not only a barricaded felon at the DeBoer residence but a hostage police lieutenant. There is no doubt as the day progressed that Frank wanted to die.

I was with Captain Dick Currier of the sheriff's department working on a case when the first calls came in. I accompanied Dick to Florence Station, where Dick set up a command post. As a newly trained hostage negotiator, I was more than eager to help in any way I could. Not to worry, Sheriff Don Scofield definitely would handle any negotiating.

In small communities everyone knows everyone. Don Scofield knew Frank well and got him on the phone. He encouraged Frank to let Lieutenant Munda go, lay the guns down, come out, and get some help. Frank would have none if it, and he made that very clear. He told the sheriff that he would come out later with guns blazing. Sheriff Scofield kept trying to diffuse him from a phone in the radio room at the Stephenson County Sheriff's Office.

Frank hung up on the sheriff, and a reporter from a Chicago News outlet called Frank's home. Frank answered and became highly agitated and hung up on him. Then the reporter made the mistake of calling the sheriff, who I'd been told by not only the sheriff but others who were there, that Sheriff Scofield told him, "You come out here, you SOB. I'll nail your nuts to a fence post and push you over backwoods." Knowing Sheriff Scofield as I do, I have no doubt that is what he said.

Don Scofield kept trying to call Frank back and keep him on the phone. Frank was having nothing to do with settling down in any way. He was bent on a shootout. Though according to Lieutenant Munda and Sheriff Scofield, he continued to say he was going out but taking someone with him. Did he mean it, or did he just want to die? That is certainly an answer none of us can give.

Several hours passed. The sheriff had coordinated with the phone company that the only calls that could go to the DeBoer phone were from the sheriff's office. Police from many area jurisdictions continued to arrive with offers of help. The home in little Florence Station was well cordoned off, and media continued to try to get close. Captain Currier had his deputies and other officers ordered to keep them away.

We had a standoff with a very distraught individual, and reports kept coming to the command post from those who knew him and family members that his mental state had become worse and worse in recent weeks. Something would happen, and it would be soon.

Sheriff Scofield continued his efforts to get and keep DeBoer on the phone, and he did all he could to settle him, and it just wasn't working.

We learn that when Frank was in the Army in the 1950s, he was injured in an accident in Germany, resulting in a steel plate being placed in his head. Frank's agitation increases through the day, and try as he would, the sheriff simply couldn't keep Frank on the phone. Frank's threats became more and more bizarre.

After a two and a half hours' standoff, Frank called the sheriff and told him he was coming out with guns blazing. Deputy Sheriff John Peterson, armed with a twelve-gauge shotgun, and Sergeant Les Davis of the Illinois State Police, were positioned just north and east of Frank's house which would face the rear entrance. The radios had all crackled, "He is coming out shooting." He did just that.

Deputy Peterson got off one shot, and Sergeant Davis fired all nine rounds from his model 39 Smith and Wesson semiautomatic pistol. Eight rounds struck DeBoer. When Sergeant Davis was asked later how many rounds he fired, he responded, "Two, maybe three." This is a very typical response in a highly tense shooting situation.

Sadly Frank DeBoer got his wish, "suicide by cop." It's the path he chose. Sadly, the issue he faced, to you and me, would be no big deal. The mind can work in strange ways. He took a permanent solution to a temporary problem.

GENE COOTS

G ene Coots was the "best of the best."

I first met him prior to even being officially transferred to Rockford while I was still on my recruiting applicant road trip out of Chicago.

It had been determined, unbeknown to me, that Jerry Nolan, the senior resident agent (SRA), was somehow going to get me transferred to Rockford. His motives, of course, would be to get his "eighth man" thereby qualifying to become a GS14 supervisory senior resident agent (SSRA) with a significant raise. It didn't hurt at all that I truly wanted the transfer and I knew I fit in well with the existing seven agents. With Bill Meincke in the front office and Jerry Nolan in Rockford, my transfer chances were looking good.

Jerry was taking me around meeting the law enforcement officers in the area; enter then Sgt. Gene (Elwood) Coots who was already a legend of sorts. Sgt. Coots was sitting behind his desk in the basement detective bureau. Gene was the Chief of Detectives for then Sheriff Paul Bengston, the Sheriff of Winnebago County.

The detective bureau space was relegated to the basement due to space issues and I at six foot had to duck. Jerry Nolan, who had a good five inches on me, literally had to bend at the waist. Jerry was pursuing a lead for the sheriff's office on what we in the FBI referred to as an 88 case, or UFAP unlawful flight to avoid prosecution, which was a local felon who was believed to have fled the state and the locals needed our help.

Gene was famous for his "colloquialisms," or clever sayings which I had not yet completely grasped.

The man we were looking for was in Coot's description, "crookeder than a barrel of guts." I tried not to chuckle but the good

Sergeant capitalized on my smirk and lit into a tirade of just how evil this "slimy bastard" was. He was wanted not only by the county but separate charges, all felonies, by the city of Rockford as well.

During our visit, I learned Sgt. Coots had small town rural roots similar to my own and we developed a friendship that lasted until his passing in the fall of 2014.

Ironically Gene and I both had our weddings in Gilman, a small burg in north central Wisconsin, and our receptions at kool-mos Ballroom. Neither of us knew this until many years later when Gene was back visiting Gilman on a weekend and thought he saw me. The story is told that he avoided me as he assumed I was on some FBI undercover or covert operation and he wasn't about to blow it.

Gene's marriage was very short lived. They did have a daughter but shortly after her birth they parted. As only Gene could relate "our marriage started out okay but as soon as the preacher finished and we turned to walk back to the door it started going to hell."

Gene's skills, rank, and notoriety continued to grow. In many ways, he became one of the best known and respected officers in Northern Illinois and Southern Wisconsin. You just couldn't talk of one of Sgt. Coot's investigations without finding some humor, no matter the gravity of the case. One of my all-time favorites was Coots sitting on a picnic table beside the house of a double murder of an elderly couple, the Lloyd Schrader's. Coots' appearance was always somewhat disheveled. He wore a Fedora hat with the brim turned up all the way around looking somewhat comical. He was being interviewed by the three local television channels and was asked the question, "Do you have any leads?" In his down-home colloquialism, he stated, "Well, we've been lookin' at several fellers, and now we are scopin' in on a couple more."

The appearance was of someone not very knowledgeable—not so fast. Coots had it all together, and his clever techniques of appearing not aware solved many crimes.

Former FBI agent Dan Doyle became the Winnebago County State attorney. Totally perplexed that a criminal had confessed to Coots after many had determined he wouldn't "crack," he asked the man what Coots had said to bring him around. Our hardened criminal stated it wasn't what he asked me or said, he just kept slobbering coffee and dribbling cookie crumbs as he walked around me talking all the time—"I couldn't stand it anymore."

When Gene retired, he came to work for me at NITE Equipment. His gift of making everyone feel like a long-lost friend was among Gene's greatest assets, exceeded only by his competence and humor.

Gene loved to talk and loved to drink coffee. Walking around with his coffee cup, slobbering coffee, just added more humor to most any situation.

Our son Jerry, on his return from college, worked regularly with Gene. The tale is repeated often that when Gene got down to about one quarter of the coffee remaining in his cup, it will have cooled to the point that he was ready for a fresh cup. Jerry swears, and knowing Cooter as I did, I know it happened regularly. Gene would be six to ten feet from the open door and attempt to toss the remaining coffee out the door. Of course only a few drops made it out the door, the balance left a path from his feet, on the concrete floor, to the doorway. It probably emphasized why Gene would have had a problem living with a woman.

Jerry brought with him from his college days at River Falls, Wisconsin, a beautiful, gentle Dalmatian "Lucas" who stole the hearts of our entire family—not so much Gene Coots.

Jerry often shares of Cooter, with a sweet roll in one hand, dribbling coffee from the cup in his other hand and Lucas just inches from and eyeing Gene's sweet roll, being in a deep conversation with a customer wanting to buy a trailer. Gene just blurted out, "F—— you, Lucas," and continued his deep conversation with the customer. Of course, both Jerry and the customer started laughing profusely. Classic Cooter!

One of Coots' biggest disappointments was the failure to solve the disappearance of two realtors, Everett Hawley and Clarence Owens, in late February 1976. The men in their "gold Cadillac," a newly painted 1966 Chevrolet four door, were last seen at a farm auction near the Winnebago / Ogle County Line and disappeared without a trace. That morning they had attended a rally for Gubernatorial Candidate Big Jim Thompson in downtown Pecatonica.

Owens at sixty-five and Hawley seventy-two were business partners and the best of friends. Every lead over Coots' many year career came up empty. What troubled Coots the most was that they simply vanished. His investigative skills notwithstanding, this case would remain unsolved and no amount of speculation would lead to solving it.

Gene grew up in rural Winnebago County, Burritt Township, where for years, specifically the thirties, forties, and fifties, the annual "Trask Bridge Picnic" was hosted. Lore had it that it started sometime in the 1920s, usually in August, with a county fair type of atmosphere. Gene spoke of it often, and exaggeration was perhaps an accepted way to discuss how it was "back then."

In the late 1990s, it was brought back with a few "diehards" such as Gene Coots to relive days gone by. It reappeared as "the Trask Bridge Picnic revisited" and was and is to this day held at the Burritt Town Hall. Plowing with horses and mules and antique tractors as well as many displays makes up a very enjoyable day for everyone who visits. Local bands play, displays are set out, and the museum is open for all to see. Local talent is always welcome.

Until Gene's passing, he was always among those getting the most attention and laughs. Gene was simply put, a fixture in the community and to spend a half hour with him at the Trask Bridge Picnic had your sides hurting from laughing, with his never ending "Cooterisms." "Hey Jim look at this. Now ain't that handier than a pocket in your underwear."

As we stared at an unknown piece of machinery, I inquired, "What do you know about this, Gene?"

His response was, "I know about as much about that as a hog knows about Good Friday."

Our conversation moved to a man of questionable ability he saw. "Well, what do you know about him, Gene?"

"Well, let's just say he's not always in gear when he tries to pull ahead."

Safe to say it never ends. I have no clue if he made them up on the fly or simply never forgot one he liked.

"He's clumsier than a cub bear with an arm load of shelled corn."

"He's so slow, if you gave him two turtles to play with one would get away."

"Well of course he's old—he's waiting for funeral prices to go down."

"That old boy is uglier than a bouquet of hind ends held together by a log chain."

"The price of that car is higher than a giraffe's hind end."

They just went on and on.

JIGS STIENER

As I write this some forty years after I worked with Jigs, I can mentally see him as if it were yesterday. Jigs was the chief of police in East Dubuque, Illinois, and had been throughout the colorful years of East Dubuque.

Yes, East Dubuque is a river town, just across the Mississippi River from Dubuque, Iowa. When Iowa closed late at night, East Dubuque came to life.

Jigs was what one would call an "old school" cop, keep the peace in town. If it was best to turn his head and look the other way he would. I believe most would agree Jigs was a good man. He fit the image of a small-town chief. He was overweight, had high blood pressure leading to an always-red face, but he knew everything going on in his community.

Jigs called me on a Friday morning. He needed to see me, and off to East Dubuque I went. He gave me a sketchy outline of a prostitute that had gotten word to him that she was being held against her will and forced to turn tricks. It was a story I was familiar with. Though at this point, I lacked specifics, Jigs would update me as soon as I arrived.

Somehow, with a very small police force Jigs kept the peace.

My previous efforts with federal prosecution of pimps transporting women across state lines in the Northern District of Illinois had met with only limited success. I contacted the Jo Daviess County States Attorney John Cox who was adamant for federal prosecution.

All I could do at this point was get the facts and hopefully talk with this very scared young woman. We could sort out prosecution later. Jigs arranged the meeting with her, and as I recall, Jo Daviess County Detective Dan Sheehan.

The story, told between tears and dashing glances everywhere fearing for her safety, is hard to put into words. This is about as good as I can do.

We'll call her Sheila. She told us the bizarre story that Jigs had previously sketchily outlined. Sheila and her friend Natasha were being forced by their man Alphons to turn tricks between beatings and being kept in a room under the watchful eye of a German Shepard guard dog. At this moment she was believed to be "tricking" by Alphons but had come to the back door of City Hall with Jigs help and that of the "John" that gave her extra money, as he felt bad for her. We got her statement and we were able to get a photo of Alphons through Jigs that he had obtained from a department where he had previously been arrested.

Jigs took Sheila back out the rear door of City Hall, confident he could get her back to the "John" who had helped her. Now it was up to Danny and I to get a warrant for Alphons and preferably a search warrant for the apartment that Sheila, Natasha, and Alphons shared.

As I feared, the assistant US attorney for the Western Division of the Northern District of Illinois had very little interest in prosecution. Here is the conundrum. At that time, with the Northern District headquartered in Chicago and the Western Division, when there were prosecutions that required an assistant US attorney (AUSA), they would travel to Freeport on a road trip from Chicago (about 150 miles). Add to that East Dubuque and you have another sixty miles.

If prosecution was forthcoming both the Federal Judge and AUSA had to road trip from Chicago to Freeport. Accordingly, crime, unless heinous, was difficult to prosecute on a federal level.

States Attorney John Cox was livid. He knew this was unequivocally a good federal case and sentence time would be far more significant than a state charge. I explained the declination to prosecute to John in a very embarrassed manner. John knew there was little I could do about it. Jigs sat quietly and listened. Dan and I tried to come up with a good way to get this clown.

I went home that evening tremendously frustrated, an excellent federal case with great prosecutive potential slipping through my fingers. At seven thirty the next morning, Jigs had me on the phone, could I come right over. I let Nolan know I was en route back to East Dubuque, and he echoed my sentiments as I left, "Find a way to get this bastard will you." Of course, Jerry—somehow!

When I arrived in East Dubuque Sheriff Marlo Specht, Detective Sheehan, and Jigs were already there as was John Cox. Marlo gave me, what I recall as a smile, as he shook my hand with a comment: "Jimmy, there is always a way." With that Jigs, coffee cup in hand, related that Sheila and Natasha were on a bus back to their small town in Tennessee. That certainly told me that Jigs had found a way to get them away from Alphons.

Of course, my next question of Jigs was "What happened to Alphons?" Jigs's response was classic Jigs: "Let's just say we encouraged him to leave town." Perhaps it's not justice at its finest, but justice it is.

No, I never did learn the details to the "rest of the story." Knowing Jigs as I did, I had little doubt that the issue was tactfully handled. I also had little doubt that Alphons had no desire to ever return to East Dubuque.

Throughout my law enforcement career, one of my greatest disappointments was having what I believed was an excellent prosecutable case, not be prosecuted. One might argue that some of the elements of successful prosecution were lacking. Sometimes you could readily see that a very overworked prosecutor's office was declining simply because more important or higher-profile cases took precedence.

Throughout my thirty-plus-year career in law enforcement, I can say unequivocally that cases readily prosecuted early on in my career were readily declined toward the end of my career. Two quick examples: when I was a new agent in Salt Lake City we successfully prosecuted a man for a single car (ITSMV) Interstate Transportation of a Stolen Motor Vehicle. When I left the Chicago Division with my retirement in 1997, we wouldn't even investigate unless it was a ring case (numerous subjects and numerous vehicles). Bank embezzlement investigations are always commonplace. Early in my career we investigated and successfully prosecuted all of them. By the time I left in 1997 unless the loss was at least $1,500 the FBI would not even become involved. I'm sure by now that the threshold is even higher.

In no way is this meant as disparaging to our AUSA's (Assistant United States Attorneys). It's simple reality—more crime, less resources to deal with them.

The following letter from JoDaviess County Attorney John Cox to US Attorney Thomas Sullivan dated May 16, 1979, shared my deep concern for federal prosecution in Northwest Illinois.

JIM SACIA

JOHN W. COX, JR.
STATE'S ATTORNEY
JO DAVIESS COUNTY COURTHOUSE
GALENA, ILLINOIS 61036
815 777-0109 — 815 777-0533

May 16, 1979

Honorable Thomas Sullivan
U.S. Attorney
Northern District of Illinois
Derkson Federal Building
300 S. Dearborn
Chicago, Illinois 60604

Re: Prosecution of Federal Crime
Laws in the Western Division
of the Northern District of
Illinois

Dear Mr. Sullivan:

I am becoming more and more concerned about the prosecution
or lack thereof of Federal Crime Statutes in our end of the
District. A recent case involving white slave trafficer in my
county has revealed to me what appears to be a rather conspicuous
lack of prosecutorial forces in this area. I have discussed this
matter extensively with local agents of the Federal Bureau of
Investigation. These agents agree that there is simply no real
contact from your office in the Western Division.

I will admit that I personally have not requested assistance
from your office on a prior occasion. However, the above mentioned
case certainly has revealed to me a need to open general communi-
cations with your office. FBI agents' have expressed to me their
deep frustration with the lack of obtaining ultimate prosecution of
cases they investigate.

When they have a case where it appears to be a clear violation of a Federal Criminal Statute with no apparent difficulty
in proof of the elements of the crime, it is only reasonable to
assume that prosecution will follow. In general, this was true
in the above mentioned case and yet, to date, there has been no
prosecution from your office. I have discussed the above case
with the head of your criminal division, Mr. McQueen, and he has
listed numerous inadequecies in the evidence. It is certainly not
my desire to be critical of one or more of your assistants and how
they would choose to handle a specific case. However, I can not
help but feel that the the reason this case was not prosecuted
lies not in the insufficiency of evidence, but rather lies in
the distance from East Dubuque Illinois, to Chicago, Illinois.

All of this points out that it may be a benefit to everyone if there were a residence Assistant U.S. Attorney in Rockford.
It is my understanding that no such position exists at the
present time.

May 16, 1979

Page 2

Honorable Thomas Sullivan

Continued,

    I must state that I, like the FBI, am frustrated and saddened by the apparent lack of desire to prosecute cases in the Western Division. If my conclusions are erroneous, I would be happy to be shown how. If my conclusions are correct, I would appreciate hearing from you on what, if any, actions you intend to take to correct this situation.

    Thank you.

Sincerely yours,

John W. Cox, Jr.
State's Attorney, Jo Daviess County

cc: Hon. James E. Carter, President of The United States
    Hon. Charles Percy
    Hon. Adlai Stevenson
    Hon. John B. Anderson
    Hon. Griffin Bell
    Hon. Edward Kennedy
    Director of Federal Bureau of Investigation
    Mr. James Scacia
    Mr. Marlo Specht

BANK ROBBERY SEMINARS

At seven thirty in the morning, I'm standing in the bank lobby facing all the Fulton Bank's employees.

Banks are required by their charters to have all employees trained regularly in procedures dealing with bank robberies. Why? Because banks will be robbed!

Though the phrase is attributed to famed bank robber Willy Sutton, when asked why he robbed banks, he allegedly responded with "Because that's where the money is." Mr. Sutton adamantly denied until his death he made that statement. According to Mr. Sutton, because of his notoriety, he attributes the infamous comment to some enterprising reporter who needed to fill copy and thereafter it stuck like glue. He did coauthor a book in 1976, *That's Where the Money Was*.

Back to my seminar. The FBI is not the required agency to provide the training, but I personally provided it to all the banks in the four counties that I covered. The banks loved it. We obviously didn't charge, I worked very hard at giving a good presentation and I believe I got very good at it.

On this particular morning, coffee cup close by, I'm really getting warmed up and my audience is very attentive. Then it happened; I noticed a few smirks, then employees nudging one another, and silent whispers followed by smiles. Any man, who has ever faced a group in such a setting, has felt that very uncomfortable feeling of "Oh my god, is my zipper down?"

Not wanting to be conspicuous for obvious reasons, I clipped my right thumb over my belt buckle, and with my index finger, I inconspicuously determined that whew! It was zipped up. By now they were all distracted, and I had no choice. I stopped my delivery and simply said, "All right, what is it?" I was greeted with hysterical laughter.

Leaving home at 4:00 a.m. for the seventy miles to Fulton, I did not wish to wake Jenny, so I pretty much dressed in the dark. I always wore western cut suits and cowboy boots. I now joined in the laughter as I realized I was wearing one brown and one black boot.

Through it all I somehow got them reengaged and commented, "Now that I have your full attention," and went on with my training, somewhat embarrassed. We had a great seminar.

I always taught actions at the bank before, during and after the robbery. Each facet is extremely important. Before hand—what the bank does in its day to day operations may well prevent a robbery. Simple things like encouraging employees to make eye contact with everyone. The number of robberies I responded to over the years, during interviews of the apprehended subject, they would say that when they "cased" this bank nobody seemed to pay attention to them. That was often followed with "We were going to rob bank X, but their people seemed to be watching us."

I had these stories to tell. I often used a short video of actual bank camera footage taken during actual robberies. My favorites, and the ones that drove the point home, were cameras not periodically checked and maintained. During one actual robbery, the camera, due to being bumped or somehow the point of arm moved, we had great photos of the robbers' shoes and nothing else. Another favorite photo I used was a very alert teller, observing a would be robber in her mind, activates the camera when the robber starts to come toward her station, only to have the film break just as he was coming into focus, due to the camera not being regularly checked and the film was old and brittle. This isn't a problem so much today thanks to modern technology but it always made a great point on the need for maintenance contracts with the camera provider.

Perhaps the following is the victim of numerous "retellings," but it remains one of my all-time favorite episodes of an actual robbery/embezzlement which occurred to a Philadelphia Bank in the late 1960s. It was a story I could not resist telling.

A longtime employee, a lady who never married, developed a peculiar habit of bringing her pet rabbit to the bank. The bank was large and employed full-time bank guards, something we didn't often see in the rural banks where I spent a great deal of time. Apparently, the guards would look in her package each day as she came to work and again as she left work each evening. To say she was a well trusted employee would be an understatement. Her duties were in the bowels of the large bank vault area of this well-known bank.

After many days the guards weren't near as inquisitive, and she left the bank, not with her rabbit but with $86,000 cash. In the 1960s, that was a great deal of money. Did she get away with it? I honestly don't know. What I do know is that it was a great example of why senior bank employees are required to take two weeks off each year and I would often use that story to make my point.

I always spent a great deal of time on opening and closing procedures and I could share numerous actual happenings of these times finding the banks most vulnerable.

Yes, I spent much time on actions before the robbery, but what if it actually happens? This was where I could really go into road gear. Thanks to numerous FBI cases over the years, I could use actual examples to get the bankers eating out of my hand.

More than anything I stressed safety. Far too many bank employees over the years have been injured or killed due to trying something heroic or stupid. I invariably shared the true story of how the term "Stockholm syndrome" came to be.

August 23, 1973

Stockholm Sweden Kreditbanken employees Birgitta Lundblad, Elisabeth Oldgren, Kristin Enmark, and Sven Safstrom were taken hostage by career criminal thirty two-year-old Jan-Erik Olsson, who was later joined at the bank by a former prison mate. Six days later, when the standoff with police ended a unique bond had occurred between the bad guys and good folks.

First; the terrifying belief that you are going to die. When you aren't killed a bond develops! These aren't such bad guys after all.

Simple acts of kindness by the bad guys such as giving some food or being allowed to go to the bathroom, the good guys no longer look at our hostage takers as bad guys but the people who will let them live.

In one of the phone calls from the bank vault to Sweden's Prime Minister Olof Palme, Enmark begged the prime minister to provide a getaway car. Enmark is quoted as saying, "I think you are sitting there playing checkers with our lives. I fully trust Clark and the robber. I am not desperate. They haven't done a thing to us. On the contrary, they have been very nice. But you know Olof, what I'm scared of is that the police will attack and cause us to die."

American Journalist David Lang visited each of the hostages a year later. They all believed they owed their lives to the pair of criminals. On one occasion a claustrophobic Elisabeth Oldgren was allowed to leave the bank vault to walk around the bank with a rope around her neck. She spoke of feeling that this was very kind of the robbers.

During an interview with Safstrom he stated he felt gratitude from Olsson who told him he planned to shoot him to show the police he meant business. He had been convinced that Olsson would only wound him and allow him to get drunk first.

As a hostage negotiator myself, I always believed in a unique transference between hostage and hostage taker.

Following the robbery the importance of securing the bank, allow no one to enter or leave, preserve the crime scene, activate the alarm and get law enforcement on the phone and don't hang up until law enforcement arrives.

Elsewhere I've shared that following the Scales Mound Illinois bank robbery in 1974, Bank President Ida Travis called the Jo Daviess County Sheriff's Office with the comment "My god, the bank's been robbed" and hung up the phone. The sheriff's office had no clue which bank had been robbed. At that time, there were nine banks in Jo Daviess County. Deputies frantically called each one. The ninth one to be called was Scales Mound.

FOUR OF THE GREAT ONES

Once I was permanently assigned to Rockford, I was to work with SA Brad Riggs, who worked predominantly organized-crime issues. Brad was a lawyer, a WWII Veteran who served in the Pacific Theatre, a great family man, and I learned volumes from him regarding the Rockford Organized Crime Family. Brad's allegiance as the organized crime agent was to Vince Inserra, the C-1 supervisor. By default, I was also assigned there for a short time. OC (Organized Crime) was good work but not exciting to a young former police officer and infantry soldier.

SA Glen McKenzie was receiving his OP (office of preference) assignment to Albuquerque, New Mexico, and his four counties—Jo Daviess, Stephenson, Carroll, and Whiteside—would be available for another agent to cover. Jerry Nolan knew of my desire to get Glen's counties and he made it happen.

The sheriffs of those four counties were among the finest men I've ever known—Marlo Specht the Sheriff of Jo Daviess, Jimmy Thulen the Sheriff of Carroll, Lester (Butch) Kimmel the Sheriff of Whiteside, and Don Scofield the Sheriff of Stephenson—were the four and no finer men on the planet. Somewhere in my archive of clutter, I have a photo of the four of them with me at a trail ride, and I'd give anything to find it, but I'm not overly optimistic.

Each had his own leadership style but each of them openly accepted me as the new FBI agent in their territory. It has been my experience that Sheriffs are very protective of their "corner of the world" and more than one FBI agent has gotten crosswise with a Sheriff by trying to come on as a know-it-all or a little arrogant, not a good way to start. To my good fortune, Glen introduced me to each one making my transition much easier.

Marlo was the epitome of a gentleman. He was calm, reserved and deeply loved and respected. Marlo reminded me of a Southern gentleman, and he wasn't even from the South. He always found time for me and was a volume of information simply knowing everyone in his county.

His wife Jane was also a class act. The two of them fit wherever they went. They were as comfortable with the jet set as they were with the good ole boys.

Marlo left a lasting impression with everyone who met him. His positive attitude just had a way of rubbing off. Sadly both Marlo and Jane have passed away.

All four of the sheriffs were great friends. That segue takes me to Jim Thulen. When I got the photo of the four of them with me it was taken at Camp Creek Ranch deep in the hills of Carroll County at a trail ride. Jim hosted a trail ride for his mounted patrol deputies and the Ranch where he lived was the perfect venue. Of course, all were invited. I think a separate book could be written about him and his down-home ways. I devoted a chapter to him elsewhere in this book, and reading it will absolutely help you understand why.

"Butch" Kimmel of Whiteside was an effervescent, easy going sheriff who expected and got the best from his men. As with Marlo, Butch has gone to the "great beyond." He was a mountain of a man, and when I learned he had a heart condition, I was shocked. No one that burly could have a bad heart. Sad to say, he did. I miss the friendly banter over coffee and discussing leads with him and his detectives. My job was made so much easier just from sitting at those coffee gatherings. To many in the county of Whiteside he is gone but not forgotten.

Getting to know Sheriff Don Scofield arguable scared me. Don had the reputation of being somewhat gruff who allegedly, I stress allegedly, threw a State Trooper from his office. When I met Don I found him in many ways to be a "gentle giant." He was also someone you didn't cross. I know those who did, in particular the media. The turnout was never good for the one on the receiving end of Don's wrath. He got the job done, and he did it well.

Don would be called by some as brash. I would call him firm and someone that you didn't push around. I would say that the exception would be his wife, Donna. Like so many good marriages, they understood each other well.

Donna was the cook at the sheriff's office, and much like my noon stops in Carroll County to enjoy Dorothy Thulen's "jailhouse fare" the lunch prepared by Donna was superb.

Getting Don talking about his "truck driving days" and his many exploits in law enforcement was always a highlight. Don enjoyed sharing and he would always have a willing audience.

Don's chief investigator was Captain Dick Currier. I treasured the friendship of this man and he certainly helped cement a great friendship that I have with Don Scofield.

Dick passed away on the same day that the Challenger exploded. I must share some of his "down-home" humor. Dick and I had gotten on the elevator on the ground floor of the Public Safety Building heading to his office on the third floor. The elevator stopped on two, and a lovely young woman came in, and just as the doors started to close, Dick stepped out saying "I'll see you on three, Jim." I was somewhat confused, but the gravity hit me as I realized he had passed some significant, odiferous gas and the time to the third floor for that poor young lady and me was an eternity. I'm sure she held her breath the entire way, and of course, she just knew I was responsible. I know I deviated from Don Scofield, but Dick Currier is simply part of the Don Scofield lore.

These four outstanding Sheriffs helped shape my FBI career. Their assistance on federal matters was always there without question. I hope in some small way, I reciprocated on behalf of the FBI and deep and sincere friendship.

ALAN WENZEL PANEL

M any times throughout my FBI career, I was asked to participate in forums, make speeches about the FBI, be a panel member or any number of "desires from the public" to discuss the agency I was so proud to be a part of. It all would be considered extra on my part as there was no requirement to participate, but I always welcomed the opportunity. Of course SACs (special agents in charge), ASAC (assistant special agents in charge), and supervisors did these "extra duties" as a matter of course.

As the only agent in the far northwest counties of Illinois (Jo Daviess, Stephenson, Carroll, and Whiteside), I was, for better or worse, "the FBI."

One of the yearly panels I participated in was the "young leadership forum for northern Illinois," sponsored and taught by Highland College Instructor Alan Wenzel. On the day of my participation, it consisted of me as the representative for the FBI, the sheriff of Stephenson County, the Freeport chief of Police, the commander of the local State Police District, the state attorney of Stephenson County Mike Bald, and a local prominent defense attorney Tim Mahoney, and as I recall a judge. Each of us was expected to explain the duties of our agency, how we fit into the overall law enforcement community and our day to day activities.

Our panel answered questions for several hours with very active audience participation and the hours whizzed by. Following a break, we were each asked by Mr. Wenzel what each of us saw in the mirror in the morning. In other words, how did we see our chosen professions. There is always friendly bantering between those charged with prosecuting crimes, defending the criminal, and the investigators. The banter between States Attorney Bald and Freeport's most liberal tenacious "defender of the masses" Tim Mahoney was absolutely about as charged as it could get when this question was asked.

Attorney Mahoney went into a diatribe of the importance of being there for the "little guy," the guy who didn't understand the system. It didn't matter whether or not the subject was guilty, it was his job to find chinks in the armor of the prosecution and get his guy off. He felt when he looked in the mirror he saw such a defender.

States attorney Mike Bald is the nicest, easiest-going man on the planet. As a prosecutor, he was loved by the police because he was seen as totally fair and unassuming. As he stood to answer Mr. Wenzel's question of looking in the mirror each morning he brought the house down with his short, to the point quip, "Each day as I look in the mirror, I thank God I'm not Tim Mahoney." Order was not restored by Mr. Wenzel for at least ten minutes. Many were doubled over with laughter.

Today Mike Bald is a highly respected judge, and Tim Mahoney remains a prominent and highly respected attorney. They remain the best of friends.

AUCTIONEER

As a boy, I was infatuated with farm auctions. I didn't get to go often, but when I did, I marveled at the auctioneer and that sing-songy chant. Perhaps it was because it captured the entire crowd's attention. Perhaps it was because they were always in the middle of "neat stuff" that they sold to the highest bidder. I think more than anything I loved their personalities and often quipped "one-liners" that made the entire crowd laugh.

To this day, other auctioneers are a study to me as I constantly work to improve my skill at it. Being licensed in both Illinois and Wisconsin and having been ever since each state required a license has given me many opportunities.

As an FBI agent, I never could have accepted payment but safe to say I had numerous opportunities to "cry" auctions at benefits and charities and I often helped gratis some of my close friends who were professional auctioneers.

I don't know the first time I heard LeRoy VanDyke do the auctioneer song, but to this day, whenever I hear it, a smile comes across my face. Many auctioneers are school trained but the "chant" of an auctioneer is often developed "behind the barn" or in the shower. There isn't much that I enjoy more than selling items at auction or attending them.

Alvin Kohnert was the most popular auctioneer while I grew up in the hills of Wisconsin. Being able to go to a Saturday afternoon auction after the calf pens were cleaned and the corn and oats or grist was hauled to the feed mill in North Bend to be ground would make my day.

Alvin, holding up a five gallon can on a bitter-cold day responding to a farmer in the crowd hollering, "What's in it?" and Alvin responding with that auctioneer humor "Antifreeze but it's froze," the crowd roaring with approval. It certainly was and is my kind of humor.

One of the farmers helping on the hay rack, strewn with items drug out of the granary, tripped and nearly fell as Alvin, not changing his chant at all, inserted the words "twenty dollars now twenty-five careful no place for a drunk. Now fifty," as the crowd again roared with approval.

In many ways, an auction is a live sitcom filled with "one-liners" if the auctioneer is so skilled and often puts great levity into what otherwise could be a humdrum sale.

Dale Devriess rapidly became my favorite Illinois Auctioneer whether selling hogs, cattle or farm machinery, his infectious outgoing personality cemented my desire to become a licensed auctioneer. The farmers all loved Dale. One particular day Dale is selling an M Farmall Tractor built from 1939 to 1952. The one selling was bought in the 1940s. Dale has one farmer slowly and reluctantly bidding who blares out at Dale, "I wish it was later," meaning of course the year. Dale responded, "Well, it's 3:05 p.m., how about we wait until 3:10 p.m.?" Of course, the crowd roared with approval. The farmer bid again and bought the tractor. That levity was amazing.

I continued to work on my chant and "one-liners," and to this day, I thoroughly enjoy not only attending but participating in a good auction.

The FBI's needs, often in undercover rolls, are often changing. Part of my motivation to become an auctioneer was just in case. Just maybe the need would arise.

I know I was kidding myself, but my life has been much richer being a part of, at least part time, of a magnificent profession.

FALLING ON KITCHEN TABLE

In police vernacular, it's often stated, "You can't make this stuff up."

Such was the case of a bank robber that we, in the Rockford RA, had been pursuing for some time. David Hogan was elusive. We had him identified as our bad guy, but he certainly was a fugitive not being seen in weeks.

Informants are, always have been, always will be, the lifeblood of the law enforcement community.

SA Phil McClanahan had a source who, out of the clear blue, asked if he was looking for David Hogan. He told Phil that if so, he knew who his girlfriend was as he was seeing her as well. He told Phil that his lady friend believed that Hogan had hidden money in her attic.

Phil played it well, as he was not aware of the want for Hogan. When he got back to the RA and asked if anyone was looking for David Hogan, all the bells and whistles went off. Lon Christianson shared that he had a warrant for bank robbery for Hogan.

Phil was able to get the lady friend's name and address, and I went with Lon to interview her.

Roscoe is a quaint little burg just north of Rockford, and our interview took some interesting twists and turns. Most importantly, she wasn't giving up information on Hogan.

Our lady was, fair to say, probably not a lady, certainly a rough talker with little, if any, respect for law enforcement. By profession, she was a dancer with no visible means of support. One might assume she was a prostitute, but certainly we were making no judgments.

We convinced her that we had been watching her and we knew Hogan had been there. We asked if we could search the house, and after convincing her of the harboring statute and its penalties for harboring a fugitive, she reluctantly agreed.

Her bedroom had the largest assortment of sex toys I had ever seen and I'm sure even made me blush. She watched me go through her dresser casting looks that absolutely would kill. I asked if there was an upstairs, and her response was "Only an attic." The opening was in the hallway and with the help of a chair and a boost from Lon, I pulled myself into the attic and began crawling across the two by four framing searching with my flashlight.

Lon and our lovely lady are waiting in the kitchen, and Lon is at the table writing up his interview. Our lovely lady comments to Lon, "You know he's probably going to fall through the ceiling," and according to Lon, it no more cleared her lips and there I was, *bam*, right on top of the table covered with plaster, Christmas decorations, miscellaneous files, but no bank robbery money.

Our lady friend was quite indignant as well she should have been. She stared at me with a quizzical look with the obvious question, "Did you find what you are looking for?" Of course, I simply picked myself up, brushed myself off and looked at Lon, and when he realized I wasn't hurt, did all he could to refrain from laughing out loud.

We gave our lady friend the proper forms to fill out to be reimbursed by the government for the damage we had caused.

The very next day, in the Rockford RA, appearing above my desk was a cowboy boot obtained from our good friend state trooper Dave Reed protruding through the ceiling. Humor makes it all palatable. It remained there until the day I retired. You just can't make it up.

FATHER GORINAS AND
THE POLKA MASS

Father Gorinas was about as pleasant a man that you'd ever hope to meet. He was the parish priest in Menominee, Illinois, a tiny berg in the hills of Jo Daviess County.

Father's history was among the most unique of any priest I had ever known, and being a Catholic myself, I have known many. He didn't become a priest until late in life. Father had been married many years as a lay person raising a family and was in the restaurant business in Chicago. Late in his life, following the death of his wife, he decided to become a priest, and the diocese gave him the necessary dispensation.

Even more interesting, Father had served in the Lithuanian Army as a commissioned officer during World War II, and I so wish that I had visited with him more about those war years and his considerable combat experience. Our meeting never allowed us that kind of levity and the chance to visit outside our professional contact.

It occurred in the mid-1970s on a quiet morning when SA Bob Branigan took a phone call from Bishop Arthur J. O'Neill, the head of our Catholic diocese in Rockford for all of Northern Illinois. The bishop was quite upset and he told Bob that he must meet with us immediately regarding an incident involving one of his parish priests serving Menominee Illinois.

Bob had no idea where Menominee was until he consulted a map.

With that, he hollered at me, "Jimmy, you're going with me!"

And off we went to the cathedral office and met with the good bishop. Bishop O'Neill shared with us a letter, which we both imme-

197

diately asked him not to handle. As he laid it out in front of us on his desk, it was like something out of a James Bond novel, with words cut out and pasted on a white sheet of typing paper stating, "Gorinas must go or rectory gets bombed."

Well, we certainly had our federal violation of extortion. The bishop told us that it arrived in the mail this morning and the envelope had a Rockford Post Office cancelled date stamp.

I carefully picked the demand letter by the corners, had the bishop date and initial both the letter and the envelope and placed them in a large envelope and further prepared it to be sent to our FBI laboratory in Washington, DC.

The Bishop stated that after advising Father Gorinas of the demand Father requested permission to hire a guard which had already taken place. As Bob had other obligations I was off to Jo Daviess County and I called Detective Danny Sheehan of the sheriff's office and we agreed to meet in Menominee. Interestingly Danny and his wife lived in Menominee and attended Mass at Nativity of the Blessed Virgin Mary Church, the Parish headed by Father Gorinas.

During our interview of Father he was totally perplexed at who could have done such a thing. Dan told me that he was popular with the parishioners and fair to say over all well-liked in the community.

After several days, Dan came up with an interesting theory. He shared with me that a prominent family in the community, certainly among the Catholic faith, had several children who had become priests and one of their daughters was a nun. I was struggling to see what Dan was driving at when he shared that the family was not real happy with Father Gorinas as he had been an obstacle regarding several situations. Dan and I sat with Father after Dan shared his theory with me. Pastor Gorinas stated that he knew the family well and recently the daughter, who was a nun, had requested to have a "Polka Mass," which he rejected. Father shared that in the old country he had attended a "Polka Mass" and the dignity of his church was not going to be reduced to some cheap musical.

It didn't sound to me like something to write such a ridiculous demand letter over but following an interview with several of the family members we determined that the nun was a good subject.

Following several interviews we determined which family member was responsible. Several other family members knew of the incident and all from the prosecutors to Father Gorinas to the Bishop and all concerned agreed that making this a public incident would serve no one. Father Gorinas was hospitalized in the middle of the investigation with a heart issue brought on by stress.

A small amount of probation was doled out, the nun returned to her community. Father Gorinas released the body guard who was recently discharged from the Marine Corps. Bishop O'Neill simply shook his head and thanked all of us for keeping it as quiet as we had. If Danny and I could have ridden off into the sunset any better, I don't know what it could have been. Sometimes the resolution of cases is somewhat bizarre.

FIREARMS TRAINING AND
"RALPH'S PLACE"

The best day of every month for every FBI agent is "the day at the range." Firearms training and qualification is as important to an FBI agent as constant requalification for airline pilots.

Shooting accurately and safely is a "perishable skill." It's a tribute to the FBI and the special agents who are mandated to carry that firearm to always keep that skill highly honed.

It was always an early morning departure. The range used by the FBI was, I believe, actually a part of the Great Lakes Naval Training Center in North Chicago, accordingly, from Rockford, a good two hour drive. Usually two or three of us would go together, maybe stop in Harvard for breakfast if we got going early enough.

Jack Mulvey, Bob Branigan and I would often travel together and arrive before 8:00 a.m. Training was often conducted by Tom Smith and Jim Gibbs who were two of the "knuckle draggers" who taught firearms, disarming tactics, and physical conditioning.

Each month, along with participating in the latest disarming tactics and physical conditioning, we would be required to qualify with our personal sidearm as well as stay proficient with the shotgun and rifle. We each carried an assigned shotgun in the trunk of our car and two or three of the agents in the resident agency carried an AR15 rifle.

We were allowed to carry a personally owned sidearm as well as our own shotgun and rifle, assuming they were inspected by the Range Guys and we qualified with them. I kept my personal 870 12 gauge shotgun and my AR15 in the trunk of my assigned bureau car.

When I left training school in 1969, my sidearm was my issued four-inch model 10 Smith and Wesson (S&W) .38 caliber revolver and a "Hank Sloan" holster. Hank was the SAC of the Firearms Training Division at Quantico and he had designed a holster especially for FBI agents.

Along the way, I purchased several hand guns that I qualified to carry that I liked much better than my issued model 10.

Midway through my career, the FBI transitioned from the revolver to the semiautomatic pistol. The semiautomatic pistol of choice for the FBI was the Smith and Wesson 10 millimeter. We had the option of an issue weapon or we could purchase an approved firearm of our choice. I purchased a SIG Sauer 9 mm semiautomatic pistol and carried that until I retired in 1997, I sold it to Jack Mulvey's son in law who was an agent in Kansas City.

At the end of the training day there were several "haunts" to stop for something to eat, often with a beer and invariable great conversation with other agents from the Chicago Division that we didn't often see.

One of our favorite stops was "Ralph's Place." Ralph was an older gentleman who catered to the agents at the range, and several days each week he could count on thirty to forty agents being at the range and enjoying his "fare."

Ralph's was basically a beer-and-burger joint, and we all loved Ralph and he went out of his way to accommodate us. Though Ralph cooked a great burger, it became somewhat humorous to observe his financial ability. By the time we would be leaving, it was up to us to recall what we had. We'd tell Ralph at the cash register, and he'd roll his eyes back and mentally calculate in his mind what we owed. This all became quite a joke as Ralph would go through his mental calculation as follows:

An agent would say, "Ralph, I had two hamburgers and two beers."

Ralph would say, "Let's see, that's"—he would take a long pause—"a buck and a half."

Next agent said, "Ralph, I had one beer and one burger."

Ralph said, "Let's see, that's"—he would take a long pause—"a buck and a half."

Next agent would say, "Ralph, I had a water and a burger."

Ralph would say, "Let's see, that's"—he would take a long pause—"a buck and a half."

Of course, we all left a substantial tip to ensure that we were fair, but I never recall any number other than "a buck and a half."

The memories and conversations at Ralph's are absolutely legendary. Whenever I run into agents of my vintage, invariable firearms and Ralph's Place come up. The first words out of that agent's mouth with a huge smile were always "Oh yeah, old buck and a half."

TONY SEIDL

Tony Seidl is an enigma. I say that with the greatest respect for an amazing FBI agent. Tony, as an agent, accomplished much. Perhaps it was his inquisitive nature, maybe being at the right place at the right time. I know better because he simply made things happen.

Tony could be undercover as a doctor one week (he had spent part of college life in premed). Soon thereafter he'd be part of a motorcycle gang. Tony was "where the action was." How he pulled it off could probably be summarized with the fact that all the supervisors knew Tony could make it happen. He operated always "on the edge." A finer agent you'd never meet.

Some of his escapades merit repeating. I missed being a part of either of the next two, but they were often repeated by those with firsthand knowledge. An all-time favorite became part of the Chicago FBI Lore.

Tony and several agents are at the firearms range for our monthly training on firearms.

Stopping for a beer on the way home was not uncommon, and Tony and his pals knew a quaint "biker bar."

Now all of us know that sometimes a certain clientele patronize certain bars. Tony and his pals walked in as if they owned the place, ordered a beer and racked up the balls on the pool table. To hear the story told reveals that the hard core patrons did not look kindly on our unknown visitors to "Their" bar. I'm sure there was an air of uneasiness among Tony's colleagues, certainly not Tony.

As one might guess, something will be said, and sure enough, a rather large, somewhat inebriated biker type announces to Tony and his fellow agents, "They call me the animal. Do you know why they call me that?"

Tony just couldn't help himself as he chalked his pool cue and responded, "Probably because you're f—— pigs."

Bam! The place went up for grabs. The bartender was on the phone to the sheriff's office, and arriving officers hauled everyone in. Of course, to this point, none of the agents had identified themselves. Apparently, they agreed to pay part of the damage, and they left the sheriff's office being admonished by uniformed deputy, "Probably not a good place for you guys to get a drink in the future." Smiles were exchanged, and off they went.

The stories of Tony never cease. Following a long night on a stakeout, he and several others decided to have a drink before they head home. At 4:00 a.m. Tony was stopped on the Dan Ryan Expressway by one of Chicago's finest, who had Tony on radar with the following words to him, "I have you on radar, sir. Do you know how fast you were going?"

Tony said, "No, sir!"

"I have you at six."

Apparently, Tony was hugging the right lane barely crawling to his exit, hoping to get home and cause no issues.

Because he was well-known, not only to other agents but many in law enforcement as well, they helped him home. Tony is one of those agents whose lore will live in infamy.

MELISSA ACKERMAN

In law enforcement vernacular, it's called past recollection recalled. You recall the incident but need to read your report or notes or otherwise locate information to help you recall the incident specific details.

I'm often asked to share my most memorable case as an agent and the one that comes to mind was not my case at all but I, like numerous other agents, and other law enforcement officers spent the summer of 1985 in the little town of Somonauk, Illinois, in Dekalb County trying to solve an absolutely heinous crime, that to this day makes my blood run cold.

It's June 2, 1985, a warm Sunday morning and seven-year-old Melissa Ackerman was riding her pink bicycle with her eight-year-old friend Opal Horton.

Somonauk is the kind of small town we'd all like to raise our children. Were it not for the events of that day it would have remained "sleepy hollow." Melissa and Opal were riding on a gravel side street next to a farm equipment business. They were laughing and joking when a small dark automobile stopped beside them. The driver jumped out, grabbed Opal, and threw her in the car. Then he pursued Melissa on foot. Melissa yelled at Opal to get out and run. Opal managed to crawl out a window and had the presence of mind to crawl into a combine grain tank at the farm equipment dealership where she hides. Melissa was dragged into the car and the driver makes a quick search to locate his original victim. Opal remains hidden until the car speeds away with Melissa a captive.

When she feels it's safe, she runs to a neighbor's house crying profusely and between sobs is able to say that a man took Melissa. This begins one of the most intense investigations of my twenty-eight year career.

Within a matter of just several hours, nearly two hundred FBI agents, state police, and county and local officers are at the command center, which was the community hall at the Catholic church.

Words cannot describe the intensity among us all as we got our arms around the gravity of the situation.

We knew we had a missing child. We knew that the car was small and dark colored. We believe it is a two-door. We believe there is only one person, a scruffy dirty white male not very old who sped off with Melissa.

Marked squad cars and uniformed offices were setting up road blocks on just about every road in the area. We were hoping that even though we had such little information of our subject someone may share some information that may be helpful.

There was no demand for ransom though many of us believed there would be. Slowly we became very well organized, and the command structure began making assignments. For the next four consecutive weeks, the command center was the heartbeat of the effort.

No one counted hours; we just continued our investigation. I was teamed up with SA John O'Rourke, a very good investigator, and we complemented each other well though this was our first time working together. John was a Chicago agent; my beat was the four northwest counties of Illinois. John was scared to death of dogs. They didn't bother me at all. As we approached a home, if a dog was barking, John would hold back a little, and I would take the lead.

Hours turned to days, days turned to weeks, and hope faded that we would find Melissa alive.

Each morning at about seven, the teams gathered, and we got our assignments. The great citizens of Somonauk and the surrounding areas saw to it that there was always food and drink available before we left on our assignments, and again when we returned. The citizens from the area were simply great. All the church groups, social clubs, and individuals poured their hearts out by providing food and any needs that any of us have. Every parent realized that Melissa could be any of their children. The heartache and sorrow was almost overwhelming. In some ways, we, the investigators, were envied as we knew what was going on, which, unfortunately, early on was not much, but at least we were a direct part of it all, and I saw how each and every person would give heart and soul if they could. Each day we worked late into the night, each day hoping beyond hope that we could find this precious child alive.

Each day at an assigned time we'd gather to discuss the results of all leads and where the investigation stood.

When you do an investigation of this magnitude in any community, you start believing the area is full of perverts. Here is why. More and more people ponder an event or a person that said something at some time and comes to us with words to the affect, "I don't know about old Joe who lives down by the old creamery. He just acts kind of weird."

The investigator would say, "What do you mean weird?"

The citizen would reply, "Well, you know just weird."

Well, you have no choice but to check out old Joe. Old Joe might be the greatest guy on the planet, but two FBI agents were going to have a conversation with him, and a report (FD302) would be created.

Somonauk and the surrounding area were full of great people, and yes, a few weirdoes, arguably no more or less than anywhere else. One very memorable knock on a door will emphasize my point. There was no dog barking, so O'Rourke was in the lead, and he banged on the door. The door swung wide open, an older white male stood there completely nude except for combat boots. On his head was one of those long skinny balloons the clowns tie into different shapes for little children. I tried to remain professional, but I burst out laughing, much to the indignation of the gentleman. He was weird, but he knew nothing of Melissa.

Within an hour of Melissa's abduction, a Mendota Police Officer checked out a man at a gas station in Mendota in a dark American Motors Gremlin. The man, Brian Dugan, could not produce a driver's license, so he showed the officer a fishing license. He assured the officer that he had a valid driver's license. The officer attempted to verify it, but the computer was down. There was no reason to hold Dugan according to the judgment of this officer. There was no evidence of a child in the car.

When the computer came up (online) and revealed that there were outstanding warrants for Brian Dugan, he was long gone.

As the days went on, Dugan became of more interest because of past serious crimes.

Some agents and officers are assigned solely to analyzing evidence. That evidence then is used to create leads to assign to teams of agents and officers. Much brainstorming continues and some of the investigative techniques used were new to me and marvelous.

One example, a highly classified technique at the time using military aircraft to fly overhead with highly sophisticated sensors to detect any isolated areas of heat. The technology is commonplace today, but in 1985 it was new and classified. The created map isolated every rotting hay bale, dead squirrel, compost or manure pile and of course assignments were given out to check out each and every one for potential of finding Melissa dead.

Leads continued to develop, and more and more Brian Dugan was more than a person of interest. He was located, arrested on outstanding warrants, and search warrants for his car and apartment are issued. Investigators analyzed each and every possible bit of evidence.

His landlady remembered him coming home early on the day Melissa was taken and taking a bath, which she remembered as peculiar as he was not known for cleanliness.

A search of his car revealed several hairs and fibers, which are sent to the lab for analysis. No one was saying it, but experience told us all that we more than likely were looking for a body.

Each day we searched, each day more frustration. No Melissa.

At about the twenty-day mark, a uniformed deputy sheriff, on a hunch, searched an area in his patrol area that he knew was very isolated. Far back in a farm field, he exited his vehicle to look into a narrow horizontal culvert crossing a creek under an unused gravel road. Yes, he found a decomposed body.

As investigators we were thankful. We knew the body and crime scene would yield evidence. I couldn't even imagine the emotions of the family.

NOT IN MY WILDEST DREAMS

The investigation continued, and fibers from Melissa's sweater found in the creek and identified by the parents as Melissa's yield fibers that were identical to those found in Dugan's Gremlin.

Dugan was charged with her murder. The high-flying military plane could not sense the decomposing body inside the culvert. Dugan played it well.

There were many unsung heroes in the FBI. Among them are the two who interviewed Dugan and got his confession. Common decency will not allow me to disclose how Dugan, in his demented mind, boasted of his deed and how this beautiful child enjoyed the final minutes of her life. For those opposed to the death penalty, it's a shame they are not familiar with the heinousness of Brian Dugan. I would love to be the one to throw the switch.

After Melissa's body was found and Dugan confessed, someone posted the following quote on the bulletin board: Substituting Dugan's name for a villain out west as Judge Roy Bean sentenced him to hang for his ill deeds. It just made us all feel better, and we so wished Dugan could meet such a fate. "Dugan was sentenced to life without parole in exchange for his confession and his involvement in numerous other heinous acts that he had committed."

This is an actual quote from the famous frontier judge of Pecos County Texas in the mid-1800s sentencing Manuel Gonzales with the name change:

> Brian Dugan in a few short weeks it will be spring. The snows of winter will flow away, the ice will vanish, the air will become soft and balmy. The annual miracle of the years will awaken and come to pass.
>
> The rivulet will run its soaring course to the sea. The timid desert flowers will put forth their tender shoots. The glorious valleys of this imperial domain will blossom as the rose. From every tree top, some wild songster will carol his mating song, Butterflies will sport the sunshine.

But you will not be there to enjoy it. Because I command the Sheriff of the County to lead you away to some remote spot, swing you by the neck from a knotting bough of some sturdy oak and let you hang until dead.

And then Brian Dugan I further command that such officers retire quickly from your dangling corpse that vultures may descend from the heavens upon your filthy body until nothing is left but the bare bleached bones of a cold blooded, blood thirsty, throat cutting murdering son of a bitch.

Oh, how this dirtbag would have deserved that.

BROKEN PIPE AND A KINKY TUB

The winter of 1985–1986 was a typical Midwest weather pattern—snow and cold. Jen and I had just returned from four days in Hawaii and we were back at our Pecatonica farm. My brother Tom, was working in Rockford, and had stayed with the boys and horses while we were gone.

It's Christmas and we were off to Jen's family in Gilman, Wisconsin with a brief visit with my parents at the home farm in North Bend. It certainly was wonderful having both of our families within a relatively short distance from us—four hours to the North Bend Farm and about five to Jen's Gilman home.

It's late at night, more like early morning, as we turned into our driveway. It had been an enjoyable trip and the boys were asleep in the back of the van. Jen and I had been enjoying a great visit discussing not only our time with our families but also reminiscing about Hawaii.

The boys were gradually coming to and we gathered our things and head for the house. We always left several lights on for security and as I approached the house it was apparent that something was amiss. Our front door had a large window which appeared to be fogged up. As I opened the door, I walked into a sauna. I was in shock and disbelief.

Hot water is pouring through the ceiling everywhere. The plants are as green as I have ever seen them. It was probably eighty-plus degrees Fahrenheit. I ran through the sloshing water upstairs to find a ruptured copper pipe which was part of the hot water furnace system. The good news was the furnace was still working. My god, the furnace—with the amount of water gushing from the pipe how it could still be working.

By this time, Jen and the boys were in the house, and it was below zero outside. They all found an area that they were not getting rained on, and I was probably approaching panic mode as I headed to the basement to look at the furnace.

In my lifetime, I believe that timing and divine intervention has played a huge roll. The next two hours were total divine intervention. The water on the basement floor was at least three inches high. The gas furnace pilot light was about at the three and one-half-inch level. Probably it was about an hour from being put out by the water.

I had to get the water shut off and the furnace shut down and then figure a way to keep the house warm. I remember calling my dad for advice. He was a gas furnace salesman and I knew he could help. As I reflect I think I called him to express my disbelief. He gave me the best advice I could have gotten, "Call your brother, Mike." Groggily Mike answered the phone at 1:00 a.m.

When we moved to our Pecatonica home in December 1972, our heating system was, at best, horrible. It was an old oil, forced air system, with no heat to the second floor. Every time it kicked on, it banged, and I think sensible people would have been scared of it. Again, I think divine intervention kept us alive and healthy (I'm sure I'm being a little melodramatic), but it was a lousy system.

Mike worked for the same gas company as my dad, Tru Gas in LaCrosse, Wisconsin. My dad was a road salesman and Mike was in service and really knew and understood furnaces. Mike had installed this furnace for Jen and I in the summer of 1973. Did I ever adequately compensate him? The answer would have to be no.

Mike got permission from his boss, Jim Senty, to take a week's vacation and bring his service truck to Pecatonica to help his brother install a furnace—no, let me correct that—to install a new furnace while Jim watched and played the role of "gopher." Mike and his young wife, Lois, gave up a summer vacation to do that for his brother and sister in law.

But I digress, what do I do on this below-zero night in Northern Illinois to keep my family comfortable and my house from freezing up? I had shut the water and the furnace off. Mike, help! What do I do? Mike is far calmer than me. He tells me that somehow I must repair that ruptured pipe and get the water flowing back through the system and get the furnace back operating.

I don't recall where Jenny got the kids bedded down, but she had that under control and was building a fire in the fireplace to try to keep the house as warm as possible. I had thought of sending Jen and the kids to a motel, but I wasn't ready to give up.

How could I repair that pipe, and why had it ruptured to begin with? The second question was easy to figure out. It ruptured where it passed through a cold area and the insulation had become dislodged.

I knew or at least I doubted that I could have gotten a hot water furnace man at this time of the night, especially when it was that cold. My old Army days kicked in as I thought of field expedience. In other words, how can I cut out the ruptured three-fourth-inch copper pipe split and reconnect it?

The lightbulb went off, and I thought of automobile heater hose. I ran to the garage, and aha! I had heater hose. Problem is, it was five-eighths, and my copper pipe is three-fourth inch. What could I slip over the copper, reconnect in a manner to take the pressure of the water through the pipe?

Where does an epiphany come from? I ran to my machine shed to the John Deere 55 combine with a cab. I knew it had a heater, could the heater hose be three fourth inch? In my mind it has always been the Good Lord who has been there for me. This was no exception. Finding hose that size that will take pressure during regular business hours would have been difficult. Having a machine with that size hose backed in the shed nearly blew my mind.

I surely didn't bother to drain down the antifreeze, I just cut the hose, let it run out, and removed the clamps from each end. I believed I had my fix.

An hour later I had a six inch piece clamped over the four inch area and I had cut out the rupture. I turned the water back on and success. I wrapped it in towels for temporary insulation and kicked the furnace back on with a great, I do mean great, sense of relief.

We went through all that and there was even a silver lining. We had, for some time, been talking of remodeling our turn of the century farm home. The ceiling, several walls, collectibles, and more had been damaged or destroyed. With the insurance money we received, it gave us a good start to our remodeling effort, which happened the next summer. With an amazingly talented carpenter Jeff Gregg, the house was expanded to become Jenny's dream home.

Throughout the process it became apparent to both Jen and me that I was willing to accept whatever her wishes were. I had no specific wishes. It was her house and the amenities should be what she wanted. I am sure I helped a little on the exterior decisions. Embarrassingly I did have one request which did become a reality. In the bathroom attached to Jen's and my bedroom, I wanted an extra-large bathtub—yes, room for two. Of course, I took a significant razzing from the carpenter and our friends who would stop by and view the progress. I decided that the best defense to the jesting was a strong offense; accordingly I referred to it as the "kinky" tub.

Throughout the years soaking in that huge tub with the water jets soothing, aching muscles has been a godsend. I just wink and smile to this day as I get zinged about "that kinky tub."

THE FBI's BLOODIEST DAY

Special Agents Ben Grogan and Jerry Dove

I didn't know either man. They both were on the Bank Robbery Squad of the FBIs Miami Field Office on April 11, 1986. Both died on that day on what's been called the bloodiest day in FBI history.

The events of that day have been studied not only by the FBI, but it has become a training vehicle for all law enforcement arguably on not only what to do but what not to do when dealing with violent offenders.

My personal recollections are of course agonizing, and I recall with amazing clarity our discussions among my colleagues, not only FBI agents but other law enforcement officers as well on that day and for weeks to come. There are always "would haves" and "should haves" following such an incident. Anyone ever involved in violent confrontation knows unequivocally that no amount of training can ever resolve the numerous issues that will confront those involved. Each of the agents involved fought and performed valiantly. Ben Grogan and Jerry Dove gave their last full measure.

The incident forever changed the FBI, some ways, rather subtly, some ways, very overtly. The most obvious change was the FBI giving up the belief that agent's sidearm should be revolvers of at least .38 caliber, fondly referred to as "wheel guns." For years, the belief had been that a revolver was more reliable and wouldn't jam. The events of that day would dispute that claim as Supervisor Gordon McNeil fired his .357 revolver striking subject Matix in the head and

215

neck. Supervisor McNeal was wounded and attempted to reload his revolver, but blood and skin from his wounded hand prevented him from doing so.

I'm getting way ahead of what lead up to this ferocious shoot out. Not having been there, all I can do is relate much that has been written of the incident.

On that April morning, fourteen FBI agents under the supervision of Special Agent Gordon McNeil conducted a rolling stakeout in southern Dade County Florida looking for a stolen black Chevrolet Monte Carlo that was known to have been involved in several violent bank and armored car robberies. This was a hunch that a bank would be robbed. At the outset the names of our bad guys were not known. They were later identified as Michael Platt and William Matix, two former Army buddies from Fort Campbell Kentucky.

Ben Grogan and Jerry Dove riding together happened behind the Monte Carlo and they notified their fellow agents. With the other agents coming to the aid of agents Grogan and Dove it was feared that the car would get out onto a major highway and a call was made for a felony car stop. As the attempt was made eight of the fourteen agents were on scene and as the agents attempted to curb the Monte Carlo Platt and Matix began firing. A total of over 140 rounds were fired by all involved in the shootout. Two agents were killed, five were wounded. Platt and Matix were both killed by Agent Edmundo Mirelis as they attempted to escape in Agent Grogan and Dove's FBI vehicle though both were already severely wounded from numerous gunshot wounds. The battle lasted less than five minutes.

Of the total rounds fired, forty-two were from Platt's mini fourteen rifle firing a .223 caliber, the very same round fired by a military M16 rifle or the AR15 civilian model. The round is extremely lethal and Platt was deadly accurate; simply put Platt and Matix had the FBI out gunned.

The FBI certainly had the firepower, but coming on Platt and Matix as they did, they were not adequately prepared with heavier weapons being readily available. As Agent Mirelis exited his vehicle carrying his model 870 twelve-gauge shotgun loaded with five rounds of double ott buckshot he was hit in the forearm by Platt's

223 spinning him and throwing him to the ground. Though badly wounded with only one good arm he was able to rack his shot gun using the ground to support the stock and he delivered deadly fire on Platt and Matix with his shotgun and .357 magnum revolver as the two were attempting escape.

Agent Dove's deadly fire on Platt early in the less-than-five-minute exchange with his 459 S&W 9 mm semiatomatic pistol struck Platt on the right side with what the medical examiner later determined was a nonsurvivable wound, but Platt was far from giving up. As Agent Dove was attempting to reactivate his pistol, which had been damaged from being hit by one of Platt's 223 rounds, Platt exited the vehicle, shot and killed Agent Grogan and then shot and killed Agent Dove. Supervisor Gordon McNeil had already been hit in the neck by one of Platt's 223 rounds and was lying on the ground temporarily paralyzed from the neck down.

As Platt and Matix were attempting to escape in Agent Grogan and Dove's vehicle, it was at this point that Agent Mirelis killed them. No, again I was not there. My written comments are gleaned from the hundreds if not thousands of documents written of the incident. At that time, I was a seventeen-year veteran and perhaps had become somewhat lackadaisical.

Every month at fire arms training our instructors warned us, be safe but be ready. I no longer kept my shot gun locked in the trunk. Though cased, it had a place of honor on the right front passenger seat. Thinking at the time of the many rolling stakeouts I had been involved in, I like most fellow agents reenergized myself to always be a little more ready.

The tragic events of that day were a wakeup call for all of us. Firearms training for any new agents going through the FBI Academy would be trained on an issued semiautomatic pistol of at least 9 mm. Those of us in the field would be issued semiautomatic pistols as well.

The argument between those supporting revolvers "wheel guns" and automatic had been going on for years. Confronting violent offenders such as Platt and Matix proved the superiority of semiautomatic pistols. Attempting to chamber rounds in a cylinder when someone is shooting at you as opposed to pressing a button on the side of a semiautomatic pistol and slamming in a new magazine of at least nine rounds is of no comparison.

The amazing thing is that we had clung to the "wheel gun" philosophy for years. The tragedy is that it took such an incident to wake us up.

Rest in peace, Ben Grogan and Jerry Dove.

UNDERCOVER

It was a summer day in 1982, and Supervisor Jan Wilhelm posed the question, "Jim, would you be interested in an undercover assignment?"

"Well, sure, Jan, what is it?"

It seemed that the FBI was requesting SACs and supervisors to query their agents for someone with knowledge of farm tractors as well as cars and trucks. The Memphis division was seeking someone to assist with a rash of "insurance give-ups" and outright thefts of motor vehicles.

This was right up my alley, but of course, I needed more information, and surely, I needed to talk with Jenny. Our family was young—Jerry was ten, John was eight, and Jesse is two. How much would I be gone? Jenny's concern was my safety. She felt she could hold down the fort.

Most importantly, we needed to learn more about the possible assignment. I talked on the phone with SA Jerry Bastin, who was the case agent and was assigned to the Jackson Resident Agency of the Memphis Division. I learned from Jerry that he and Joe Rasberry were the only agents assigned to the RA. During our conversation I liked what I heard, and I thought Jerry was reasonably comfortable with my background. We agreed that I would travel to Jackson and meet Jerry and the "cooperating witnesses," as Jerry called them.

The next day I talked Jack Mulvey out of his "bureau steed" as mine was getting high mileage and Jack's full-size Chevrolet was a nice road car, and I was off on a 650-mile ride to Jackson, Tennessee. I met with Jerry and Joe at the RA, and we agreed to meet their guys out on large boat in a lake I'd long ago forgotten the name of. It was apparent that it was a great place to meet informants or witnesses, and we spent the day simply bullshitting, and it was apparent I was the subject of much scrutiny as they decided if this guy would be "their guy."

I apparently passed with flying colors, and Jerry asked me to get my affairs together in Rockford and be back in Jackson as soon as possible.

I was excited. I wasn't seeking an undercover assignment, but I knew I could do the job. I had many issues to resolve in Rockford as I had a large caseload that someone will need to pick up; most importantly, I need to work things out with Jen.

As an FBI Field agent, I often felt like a thirteen speed semitractor locked in about second gear as more and more "approvals" were being required in our day to day investigations.

If as I perceived from my meeting with the cooperating witnesses and Jerry, I'd have very much a free hand. The two witnesses who were facing heavy federal time were to help me get introduced around and one of them Dave would actually work with me as much as I'd need him. The other one Syl was a business owner and needed to be running his business.

I volunteered my rollback implement and car hauling truck as it would fit in well with our scenario if we could title it as if it had never been in the name of Jim Sacia. The Illinois Secretary of State was great, and I was hooked up with one of their senior investigators, Ken Blunt, who worked his magic and retitled my truck into my undercover name. I kept my first name which always makes good sense for any undercover situation other than that I had an entirely new identity.

Off I went to Tennessee with my rollback truck, all set to hopefully put together some big cases.

One of the guys we knew to be a big car thief and master of the insurance give-up was, we'll call him Marty, introduced to me by Dave, and it was apparent he was a little leery of me, and he had no problem telling me, and I was sure it was because Dave had told him "Jimmy's a good ole boy," that he has a new '82 Chevrolet Diesel pickup and a new Corvette that he'd sell for $1,500 cash for the pair.

Not often that I'm quick on my feet, but I came back with "I want to visit with Syl first." It was my way of telling him that I didn't want him setting me up. The reality was, I didn't have $1,500 cash. This all happened so fast I hadn't made arrangements through Jerry how I'd have cash readily available. I bought myself a day telling him I'd meet him at the lot the next night at five.

The lot was ABC Motors, a "buy here, pay here" joint in McNairy County very near the Shiloh Civil War Visitor Center and just north of Corinth Mississippi. We proudly displayed on our marque "we tote the note."

Dave had arranged to rent the lot weeks earlier and it consisted of a two-bedroom trailer converted to an office and it's also where I stayed. The trailer house, or "mobile home" according to Dave, was about what you would expect. Though it had a bathroom, it had no shower facility. Dave, with the help of his son Michael, built one off the corner of the living room. It was truly a jewel. It consisted of treated plywood walls. The drain consisted of a pipe under the floor carrying the water about twenty feet out the back onto the ground, not much zoning in rural McNairy County.

My sleeping facility was a thin mattress in my office that I rolled up each morning and readied the room for the day's activities. Our technical support guys had prepared the room for me to record everything I wanted to with a button under my desk

The next morning I met Jerry near Jackson, and we both knew I needed the cash now and the bureau doesn't work that fast. Jerry thinks like I do. "Don't worry, Jim, I'll get it out of my savings and worry about the paperwork later." Jerry truly is my kind of agent. We can field expediently do anything. He went to the bank and got me twenty one-hundred-dollar bills, and tonight I met Marty. I told him Syl said "you're all right, and I count out fifteen large bills with the understanding that they will be behind the trailer by morning."

At about 2:30 a.m., I heard the rattle of the Chevrolet Diesel pickup and the purr of the Corvette. By 4:00 a.m., I had the Vette loaded, and I was headed for the Joliet Army Arsenal in Illinois, where the FBI had a building we could use to store our purchases. I, of course, had fake paperwork, and the vehicles wouldn't be reported missing for at least twenty-four hours, plenty of time to move them out.

These were both classic insurance give-ups. A prominent Chevrolet dealer in Alabama conveniently left the keys in them that night, and Marty and his guys simply drove them away. He was paid $500 large for each one he took plus the $1,500 from me, not a bad night's take, to say the least.

Marty was now sold on Jimmy. I am not dark complected. In no way can I pass myself off as a mobster. Dave had done a good job of convincing Marty that I had "Chicago connections" with the insinuation being mob ties.

My attire was always western boots and jeans, which fit well for my roll. In my left boot was the Nagra recorder. In my right boot was my ankle holster and .38 special.

I disappeared for five days and got to spend four at home, for the next eighteen months that became a pattern, three to five days at home with my family the rest of the month at ABC Motors.

To Dave and Syl and now Marty, I was just a good ole boy. Certainly, Dave and Syl knew my true identity, but to Marty, I was an ole boy with Chicago money connections, which was something he had wanted for years. Marty developed deep confidence in me, and he got me more introduced around.

I ate, drank, and slept in McNairy County. Think back to the movie *Walking Tall*. Yes, Sheriff Buford Pusser patrolled the very area where I had become a "bad guy" buying stolen vehicles and insurance give-ups.

Marty worried about me, "Jim, you need you an ole gal."

I told Marty I have my "Jody." He'd never met her, but to assure him I'm not gay, I talked of my Jody often. He knew I went to Memphis to see her. Her name was JoAnn, and she was an FBI secretary who had agreed to be my girlfriend should I need one to cover my ruse.

My trips to Memphis, in reality, were my at least biweekly debriefings with Jerry, the undercover supervisor, and the agent who had built the case against Dave and Syl. I would stay overnight, and Marty knew, at least according to me, that I was meeting my Jody.

Marty and I ran the streets of Corinth where Marty was well-known. We drove around drinking while he sized up leads for insurance give-ups and potential steals. I enjoyed my beer, but this was getting hard on my liver.

Law enforcement where I was at was very suspect. My closest cover was SA Jerry Bastin, some seventy miles away in Jackson.

Should you talk with an FBI agent today and share my charade, they might not believe that an agent would be left out there with no backup. Safe to say, Jerry and I were "pushing the envelope." I convinced him Marty was harmless and I could handle myself.

We had built quite a case against Marty, and I was pushing him to introduce me to others. Marty told me he had a "friend" in Florence, Alabama, who needed an outlet for some of his cars.

It never ceased to amaze me. In this part of the South, Granddaddy was a horse thief, Daddy was a car thief, and so was his son, Alfred. It truly was a way of life.

Marty and I drove to meet Alfred, and his lady fixed us quite a meal. Alfred then took us to his shop, which he was very proud of along with his ability with the torch. He was about to strip a new foreign "insurance give-up" and as he opened the door, a voice inside the car stated "passenger door is open" to which Alfred responded "that's okay I'm cutting it off anyway." It simply struck me funny as I learned the humor of Alfred.

Alfred agreed to get me cars and soon I was hauling his give-ups that he delivered to ABC to the Army Arsenal as well.

I always got Marty and Alfred to come into my office as I paid them. Of course, the office was video and audio monitored and our case continued to build.

While I was in my undercover roll, we needed a way for my "bad guys" to contact me when I wasn't in their area. We had set up a "hello phone" at the FBI office in Rockford. Though it speaks volumes for our "bad guys" not being the "brightest bulbs in the circuit," Alfred called for me one day when I was not at ABC motors and Dave had told him "Jimmy is up by Chicago" Alfred had the hello phone number and called it. A Chicago agent who had been sent to Rockford to pick up my urgent cases answered the phone

"FBI" and immediately realizing his mistake hung up. Apparently the office was aghast. Believe it if you will, Alfred called right back. Lon Christensen answered the phone, "Hello," Alfred laughingly stated he had just misdialed and got a hold of the FBI. One could say "we missed a bullet."

Every other day, I'd drive the 105 miles to the Memphis FBI to give the stenos my Nagra tapes. One day one of the gals who was typing my recording had the others gather round as you hear Marty say, "Jim, I've got to P——."

"So do I, Marty," I responded.

You hear the car doors shut then the Nagra picked up, my zipper noise, then the splashing upon a rock. The girls were having a good laugh, and I was a little red-faced.

It wasn't a week later, maybe 10:00 p.m., and Marty and I had been driving and drinking.

Marty said, "We're going to burn a house."

I concealed my panic as he explained he needed to find this place to torch. I knew I couldn't allow a house to burn. I was seventy miles from Jerry. This was before the day of cell phones. I was stymied. I simply knew I couldn't allow Marty to burn a house.

The good news is, Marty was hammered and wasn't quite sure where the house was. I played the part well, "Yeah, Marty, that will be cool. We'll fix that MF," all the time praying we wouldn't find the house.

Marty drove and drove and drank and drank. I was faking my amount of drinking, and by 2:00 a.m., Marty gave it up. Was he testing me? I never knew. I only knew I never would have allowed a house to be torched. I couldn't even imagine the ramifications. I didn't think Marty carried. He surely knew I did; part of my role as a guy from up by Chicago with connections gave me the privilege.

It was two nights later, and Marty showed up about ten, pretty much our time to start canvasing Corinth and surrounding areas. He came in my office with an obvious "lady of the night," saying, "Jim, this here is Beth. She's going to stay with you."

224

I quickly responded, "Marty, don't you remember the day before yesterday I told you I'd be going to Memphis tonight to see my Jody?"

I knew he had been too hammered to remember anything. He stared, puzzled at me, then put his arm around her neck and pulled up her sweater as she giggled. "Ain't she got some purty titties, Jim?"

"She sure does, Marty. I'm off to Memphis."

Jody deserved more than just to be mentioned as my make-believe girlfriend. She was, in fact, a single lady who was one of the FBI secretaries. We often visited, and I developed the deepest respect for her. As life moves on, you often wonder what happened to those friends met along the way.

During my entire stay of many months as Jerry and I build our case, the undercover FBI "sting" operation ABSCAM in New York had recently culminated. An FBI agent operating undercover as an Arab Sheik was spending huge sums of money wining and dining influential people, which were part of his role. Conversely mine was living in a rat-infested mobile home, eating baloney sandwiches, meeting dirtbags in the middle of the night to buy stolen vehicles. I had great fun shooting rats at night inside the trailer with a flashlight and pellet gun. All in all it was my kind of role.

I was really missing home. One morning at 4:00 a.m. I got a call from Skip, the squad supervisor, "Pull the monitoring equipment and get out now."

By five thirty, I was in my 1970 International Cab Over 4070 rollback truck with the sleeper full of monitoring equipment headed for Jackson. Jerry would explain when I got there.

The inspection team for the FBI was in Memphis and polygraphed Dave and Syl. Dave admitted telling at least thirty people what was going on and who I really was. By the grace of God and great work by the inspectors, I got out in the nick of time, which we later learned.

My operation in McNairy County and a similar one in Georgia were setting off all the bells and whistles back at FBI Headquarters.

Though I never verified it, the one in Georgia, also an undercover agent buying "hot" and give-up vehicles, was compromised. He apparently was severely beaten, thrown unconscious into the back of a pickup and was to be disposed of. He regained consciousness as the pickup negotiated through a densely wooded area at night. He threw himself out and somehow found his way to a highway and some help. Yes, that could have been me.

As I returned to Rockford, I would of course need to get my truck titled back in to my real name. Only in law enforcement could this have happened. Ken Blunt, the secretary of state senior investigator who handled all the identification change, had been killed helping a stranded motorist the previous winter. No one else in the secretary of state knew anything about it. It took Jan, the SAC, and Jerry Bastin to undo the tangled web. After several months, I could legally drive my truck again.

As I settled back in to the Rockford resident agency, I was contacted by FBI headquarters, to see if I would consider being part of a similar operation on the East Coast.

In our master bedroom of our Pecatonica home, Jenny had hung a picture of two little puppies snuggling. It is captioned "together is the nicest way to be". It hangs there yet today. It answered the question. My voluntary undercover days were over.

DID MY BADGE SAVE MY FAMILY?

Albuquerque, New Mexico, 1984, Jenny and I and our three sons were coming into town in a van I had purchased in El Paso, Texas, while I had been on a short term undercover assignment. I left El Paso where I had been for three weeks. Jen and the boys flew to Phoenix, from our home, where we spent a couple of days with my sister Mary, her husband Bill and their children.

Albuquerque was on the way and my old friends, FBI agent Glen McKenzie and wife Nancy, were now enjoying their retirement years.

It was about two in the afternoon, and we were traveling from the west on Interstate 40, just coming into Albuquerque. We were moving along with the traffic when suddenly I saw an amazing sight. A petrified young lady in a Pontiac Firebird was crying profusely as somebody in an old pickup truck kept ramming her from behind. We were all traveling about seventy miles per hour; he would back off then speed up and ram her again. Well, the white knight came out in me and I decided you can't do that, so I pulled alongside him as I was in the far-left lane and he was in the one immediately to my right.

I yelled, got his attention, and I shook my finger at him. Jenny didn't know what to think, and the boys, who were twelve, ten, and two, were scared of the whole situation.

Two things happened almost immediately. My friend in the pickup gave up chasing and ramming the young lady and decided to direct his wrath toward me. The next thing I knew Jenny was screaming as he pointed a pistol at the side of her head.

Talk about a situation going from bad to worse, this one just had.

Fortunately my credentials and badge were laying on the dash and I grabbed my badge and held it toward him, had it not been for his passenger, I don't think it would have made any difference. I base that on the look in his eye. He just seemed bent on raising hell with someone. His buddy grabbed his arm and pulled the gun down. I have no way of knowing, but I do believe he was crazy enough to do something. By now my whole family was crying and wondering what we had gotten ourselves into. I will always believe my badge got us out of that. Thankfully his buddy didn't want a confrontation and they got off the interstate at the next exit.

I exited several exits later and reported it to the state police. I don't know if they ever found the guy, but my initiation to Albuquerque was something to remember. I never saw the young lady again, but I hope she was safe.

228

DETECTIVE LADON TROST AND BONES

Having the privilege of working with many detectives over the years, I would be remiss not to discuss LaDon. With the resignation of Dan Sheehan, an investigator for the Jo Daviess County Sheriff's Department, I personally felt a loss. Dan had become a great friend and had proven himself to be an exceptional investigator. It was his mental depth that had solved the extortion of the Bishop of the Rockford Catholic Diocese and the threats on Father Gorinas.

Dan was an exceptional mechanic and he and his wife Donna decided to open an Automotive Electronics shop in downtown East Dubuque. Hereafter my leads in Jo Daviess County would be with newly appointed detective LaDon Trost. Sheriff Marlo Specht advised me that LaDon was a "bull dog" and when he got hold of something he simply wouldn't let go. I looked forward to working with LaDon though I knew I'd deeply miss my close association with Dan.

LaDon was everything the good sheriff told me and then some. Our friendship has grown over the years, and I hold him in the highest esteem and at this writing he is still "on the job" to quote law enforcement vernacular and is now the Chief of Police in Stockton, Illinois.

LaDon and I worked many cases together, and it's fair to say we complemented each other with our investigative techniques.

One of our cases, that unfortunately remains unsolved, was the bank robbery of the Hanover State Bank in rural Hanover, Illinois in Jo Daviess County. It was midday and three masked persons entered the bank with the one and only Hanover marked squad car parked directly in front of the bank. They were all brandishing weapons and made off with a large amount of money.

This is one of those cases I will go to my grave knowing who committed it. LaDon and I had exceptional evidence but lengthy conversations with the Assistant United States Attorney and the local Jo Daviess County States Attorney, helped us realize there wasn't enough for an indictment or the authorization for an arrest warrant. Maybe someday a cold case investigator will take a look and bring the case to its logical conclusion. Throughout my career LaDon and I would discuss "what did we miss." I won't name the culprit but I know and LaDon knows.

On with our investigation, a bank robbery anywhere is big news but in a small rural community in a county of 25,000, it's huge. An hour following the robbery as LaDon and I and other FBI agents from Rockford office, the Illinois State Police, and others are interviewing witnesses, canvassing neighborhoods, and going through all our investigative techniques. An abandoned vehicle is located on Gold Mine Road north and west of Hanover.

We use the Illinois State Police evidence technician to process the crime scene at the bank and LaDon and I head for the abandoned vehicle as it matches the description of the vehicle used in the robbery. The State Police were always more than accommodating and I for one will never be able to adequately thank them.

Marked squad cars from neighboring agencies including the Illinois State Police, are surveying possible get away routes, now an hour and a half after the robbery, chances of locating the vehicle still occupied and traveling rapidly dwindles. It doesn't take us long to know that the car parked in a secreted area on Gold Mine Road is our getaway car and is stolen from a small town south of Dubuque, Iowa. A quick search turns up nothing. We notify the state police evidence collection guys to process the car, and we leave it secured by a uniformed officer, and LaDon and I do all we can to coordinate our continued investigation and hopefully get our bad guys and soon.

Some interesting events have occurred in the past twenty-four hours in Hanover, and we learn much as all the investigators gather in the back of the bank to discuss our next move.

Several days earlier during the Village Council Meeting, the Village's only police officer, Gary Budde, was terminated. Seldom would an officer be on duty during the day and the squad was typically parked as it was today, as city hall is next to the bank. The city officer's principle duties were mainly to patrol during the night and the sheriff's office would randomly patrol during the day.

When the bank was robbed, the three burst through the front door, brandishing weapons, faces covered with masks and two had vaulted the tellers counters and grabbed a large amount of cash as the third, the smaller of the three, stayed in the lobby to cover the entire area.

Upon leaving the bank senior teller Reynold Nolan got what he felt was a decent look at the one in the lobby and thought it possibly was a girl.

The day turns to night and like all crime, the longer it takes to solve the harder it is. Evidence grows cold very quickly. I have "the bulldog" with me, and we resume our investigation the following day. It's now pretty much up to LaDon and me to solve this thing. The days turn into more days, and the leads are fewer and fewer.

LaDon's unmarked squad is a Plymouth Volare and is about the ugliest car I've ever seen but LaDon loves it, so who am I to be critical of a car with a top speed of maybe eighty.

LaDon and I would often team up and ride together. I always pushed to take my FBI assigned full-size Chevrolet which was fully police equipped as was LaDon's Volare. He had the Jo Daviess County radio or fondly known to LaDon as "the wireless," which gave him a definite advantage. I so appreciated the power and comfort of my Chevy and we had ISPERN (Illinois State Police Emergency Radio Network) which would always keep us in contact with all police agencies in both of our vehicles. The Volare was a vehicle which simply did not fit the image of Detective LaDon but again he loved it. He would come rolling up to a scene using the red light and siren, and out of the driver side door exited this large intimidating detective from little more than a pregnant roller skate—Detective LaDon Trost.

Late one day, Sheriff Specht calls me to let me know of a possible homicide in a cabin deep in the wooded hills of Jo Daviess County on Good Hope Road. Of course, the FBI has no jurisdiction in a homicide, but Sheriff Specht and LaDon have reason to believe it could be our bank robbers as there are three at the cabin counting the deceased—maybe a fight over the money. One in the cabin is a small-framed girl.

Arriving at the cabin, this place looks to me like it is right out of the movie Deliverance, it is secluded and spooky.

LaDon and I along with Rick Cass the State Police Crime Scene Tech busy ourselves attempting to determine what happened. Lying flat on his back on the floor in the main part of the cabin is our homicide victim "Bones," a young rugged looking man with what appears as gunshot wounds to the chest.

LaDon has interviewed both the remaining male and the young woman. Apparently the two males got into an argument which turned physical and they began wrestling over a 22 rifle. Our deceased male was apparently holding the barrel end while the shooter was controlling the business end. Not a good place for Bones to be.

A later autopsy reveals the first shot penetrated the lung but was survivable. The young woman ran into the room to witness the second shot which penetrated the heart and was not survivable.

LaDon was not comfortable at all with their story, and he and the sheriff felt that I should be called so we could pursue the bank-robbery angle.

As the investigation continued through several hours, LaDon ran out of cigarettes and was growing increasingly agitated. In the brown T-shirt worn by Bones was a fresh pack of Winston's, visible in the breast pocket. Bones is flat on his back having several hours earlier passed from this world.

Rich Cass had completed his investigation, and we are awaiting transport for Bones.

LaDon, as only LaDon could do, bends over Bones and says aloud, "Excuse me, sir, could I have a cigarette? Oh! I can have the whole pack. Why, thank you." LaDon has his smokes, and we continue our investigation with a much more requited LaDon Trost Detective Jo Daviess County Sheriff's Department.

Ultimately it was determined that these were not our bank robbers. LaDon continues with his homicide investigation. As the days go on we work on our bank robbery.

As I wrote at the outset, there is little doubt in LaDon's mind or mine who committed the crime. There is a huge difference between knowing and proving.

CCQE

How could such a significant organization that affected an entire community for so long and so positively not be written about?

The year was 1986 when Citizens to Continue Quality Education (CCQE) was born. The reality of it all, in my opinion, is a story that needs to be told. At that time, I was forty-two years old and Jen was thirty-nine. Our three boys—Jerry was sixteen, John was fourteen, and Jesse was eight. Not realizing it at the time, but what becomes somewhat significant is, Jen and I are a little older than parents of similar-age children.

We lived in rural Pecatonica, but our children attend school in the small community of Winnebago because of the drawings of school district lines. Like all of us with school-age children, we are involved in our work a day worlds and ensuring that our kids are receiving a good education.

Certainly we weren't up to speed, and don't think many parents were, when we received devastating news that our school district was in significant financial difficulty following a failed education referendum. It was proposed by our superintendent, Bob Colborn, with the backing of the school board, that nonstate-required courses would have to be eliminated in order to adequately fund the district with tax money available. Most citizens, especially those of us who have school-age kids, were seeking some type of an answer.

Our boys were actively involved in sports and music, not required state courses, they would be gone. So would computer classes and back then they were a new concept and could be done without as not state required. Other courses, not state required would be gone.

Citizen groups were beginning to form to discuss the alternatives, and I recall Jen and I attended them. One evening, Tammy

234

and Rick Westlake, ironically with three children the same ages as our boys, came to our home. After some pleasantries, Rick suggested I should become the Chairman of CCQE. I'm sure I was somewhat standoffish, or at least trying to digest it all, when Tammy blurted out, "Jim we need you because, you know, you're so old." Well, I'm sure I was flattered to be asked, but the four of us had a good laugh at the "you're so old" comment. It elicits a significant chuckle to this day.

CCQE became a fantastic organization due to a very hardworking core group. Each of us simply wanted to keep our school district afloat and the great district we were known for.

So much occurred over the next two years! Certainly the most significant occurred at a school board meeting which was packed with concerned citizens. We asked the board to articulate the cost in dollars, what it would take to save the programs that were scheduled to be eliminated. Understand that Winnebago is a small district in a small community with about nine hundred total students in grades K through 12.

The figure Superintendent Colborn shared was in two words "nearly impossible." The key word there is "nearly." He stated that in fourteen days the school district must have the sport programs listed for the following year, the same was true for music competition.

The staggering figure shared by Mr. Colborn "$150,000." You could watch the citizens drop their heads and shake them in disbelief. Not possible! Never say never!

We know the parameters, fourteen days to do the nearly impossible for such a small community.

The community mobilized, the local newspaper did their part, and many contacted relatives and friends. This of course was long before social media and "go fund me" efforts.

The school board's next regularly scheduled meeting was a short eleven days later, and we hoped to give them an update on any progress we might have made.

There is a real twist to all this. Winnebago is a combination of a bedroom community for folks working in Rockford. A large segment of the population is made up of farmers. The education referendum hits the farmer the hardest as it is a property tax really hammering farmers who own farm land. Farmers are deeply conflicted; they surely want to support kids. They surely want to financially hold onto their farm land.

Things are contentious but good people working together create amazing results. The CCQE secretary/treasurer carefully calculated the money that people are donating. Some of the businesses in Rockford agree to do matching funds for their employees—if a citizen employee donated $1,000, the company will match that amount, which really helps the funds begin to grow.

Donations start pouring in from as far away as California. Two California school age kids, maybe or maybe not related to some Winnebago kids, send us twenty-one dollars. A local business man, who was in a difficult situation as he sold products to farmers, some of whom were opposed to the effort, donated $5,600 as long as we promised to keep his name a secret. Thirty years have elapsed and I feel we must still keep his secret as he remains in business today.

The eleven days rolled around and again the school board meeting is a packed house. When the segment for public comments came around I had the privilege, on behalf of CCQE, to announce that not only did we raise $150,000, we had raised $186,000. The room became electric and I actually watched Superintendent Colborn choke up and cry.

When good citizens unite, the impossible can happen.

The reality is the $186,000 was simply a stop gap. We must pass an education referendum to keep our school viable into the future. By now CCQE had some credibility and we worked as likeminded citizens to again pass the referendum at the November election in 1987, and we did just that.

We started holding more and more public meetings trying to get all sides of the issue on the table. When you see so much greatness come from a community banding together, it's hurtful to see the other side with opposing views take it personal.

I've always believed if I have an issue with someone I should speak to them directly. Sadly not everyone feels that way.

Of course this is before cell phones and our home phone rings. One of my boys answered, only to be told by an anonymous caller that their father is an evil man. I could never quite understand that kind of mentality. The entire core group of CCQE received similar calls.

The good news is that in November the referendum passed. Yes, everyone had their property taxes raised which is always a hard pill to swallow. The public meetings, the fund-raisers, the efforts by so many to discuss their opinion with their opponents had a very positive effect.

Winnebago remains a great school district to this day. The reason I had such an opportunity to be directly involved with the core group was because "you know Jim, you're so old," it still makes me smile.

CCQE is now FEE (Foundation for Educational Excellence). The organization raises money with excellent fundraisers and currently has over $750,000 in the endowment fund. They make grants to teachers for classroom needs, not otherwise funded, and other needed projects.

RACE HORSE

It's the early morning hours as I sit at my desk, and I'm disturbed with the ringing of my phone. On the other end of the line is a fellow agent from another RA who needs a favor. It is October 1991.

"Jim, I understand you live on a horse farm. I need a place to put a racehorse."

A fellow agent with a unique need, of course I'll help. Dave tells me of his investigation into insurance fraud wherein racehorses, of dubious ability, are insured for large sums, mysteriously dying. A veterinarian certifies the death and the insurance company is forced to pay huge sums to the owner. All that is required is a broken-down racehorse, a crooked owner and a veterinarian gone sour. Dave is working a "ring case" wherein several owners and a veterinarian are conspiring to kill well-insured horses on a significant scale.

Through excellent investigation techniques, Dave learns the weak link is the vet. He becomes a cooperating witness.

Dave instructs him to advise the owners that Race Horse has been disposed of, and Jenny and I meet Dave and the vet at an isolated stable, load the horse, hereafter known only as Race Horse, and take him to our farm. For the next three months, Race Horse is just another horse on our small farm in Pecatonica. When friends inquire of our new horse we answer with a simple, "We are just keeping it for my brother who lost his stable." We fall in love with Race Horse and he becomes part of the family.

I've always thought of racehorses as high-strung animals. I'm sure many thoroughbred owners and trainers would take great issue with that and in fairness, after coming in contact with "Race Horse" I feel very different as well. He was as docile as a mouse and I'm guessing the reason he was being "eliminated" was he did not have that killer instinct to be a winner. No matter, Race Horse was a joy and fit in well with our registered paints. He ended up only spending the winter months with us.

My three boys, Jen and I are all suckers for horses and dogs and Race Horse was a big lover, making the joy of having him around even more palatable.

Though this is not my case, I admire Dave and all he is doing. Like so many investigations they sometimes just mushroom.

Throughout my life, even with a degree in psychology and thirty years in law enforcement, I marvel that someone can be a horse owner, trainer, or veterinarian and intentionally inflict pain on these magnificent beasts. You don't get involved with animals unless you love animals. I recognize that money and greed push many "over the edge." I guess I'll never understand, like so many, that it's easier to have more compassion for animals than for humans. Perhaps it's because they communicate with their eyes, and can't really tell us what they are thinking. Maybe it's because they are totally subservient and rely on us for all their needs. They simply give so much in return.

During my most recent life as an Illinois state representative, I received the reputation of an "evil horse hater." Illinois was the last state in the Union to allow "horse slaughter." Just the sound of that, I agree, is repulsive. Here is reality. The United States is one of the few countries in the world that does not allow horse meat for human consumption.

It is so easy to have that mental image of these magnificent animals being slaughtered. Horses grow old, became injured or unwanted. The reality is that it is a viable alternative to the extreme cost of euthanasia and carcass disposal. The emotion attached to this practice, cause some to lose any sense of perspective.

Because I was such a strong supporter of the process, which I will explain further, I caused a constituent lady to email me, "May you rot in hell, you despicable vermin." Among future favorable voters, I listed her as "doubtful."

In Illinois, in early 2004, there was a significant push by the Humane Society of the US (HSUS) and the American Society for the Prevention of Cruelty to Animals (ASPCA) to close the plant in DeKalb, Illinois. The plant was owned by a Belgian firm that butchered horses and shipped the meat to their country for human consumption.

The reality is this: the DeKalb plant was completely "state of the art." A US Department of Agriculture Veterinarian observed every "kill," which is done with a captive bolt to the head. Death is instantaneous. No it's not a palatable thought but it is very humane.

Because they were successful in their efforts to close the last remaining slaughter plant in the US, here is reality today: Killer buyers still attend the auctions. The value of a "killer" horse dropped to pennies compared to a good value when America allowed slaughter plants. The unwanted horses are shipped, crammed in trailers for over forty hours to the Mexican border with no food or water, then on into Mexico where their end of life is anything but humane in many cases. The old slaughter houses used an end of life procedure that would sicken you—it's a spear from the ceiling into the spine to incapacitate the animal. While it is still alive, the animal is hoisted by its hind legs and is skinned as it dies. The HSUS and SPCA accept the fact that this happens. They succeeded in preventing slaughter in the US.

Sadly, it causes much more heartache as many unwanted horses are simply "dumped." They are left in parks, along lonely roads, at auction barns, wherever, to be disposed of as humane as possible by whoever will accept the responsibility.

Why those who profess to be humane can't see the forest for the trees, I will never understand. There are often between fifty thousand and one hundred thousand being disposed of over the border each year. Those that end up in the Canadian plants are more humanely disposed of.

I had told my boss Jan that I was keeping the horse for Dave and it should be for just a few days. He had that look of concern but had no problem as it will only be for a "few days."

After two months Dave and I agree that I should be compensated for the care of the horse as the case is developing bigger and bigger and we cannot yet divulge that racehorse is really alive. It's a great undercover case and Dave is getting more and more subjects involved. I determine that in actual feed costs, with no regard for the care and time, I can support racehorse for three dollars per day.

At the end of the third month, I submitted my voucher for ninety days care of Race Horse at three dollars per day. Jan went ballistic. He had pretty much forgotten about the case. He assumed that Race Horse was gone and there was no way an agent could receive money for "caring for evidence."

There could be the appearance of impropriety on the part of an agent receiving compensation that could be going to a regular citizen. I explained to Jan that I was caring for Race Horse at a cost no one could argue that I was "making money on the bureau." Jan had gotten word from the front office that Race Horse had to go.

With hindsight, I so regret not simply waiting until the entire case was over and submitting a voucher at that time.

The bureau hired a vet to come to our farm, at significant expense to the US government, haul the horse to that vet's stable, pay the going rates for stabling the animal until the case was disposed of, $400 per month. The case was disposed of in June of 1997, four months after I retired.

Your tax dollars at work, you figure the cost, I'm too frustrated!

BARTELS

As a boy, I loved the Sunday night television show *You Are There*, hosted by famed commentator Walter Cronkite. I'm talking the mid to late 1950s when our one television channel received in our rural farm home two miles outside of unincorporated North Bend was channel 8 out of La Crosse, Wisconsin. There was normal broadcasting from 6:00 a.m. until 10:00 p.m., at which time for the next eight hours, it was "test pattern and tone." But I digress, Walter's deep announcers voice would always introduce that evening's series as follows after announcing the date we would go to "What sort of a day was it—a day like all days, filled with the events that alter and illuminate our times. All things are as they were then except "you are there."

I was there June 9, 1990. I don't recall who made the call to the Rockford Office of the FBI. I and seven colleagues under the leadership of SSRA Jan Wilhelm were working on our reports from previous investigations basically readying to "hit the street."

Jan ordered us all to Shiloh Drive in unincorporated upscale Winnebago County regarding the kidnapping of an infant boy.

It rapidly became apparent that we had a legitimate kidnapping as almost simultaneously with our arrival in the vicinity of the residence the father of the infant, Dr. David Bartels, received a call from a male voice stating he had his child and to await further instructions.

Inside the home babysitter, Katherine White, age twenty-seven, and Brad Bartels, the six-year-old brother of eleven-month-old Douglas (Doogie), were struggling to free themselves from their ties. Bradley was the first to get free and he was able to help Katherine free herself but only after he notified police.

About one half hour prior a knock at the door was answered by Bradley as Katherine, carrying little Doogie, approached the door to see who was there. A flower delivery man carrying red roses produced a pistol and ordered Katherine and Bradley to the basement. He handcuffed Katherine to a pole and Bradley to the leg of a sink, picked up crying Doogie by one arm and ran up the stairs, and was gone.

One of our most telling fears was the indifferent way he had picked up the child. He simply grabbed Doogie by his little wrist and carried him away. It told us that the abductor had little regard for the life of the child. Herculean efforts were used to keep that from the press as the day unfolded.

A series of phone calls come to the home, where Dr. Bartels now is throughout the day, all traced as coming from different pay phones throughout the Rockford area ordered Bartels to produce $100,000 and await further orders.

Case agent SA Phil McClanahan working in concert with Winnebago County Sheriff's Department provided the leadership as FBI agents, plainclothes Sheriff Deputies and other Officers provided the network of coordination necessary in a fast moving case of this magnitude. I'm sure with the agents from Chicago, the surveillance teams and "eyes from the sky" agents totaled well over 100.

Throughout the day, we chased every possible lead, every hypothesis was analyzed and eliminated, even the potential that a former disgruntled boyfriend of Katherine could have been involved.

The behind-the-scenes legwork of any major investigation is always the rest of the story.

By late afternoon, the waiting game progressed and we still had not identified a solid suspect. There was no doubt that the family was frustrated and fearful for the life of little Doogie.

Families are always the deciding factor as whether to deliver a "dummy package" when a drop site is determined. Dr. Bartels and Carol arranged through their bank to obtain the necessary $100,000 fearing any dummy package, should it be compromised, could jeopardize Doogie's life.

Our bad guy was being very cagey and perhaps hinky, and it was apparent he had given much thought to his dastardly deed. A series of calls in rapid succession from a series of pay phones was obviously his effort to compromise any surveillance that might be on to him.

Finally he ordered that the package should be dropped at a pay phone in Alpine Village Shopping Center. Dr. Bartels was to make the drop not being followed nor having any passengers.

The drop is made and from out of nowhere appears a high powered Japanese motorcycle often referred to as a "crotch rocket" and our bad guy grabs the package of money and leaves reaching speeds in excess of 130 miles per hour.

This is where the agents in pursuit truly were heroes. If you ever question whether your tax dollars are being wisely spent on the FBI, don't. These surveillance agents were phenomenal. SA Mike Hannah directly behind the speeding motorcycle in his high powered Mustang in my opinion was the hero of the day and here is why.

Agents are well paid, among other things, for our ability to make split second decisions when much is at stake. Mike will always be an unsung hero but in my opinion he should have to carry his gonads in a wheel barrow.

As the bad guy on the motorcycle wearing a helmet and tossing tire flattening devices slows at a T intersection, Mike makes that split second decision. IF he rams him the guy will be hurt but with the helmet he should be able to communicate and tell us the location of Doogie. If the bad guy makes the corner Mike knows he won't be able to stay with him in traffic. He literally lays his career on the line; if the bad guy is hurt bad enough or killed we will never get Doogie. If the bad guy gets away, Mike's computer brain tells him we'll never hear from him again anyway. He rammed the bike, upending it. We have our bad guy, and he is not hurt bad.

Now our second hero of the day. After several lengthy attempts at interview, SA Gary Fuhr asks for a chance. Our kidnapper's name is Mark Laliberte, age twenty-seven, a cook at a mental facility. Lying on the ground, surrounded by FBI agents and police officers, he is highly indignant. When asked about the location of Doogie his response "fuck you I want a lawyer." He is checked over for injuries by a first responder then placed in the back seat of a police vehicle. Over the next forty minutes, he asks repeatedly for a lawyer. "Tell us where the baby is, you'll get your lawyer."

In the back seat of a Rockford City Squad Car Fuhr, a former Saint Louis, Missouri, Police Officer, makes it clear to our now identified Mark Laliberte what happens in prison to child killers. At about 10:00 p.m., he tells Fuhr he will take us to the infant.

We travel to a wooded area several miles North of Rockford and agents and police form a line to walk the woods. I am right beside Lt. Jerry Heisler of the Winnebago County Sheriff's Department, and I will never forget and it is frozen in my mind's eye as Jerry hollers "here he is" and his flashlight is cast on nearly nude infant lying on his stomach pushing himself up and his badly bug-bitten face stares into the flashlight.

The rest of the evening is a blur until several hours later when I get home I remember sitting on the edge of my bed and profusely crying.

Perhaps I shouldn't admit that, but all the emotion just drained out of me. My thoughts went to my own young family and how blessed I was.

Laliberte was convicted of aggravated kidnapping for ransom and sentenced to thirty years imprisonment. Of course, he appealed his conviction (which, in my opinion, was far too lenient). His biggest issue of course was his repeatedly asking for a lawyer and Special Agent Fuhr stalling.

In his appeal *People vs. Laliberte* in the Appellate Court of Illinois, Second District, dated June 16, 1993 Laliberte argued that his Fifth Amendment rights of self-incrimination had been violated by Special Agent Fuhr, who continually talked about the whereabouts of the child and avoided his request for an attorney. To read the entire appeal and also why the conviction should stand, your eyes will glaze over. The trial court framed the controlling issue as "whether the life at stake here overrides the rights at stake." The public safety exception withstood that test.

The bottom line is, I hope that sleezeball is still incarcerated.

LIFE CAN BE VERY UNFAIR

B obby

Rolling back toward the RA in midafternoon, the radio crackled as I'm coming into Rockford on West State Street. The bank on Harrison Avenue has just been robbed is the summation of several radios putting out the information simultaneously.

I throw the red light on the dash and I acknowledge Karen, office secretary, and let her know that I am en route with an ETA (estimated time of arrival) of about fifteen minutes.

We had only recently completed a major drug investigation headed up by our own Brian Barthelmy that was a coordinated effort with the Rockford Police, the Winnebago County Sheriff's Department and DEA (Drug Enforcement Administration) involving the Gangster Disciples street gang.

The investigation involved numerous investigative techniques, including a Title III, which is a legal wiretap and resulted, to the best of my recollection, in twenty-three really bad folks going to prison for a long period of time.

Brian's coordinated efforts were exceptional, and there wasn't a person involved in the investigation that didn't marvel at his astuteness to detail and simply putting it all together. It wasn't a month after the investigation culminated that the bank robbery occurred.

I ended up working with Rockford City Detective Bob Redman and we were responsible for arresting, what had been described to us as "the smaller one of the two black males." The terrified bank teller told us he was the one who definitely had a gun.

We arrested "Bobby" who turned out to be twelve years old. Bobby's only goal in life was to be a "GD," gangster disciple. At the time of the arrest, he was carrying a 9 mm semiautomatic pistol that he used in "the job."

I found myself marveling at Bobby because he was the same age as my youngest son, Jesse, who, safe to say, had a far different start at life from Bobby. Each night as I got home, Jess had a big hug for me. I got one in the morning as he headed to the school bus. For Bobby life wasn't quite as fair.

Detective Redman and I had determined that Bobby had spent a total of 123 days attending public school since kindergarten. It is safe to say that he had a PhD in street smarts. Bobby knew the lingo and knew the street. He lived with his prostitute sister and the only life he knew was one of crime. The G D's were what life is all about.

Throughout our interview of him, I kept thinking of Jess and how life can be so unfair. Bobby was just fine. He loved the roll. Getting sent away would get him more "status" and that was what it was all about.

We took his statement and what I remember verbatim to this day was his response to Detective Redmond's question of "Where were you last night, Bobby?"

His response was, "Me and my girlfriend was layin' in the crib watchin' video games and fuckin'."

It took me a while to get my arms around that, with a young son the same age at home.

After reading the statement back to Bobby, we asked him if it was all correct, and he said it was. It took him perhaps two minutes to methodically sign his name. He could write, but just barely.

Bobby and Jesse are thirty-four now. Jess is married with three wonderful children. He has a college degree and a good job.

No, I have no idea what happened to Bobby. Somehow I don't think that I want to know. Even that saddens me.

The bank robbery by Bobby and the reflection on my life and the cards that life deals one takes me back to those great growing-up years on our thirty cow dairy farm two miles from North Bend Wisconsin.

My parents moved to that farm in 1952 when I was eight years old and my youngest brother Tim was a new born. At eight years old you don't grasp the big picture but it became apparent, as the years went on, just how we ended up on that farm. The buildings were (and are to this day) amazing. The house being large and well-built, suited my mother, as Tim was her sixth child.

Dad was excited about another farm near Ettrick, but the house left much to be desired. The crop land lay nice and the barn was even nicer than the one on our North Bend farm. Mom had put her foot down. She knew farmers well and I'm sure my dad was no exception. If money needed to be spent on the barn it would happen. Dad would be able to "make do" in the house. Mom wasn't about to let that happen. She demanded and got a nice house.

Both my parents loved kids. Had mom not had a hysterectomy, I'm sure I'd have more siblings, but I think God had something else in mind. St. Michael's Orphanage in LaCrosse always needed foster parents. My mom couldn't resist.

Throughout those growing-up years, a total of twenty babies to young children became part of my family. It was not uncommon to come home from school, and once again, a baby bed was set up in the sunporch, which doubled as the entryway. The frustation was that new baby or child would be reunited with their parents or adopted out after varying amounts of time and invariably it broke my mom's heart.

Mom and dad made sure we understood the importance to give these kids a home and often the first real love they ever experienced. It became a way of life to us. There were always at least twelve around the dinner table. The six of us kids, mom and dad and at least four from St. Michael's.

Three of them, though never adopted, stayed with us through their high school years. To this day, with the exception of one who passed away, they remain part of the family.

Bobby was never so blessed as to have a Katherine and Jerry Sacia to give him a start that would lead to so much more than being a Gangster Disciple.

Everyone in our home had chores. In the house of course cleaning and cooking for the girls. In the barn, there was always plenty to do in caring for cattle and hogs. All in all, none of us suffered and there was always plenty of love to go around.

Bobby had his video games, his crib and his girlfriend. Sadly, no family love, only the Gangster Disciples.

I wrote that I had no idea what happened to Bobby. Well, google got the best of me. Bobby, black male, same age as Jesse, arrested in a Rockford, Illinois, drug bust in February 2011 by SLANT (State Line Area Narcotics Task Force) with three others. He was in possession of a loaded semiautomatic pistol and packages of cocaine and marijuana packaged for resale. Bobby continues to do what Bobby does best. Life can be very unfair.

PETERS GUN SHOP—FREEPORT

Bob Peters Sr. was a good and decent man who owned a gun shop in Freeport, Illinois. Sadly that was also his curse.

It was November 12, 1992, and I'm en route to the Freeport, Illinois, Police Department to meet with my good friend Chief of Detectives Lieutenant Bob Smith. The day turned out very different from my anticipated visit. It was to be on an 88 matter (UFAP— unlawful flight to avoid prosecution) regarding a criminal that the Detective Division had determined had fled the state. Investigation by the police department determined that our bad guy was in Milwaukee, Wisconsin. UFAPs were and probably are to this day the "meat and potatoes" cases that allow the FBI to search for felons who have fled local jurisdiction.

On this day, our case is never even discussed. Arriving at a nearly deserted Police Department, I quickly learn they are at Bob Peters Gun Shop, where he had been found by a customer, murdered and robbed. Murders are not commonplace in Freeport, but curiosity and a willingness to offer any assistance that I can, on behalf of the FBI, has me en route to Bob's Gun Shop.

I had never met Mr. Peters, and if there were anyone who was ready for a robbery, it was Bob, according to those who were his friends. Of course, I learned this over the course of several days.

As the crime scene technicians were doing their crime scene investigation, Lieutenant Smith brought me up to speed. The witness who had found Mr. Peters was his friend and ironically a former FBI agent and longtime Freeport attorney Burt Snow. He and Bob apparently met nearly daily for coffee. Lieutenant Smith shared with me that Bob had an absolute phobia of being robbed. He truly felt he could handle one as he had handguns secreted in numerous places, known only to him, throughout his store. He also kept one in the small of his back.

Perhaps our bad guys knew this. What we now know is the three holdup men entered the business acting as customers, William Keene, Anthony Ehlers, and Michael Hoover, three ex-cons who served time together and planned the robbery while in prison. Hoover, who was the only one from Freeport, believed they had the perfect crime.

While one of the men asked Peters to show him a knife, as Bob bent to retrieve it, he was shot in the chest, failing to fall, he was shot in the head and Keene used the knife to cut his throat.

Keene ultimately received the death penalty but it was commuted to life in prison by Governor George Ryan when he left office in 2003. I'm getting way ahead of myself. On that November 1992 day, the Police Department had no idea who the bad guys were.

Many guns were missing as was a large amount of ammunition and knives. The getaway vehicle was ultimately determined to be an Oldsmobile Bravada which the three had rented in Tinley Park, Illinois where Ehlers had a girlfriend.

Bob Smith, then the chief of detectives, now the chief of police in Pecatonica, Illinois, has a near-photographic mind of this murder and robbery, right down to how they happened to choose Peters Gun Shop. As Bob recalled the crime, he talked of the storage units that were behind the gun shop. Apparently Hoover had one rented and he had developed the habit of driving back to it by crossing the lawn at the Gun Shop. Apparently, a Gun Shop customer was parked, blocking his passage, making him angry. He walked into the Gun Shop, berated the Gun Shop customer and Bob gave him "holy hell." Hoover apparently decided he'd get even. One could argue he certainly did.

1992 drifted into 1993 and Bob and his detectives have no leads on the Gun Shop. The Freeport Police Department is under great community pressure as 1992 had five murders. That number is uncommonly high in Freeport and Bob feels the pressure. Four are solved but the Peters murder, robbery had them greatly frustrated.

Bob recalls that on March 15, 1993, he received a call from the Hobart, Indiana Police Department and Detective Ron Wagner asks

Bob if he knows an Anthony Ehlers. Bob responds negatively. He then asks about William Keene. Bob again responds with a negative. Then he asks about Michael Hoover, and Lieutenant Smith responds with an "oh yeah." The events following, arguably makes Bob's day, as Detective Wagner asks of any unsolved gun shop robberies and murders. The bells and whistles are going off in Bob's head.

Wagner convinces Bob that he has a source who is singing about the crime. Detective Brian Kuntzelman accompanies Bob, and they head out for Hobart. Following their meeting with Wagner, they are introduced to the estranged girlfriend of Hoover, who lays out what she has been told by Hoover about the crime. She brings with her a piece of paper with the serial number of a hand gun that she knows is one that Hoover kept. Bob has the entire file with him. As he goes down his list of some 250 guns; Bingo! There it is.

The details match what is known by the Freeport Police, and Bob gets on the phone with Mike Bald, then the States Attorney of Stephenson County Illinois who authorizes a two count murder warrant for Hoover, and goes before a judge that afternoon and a warrant is issued. Elsewhere in these memoirs I write of my great respect of Mike Bald. This is just one of the many reasons why. He had the balls to go out on a limb when others would cower.

Back to Hobart—Bob and Brian accompany the Hobart Police to arrest Hoover, who perhaps realizes that the "jig is up" when he sees Bob, who previously sent him to prison following a series of Southern Wisconsin burglaries, perpetrated by Hoover.

Hoover is not talking, and he is placed in the Hobart Police temporary lockup in the basement of the Police Department. This proves to be a positive as Hoover sits alone with only his thoughts.

Bob and Brian are operating on no sleep but they decide to travel to a Sturtevant, Wisconsin where Ehlers is incarcerated. Based on the girlfriend they believe that he will talk.

Hoover has been told by Bob and Detective Wagner that Ehlers and Keene have fingered him as the shooter. As he sits with only his thoughts for about four hours in the deserted lock up, he asks to see Bob. Kuntzelman and Bob are literally in the parking lot ready to head out when they get the word. They sit with Hoover, who isn't going to take a murder hit, so he coughs up Ehlers and Keene as the shooter and the stabber.

The crime is unquestionably heinous and after four months of no leads they now feel that they definitely had their criminals.

The girlfriend of Hoover told Lieutenant Smith and Detective Kuntzelman that the guns were sold to bikers in the Riverdale area. Some will unquestionably surface as time goes by and they get used in crimes and confiscated. It would have been a matter of time, but NCIC (National Crime Information Center) would tie a criminal to a serial number of a gun. NCIC was new when I became an agent. Throughout the time I was in Salt Lake City, the terminal was being installed in that FBI Office. That technology at the time was a marvel. A gun stolen in Maine turns up at a shooting in California and bingo, instantaneously we tie it to Maine and backtracking leads us to many bad folks.

So often police agencies are underrated. Throughout my years of association with the Freeport Police Department and Stephenson County Sheriff's Office, I was always impressed with their professionalism and competence. In fact, I can't think of a police agency that I worked with throughout those many years that was anything other than professional. I believe it's a testimony of police officers in general. They are forced every day to be a psychologist, a medical professional, a pastor with a sympathetic ear and yet have eyes in the back of their head and be prepared for any contingency. Detective Dave Snyders and Detective Jerry Whitmore, who both went on to excel in law enforcement, did yeoman's work on the murder, armed robbery of Bob Peters and Peters Gun Shop. Lieutenant Smith and Detective Kuntzelman and the Hobart Indiana Police Department were the ones who broke the case wide open. Again, a classic example of great cops working together to get the job done.

RACIAL ISSUES

Swanson was a new black FBI agent serving in the Chicago Division. He was a former police officer, and he seemed to have a good sense of humor. Like all newly arriving agents, he got the usual "jerk around" with attempted humor.

The bottom line is, Swanson carefully documented each incident then claimed racial prejudice and before you knew it several good agents were on the carpet for the perceived ill deeds against Swanson. Of course it ended in a settlement.

This never was a racial issue, but Swanson knew how to make it one. Had a white person been Swanson, he would have been treated exactly the same until the suit was filed. Then he simply would have been laughed at for the buffoon that he was. It hit the Chicago Office like a ton of bricks. It was probably the first time many agents came face-to-face with racial sensitivity. Swanson used the system and the tempo of the times to achieve his ill-gotten gain.

Throughout my lifetime, both in the military and in the FBI, I have served beside racial minority persons, my respect for those who performed in a manner necessary to get the job done has never wavered any more than my lack of respect for a deadbeat, be they black or white. I have come to believe that most men and women of a racial minority simply want to do their job and be respected for that. As I see it, that is how it should be. Color does not determine a soldier, an agent or any other person, character does all that. Two of the finest supervisors I've ever worked for as an FBI agent are black. John Housley, now retired bank robbery supervisor in the Chicago Division, and Ray Jones, one of my supervisors during my assignment as a field counselor for class 96-12. Ray is one of those rare persons who has the charisma and capabilities of the finest. What absolute pillars these two gentlemen are. They made their mark on merit. Race never played into the equation.

I would be remiss not to mention Staff Sergeant Johnson, my drill instructor while I was in basic training at Fort Leonard Wood, Missouri. Again, my first contact with a man of color and one of the finest persons I ever knew.

Jan Wilhelm Shooting

The cold morning started calm that December day in 1987. Arriving at the FBI Office, I decided to take the afternoon off to take care of some unfinished business at home.

I signed out on leave and was at a salvage yard in South Beloit getting some transmission parts. Karen paged me to call immediately. I contacted the RA and thus started several days that, to this day, remain a blur. "Jim, Jan's been shot. He's bad." I was dumfounded.

Apparently shortly after I left, the Little Rock Office of the FBI shared with Jan telephonically that a fugitive from their division was believed to be in Rockford. They shared an address known to be "Concord Commons," an apartment complex on Rockford's west side. Apparently Jan learned and confirmed with teletype information that fugitive Undra Furlow was holed up there with his ex-wife, Evelyn.

Jan gathered the available agents and off they went to locate and arrest Furlow. As they traveled, Jan shared information he had that Furlow was wanted for the armed bank robbery in Strong, Arkansas on July 24. He was wanted on charges for several other bank heists as well.

There was little doubt that our bad guy was "A&D," armed and dangerous, and the utmost caution should be exercised.

With the benefit of hindsight, I'm sure Jan would have notified the Rockford Police. The number of times I left the RA to do a routine arrest (which is never routine) leaves me an easy understanding, "we'll just go grab this guy, get him locked up and move on." Again with hindsight, this time that was a big mistake.

With the exception of me (which I will never forgive myself for) Jan had the entire complement of the RA with him, no need to call

Jim. He took annual leave. Phil McClanahan and Lon Christensen were covering the rear of the building. Jan, Jack Mulvey and several other agents were at the front door.

Apparently as the agents announced themselves at the front door, telling Furlow to give himself up, Furlow pulled the door open exposing his wife Evelyn and shot her in the back as he pushed her through the doorway. He continued to fire his .357 magnum revolver striking Jan in the left cheek bone which passed through his right cheek. The next bullet creased the top of Jan's bulletproof vest, crashed through his sternum disintegrating the bullet with half of it entering and passing through his heart, while the other portion of the bullet slammed through his right lung and exited his side. The third bullet hit Jan in the arm and passed through it and entered Jan's side where the front and back of the bulletproof vest come together.

Jack Mulvey immediately returned fire, after pulling Evelyn out of the way, and his excellent accurate fire had one of his bullets strike Furlow's iliac artery in his upper leg. Furlow's momentum propelled him through the back window and Phil McClanahan fired and hit him in his left shoulder as he charged through the window, dropping over in a pool of blood from the massive bleeding of his iliac artery. He never regained consciousness and was later pronounced dead at the hospital.

As a trained crime scene investigator, I am now facing the most important crime scene investigation of my career. To my good fortune the Rockford Police Crime Scene guys were right there to help me.

As the blur continues, the rapid response of Rockford Fire Paramedics unquestionably save Jan's life. He and Evelyn are both critical and throughout the night it is touch and go, if Jan will make it. To his good fortune the paramedics put squeeze pants on Jan to keep as much blood as possible in his torso.

We later learn that Jan has seven entrance and exit holes in his body. Cardiologist Dr. Marx, believed to be the finest in Rockford, is just closing a patient, hands it off and takes Jan's case on. His surgery lasts for hours, but they do finally get him stabilized.

The next day Sgt. Denny Johnson and I complete our crime scene and evidence collection and take three large bags of evidence and fly to Washington, DC, and hand deliver it to the FBI lab for analysis.

Jan has issues to this day but is a tough old German and hangs in there.

As he was recovering he developed leukemia and somehow beat that. All of his teeth have died yet he perseveres without complaint. Only by the grace of God and very competent medics and doctors is Jan alive.

Evelyn made a complete recovery, and I have no idea what ultimately happened to her.

All of us have long retired, but seldom do we gather when Jan's shooting isn't discussed. It was one hell of a time.

TFIS
(THEFT FROM INTERSTATE SHIPMENT)
FBI CLASSIFICATION 87

The number of TFIS cases I worked throughout my career would be many. The crime is constituted when a shipment of goods is consigned from one state to another. Most cases are cartage theft typically semiloads. If a semitrailer is loaded with a commodity, but being shipped within a state boundary, it is strictly a matter for the police agencies within that state.

Once that load is consigned to another state's destination, it is a matter for the federal government, specifically the FBI, if it is highjacked or stolen in any way. Depending upon the commodity the value can be significant. As you meet or pass semis on the road, you could be beside millions of dollars. The good thieves have certainly figured that out.

It is another of those crimes where local authorities have jurisdiction as well, but one of the better examples of where the nationwide network of the FBI can best follow leads and hopefully resolve the case successfully. Good working relationships with local police are imperative. Prosecution is typically through the US Attorneys Office and typically before a federal judge.

The Chicago Office of the FBI in my day devoted an entire squad to TFIS. We, in the Resident Agencies, for example me in Rockford, would coordinate closely with the squad supervisor as very often these would be ring cases. That is a similar modus operandi (MO) as other thefts and coordination is essential.

One TFIS case stands out from my career and merits a chapter in this book. How I initially got to know Mike Dunn, the owner of Miller freight line I no longer recall. Safe to say we had become friends. Mike called me early one morning to let me know that one of his trailers, with a load consigned in interstate shipment, had been stolen.

Miller Freight Line had a contract with the tire manufacturing plant in Freeport, Illinois, Kelly Springfield, to haul many of their tires from their plant to their destinations. The procedure was to load a semitrailer with a specific number of tires, seal the trailer, and spot it at a parking area next to the plant.

Bad guys are always on the prowl for crimes of opportunity. So frustrating to the law enforcement community is when the good guys simply grant those opportunities.

The obvious question should be how they got to the trailer; surely the lot was secure. Sadly, it wasn't. All our bad guys had to do was back their tractor under the trailer hook and go. A competent trucker can do that in about five minutes.

As I've written elsewhere, thieves aren't always the brightest bulbs in the circuit. Typically and arguably, they are all opportunists. Imagine our bad guys observing semitrailers being loaded at the tire plant then being spotted in a deserted, unlit parking lot; almost like candy to a child.

Mike's driver arrived at the lot at about 5:00 a.m. but could not locate his loaded trailer. It didn't take a great deal of investigation to determine that it was missing. The police were notified, Mike is contacted and both the sheriff's office and Mike Dunn called our FBI Office in Rockford within minutes of each other. Our ending scenario would have been very different had the trailer our bad guys grabbed had been loaded with common size automobile tires as opposed to large farm tractor tires.

When they arrived at their destination, a large truck stop off I-90 and I-80 just inside the Indiana line, they parked the trailer with a plan to sell the car tires. They were perplexed and angry when they broke the lock off the trailer, swung open the doors expecting to sell out their car tires in a few hours and the thought of course is, "What the hell do we do now?"

Now remember these guys aren't rocket scientists. However, they do know that the only tractors going in and out of this parking area by the tire plant were Miller Freight units. They hatch a plan to sell the load back to Miller for $20,000.

By this time I am fully involved in the investigation having met with the Sheriff's Police, gotten a copy of the Police Report and I am on my way to the Miller Truck Terminal to meet with Mike when I am paged to call Mike Dunn. Mike told me what has been proposed to him by the bad guy. He is more than willing to pay the ransom as the load, according to Mike, is worth $84,000 and he absolutely doesn't want an insurance claim.

Mike told me he is expecting a call back very soon as he had advised them he must gather up that much cash. I suggested to Mike that perhaps when they call back tell them all he could round up is $10,000. Mike took that suggestion and as I continued to Mike's terminal I contacted the US attorney's office to get authority for an over hear devise on Mike's phone.

Fortunately we received the authority and fellow agent Lon Christensen left for Mike's Terminal to install the listening device. Shortly thereafter I arrived at the Terminal and Lon and I instruct a nervous Mike Dunn on how to activate the recorder when the bad guy called back. Lon and I along with Mike Dunn now awaited the call and it didn't take long.

Mike played his part very well and with Lon and I listening Mike convinced our subject that all he can come up with is $9,000 in cash to which they readily agreed. Mike described his tractor to our bad guy and gave a vague description of me who would be driving the tractor and that he would be the passenger with the cash.

My much younger years of obtaining my (CDL) Commercial Drivers License, required for driving a tractor trailer unit, paid off. Shakespeare wrote that old men remember, with advantages, the deeds they did as warriors. I was no warrior but I can give a blow-by-blow as I was behind the wheel.

Mike agreed with the bad guy that we would come to the truck stop and back up to the stolen trailer. When they were convinced that we were alone, one of them would come to the passenger door and Mike would accompany him to the back of the trailer to ensure that the tires were still there.

This would not happen according to the bad guy until he was convinced that we were alone and that there were no cops around. Mike assured him that it would only be him and his driver (me) and that no police had been notified.

The reality was that Agent Lon Christensen was in the sleeper and several members of the Chicago surveillance squad were prepositioned at the truck stop and, as I recall, all our available Rockford agents were nearby. I was behind the wheel of Mike's cab over sleeper semitractor, so I was somewhat concerned that I would miss most of the action which is exactly what happened.

The great news was it worked exactly as planned, something that is often not the case. Again I must reiterate that often dumb luck trumps good investigation. When the bad guys readily agreed to accept $9,000 I had the feeling this would work out well.

The only bad guy I got to see initially was the one who walked to Mike's door. I stayed in the tractor as Mike accompanied him to the back of the trailer at which time the bad guy's friend joined him and our nearby agents placed them both under arrest as they were counting out the $9,000 that Mike had given them.

If only all our cases could have been this text book but such was usually not the case.

Mike had to leave his $9,000 with the arresting agents until the following day after it had been processed as evidence.

As the bad guys were taken away, our evidence technicians processed the trailer and its contents and then I pulled Mike's load, again with him as the passenger, back to his terminal in Rockford. Mike loved how it all went down. Throughout the three-hour drive back to Rockford, he promised numerous times that he would get his lot in Freeport fenced, lighted, and cameras installed. He was true to his word.

We recovered an $84,000 load and got two significant thieves out of circulation. (They both had extensive arrest records).

Mike Dunn and all who would listen to him were convinced that the FBI walked on water. Of course, we were modest, but a pat on the back always feels good.

SUICIDE BY COP

I'm extremely proud of the schools I attended as an FBI agent. The one most meaningful was being trained as a hostage negotiator. Candidates, that the hierarchy of the FBI wanted, were agents that had a police background and training as a sociologist or psychologist. This being right up my alley, as I was two years a River Falls Wisconsin Police Officer and had a degree in psychology and speech from the University of Wisconsin at River Falls.

The intensity of the training centered on the importance and the ability to win over the hostage taker, whenever possible. The importance of establishing rapport was the key.

A call to the Rockford Resident Agency of the FBI from Detective Dave Ernest of the Belvidere Illinois Police Department on October 6, 1994, which would be my first test as a hostage negotiator.

Dave got me on the phone and asked if I could help with a hostage situation in their city. Of course, I advised, and after I briefed Jan Wilhelm, our supervisor, he authorized the entire office of agents to be en route to Belvidere, only twenty minutes away.

From the command post, Dave and I and the others discussed our options and situation—Robert Rickey Arthur was holding his girlfriend, Suzy and infant son, threatening to kill them both. Dave told us officers were called by a distraught Suzy, wanting Robert arrested and a domestic issue was getting critical. Responding officers were ordered off the property by an armed Robert who threatened to kill them both and the officers, if the officers didn't leave. The officers, of course, backed off and called for backup.

The Belvidere swat team was in place as we got briefed, and it was evident the situation was bad and deteriorating rapidly as Suzy continued to goad Robert. Dave told us he had telephonically spoken with Robert and he could hear Suzy in the background insulting and humiliating him.

I learned from Dave that Robert was small in stature, was a volunteer fireman and wanted to become a full time fireman or policeman. This is what I knew when Dave called him back and Robert did answer. Dave told him that he wanted him to speak to me as I was an FBI agent and could help.

When Robert got on the phone it was apparent he was highly agitated yet wanted to talk. Thus began a seven hour effort to get Robert to release Suzy and their infant son.

Of course we are trained to do all we can to defuse the situation. I could tell from the get go that this was not going to be easy. I knew Robert was armed, as responding officers who had been at the door had indicated they believed he had a .357 magnum revolver.

Robert and I established a good rapport. I simply kept trying to keep him talking about what was troubling him. Apparently, as he and Suzy were no longer living together, Robert had learned from friends that she was trying to give up their infant son for adoption. She had told the adoption agency that she had no idea who the father was and she no longer wanted the burden of being a mother.

As Robert is sharing his tale of woe, I hear Suzy continually humiliating him; simply put I can't believe it. She is telling him constantly what a worthless piece of s—— he is and could never be a good father, getting Robert more and more agitated.

My thought process is she knows he has a 357 and is threatening to kill her. Why in the hell doesn't she back off, but she doesn't. The torment continues over my efforts to calm Robert.

Of course as the hours progress, I'm surrounded by agents and detectives handing me suggestions. Though I don't want to lose my momentum with Robert, I ask him to put Suzy on the phone. I strongly admonish her and ask her to back off and quit agitating him, her response, "This yellow m——f—— doesn't have the balls to kill me."

"Are you kidding me, lady? Goddamn it, back off, and you're going to jail if something happens."

Somehow that seemed to get her attention, and for the next hour, she remained somewhat calm.

Robert couldn't believe that Suzy would give away their baby.

For several more hours I attempted to defuse Robert and I truly am gaining ground when Suzy turned on the TV with "Oh, look, Robert, we are on TV."

Of course, through the course of time, more and more news outlets arrived. The police have the area well cordoned off but the media has bits and pieces of information and it truly is the "only" news during the entire standoff. Once again Suzy feels her oats and is excited that all this is causing such a big deal. News trucks from as far away as Chicago and Milwaukee are several blocks from the scene, which sadly will culminate soon enough.

I continue to win over Robert, day is moving into night. He tells me he is going to jail and his chances of ever being a full time firefighter or police officer are ruined. I assure Robert and tell him that I will stay right with him and even appear before the judge with him to explain the gravity of the situation. By now I've concluded that there is only one bad person here and it sure as hell isn't Robert. I continue to encourage him and assure him that I will stay right with him and help him through this.

After my numerous attempts, I get his assurance that he will put the gun down and let Suzy and the baby go. He finally concedes if, as he put it, he can come out with them. I assure him that will be fine and both he and Suzy must both come out unarmed, he with his hands in the air and she carrying the baby.

Robert tells me, "We'll come out," and I alert the others who notify the swat teams covering the house. Suzy and the baby step out first. I have no idea how many high powered 308 scoped rifles were trained on the exit door. Though I don't see it from my position, I learn Robert steps out with his hands in the air. The next thing I hear is a loud exclamation "gun," then several high-powered rounds ring out, striking Robert in the temple and between the eyes. He dropped his right arm I'm told and pulled a gun from his right rear pocket aiming it to Suzy's head only to die in a hail of swat team rounds. Robert was armed with an unloaded pellet gun.

I am stunned. I had gotten Robert to promise me he'd leave the gun behind and not do anything stupid. My elation crashes to profound sadness. I was so looking forward to sitting with Robert, reinforcing him and continuing my efforts to convince him he had so much to live for, most of all his son.

And so on a suburban lawn in Belvidere, Robert Rickey Arthur lies in his own blood as investigators conduct their crime scene investigation and canvas the neighbors for more information. The drama ends with a classic example of "Suicide by Cop".

Dr. Bob Wolford, the Rockford Illinois Police Department Psychiatrist who had joined us at the height of the negotiation, leads me into a small room. We are alone, and he simply says, "Let it go." Seven hours of intensity, then elation, then bang Robert is dead.

Yes, I cried like a baby. Dr. Bob perceived my anguish and sat with me for perhaps half an hour as I composed myself. I couldn't go out there and face my peers with teary eyes.

Jan, to his great credit and Chicago ASAC Tom Duhadway took me to a restaurant and just sat and talked with me. I think they had perceived my distress prior to Dr. Bob taking me into the small room.

So my day ended like many, I headed home to my wonderful family, simply thanking God that I had been so blessed.

The following day area newspapers praised our poor young victim so traumatized by such an evil man. Yes, she got her fifteen minutes of fame. I'm thankful I was not asked my opinion.

Then Detective Ernst today is the Sheriff of Boone County with the County Seat being Belvidere, not surprised at all, one hell of a cop.

U.S. Department of Justice

Federal Bureau of Investigation

Office of the Director   *Washington, D.C. 20535*

December 9, 1994

PERSONAL

Mr. James G. Sacia
Federal Bureau of Investigation
Chicago, Illinois

Dear Mr. Sacia:

I am pleased to have this opportunity to commend you for your special efforts in connection with the Domestic Police Cooperation case involving *Robert Rickey Arthur.* Furthermore, I approved a cash award for you which will be forwarded separately.

You displayed tact and extreme determination during this tense hostage situation. Despite the commotion and excitement, you maintained negotiations with the subject and *provided invaluable assistance* and professional expertise. Throughout this stressful ordeal you responded appropriately and immediately which was exemplary. Your keen leadership was a contributing factor to the investigative efforts, and I want to thank you for your services.

Sincerely yours,

Louis J. Freeh
Director

THE US ATTORNEY OFFICE AND THE FBI

Rockford was blessed with some great assistant US attorneys. In the 1970s, there was no full-time assistant US attorney assigned full-time to Rockford. Rockford is in the "Western Circuit" of the Northern District of Illinois. The Northern District is headquartered in Chicago. We in the Western Circuit were at least one hundred ten miles from Chicago with the court house in Freeport, Illinois.

It was a struggle for years with AUSA's coming to the Rockford RA or to the court house in Freeport to discuss the prosecution of our cases. It's fair to say that at that time the Assistants nearly always prefaced their decision, "Is it possible to get the local States Attorney to prosecute this matter?" Needless to say, we in the FBI did not want to hear that and we would push hard for federal prosecution.

I think back to AUSA's like Tom Durkin, who today is a sitting Federal Judge in Chicago, who was in the forefront of helping us get a full time office for the US Attorneys in the Rockford area. Tom was one who was always willing to come to Rockford before the office was established.

The FBI can do an amazing job of investigating federal crime, wrap up the conclusions but without a dedicated and diligent Assistant US Attorney the case can die on the vine.

When the office was established it was headed by AUSA Keith Syfert and shortly thereafter he was joined by AUSA Jim Zuba. These two were the best, both dedicated and hardworking.

Shortly before my retirement in 1997, I was somewhat floored when AUSA Zuba took issue with how I handled a "pre-sentence report." A pre-sentence report is compiled by a probation officer and is relied upon heavily by Judges, especially in white-collar cases. I had conducted a lengthy investigation of a con artist attempting to scam The department of housing and urban development (HUD). We utilized many sophisticated techniques and Mr. Zuba had been very successful in prosecuting the subject. He, like me, believed the guy deserved the high end of the sentencing guidelines. The following is from my notes on November 7, 1996:

Yesterday Jim Zuba asked me to come to his office regarding the Clinton matter. This seemed a little odd as Clinton was already convicted in a difficult trial that I dealt with in late August. Clinton is to be sentenced in December.

Mr. Zuba handed me a pre-sentence report which had been prepared by a probation officer.

I read my interview with the officer wherein she interviews the investigating agent, that would be me, for information she needs to prepare a "pre-sentence report" for the judge who will do the sentencing.

The thing I remembered most of her interview, was how strongly I stressed that Clinton showed no remorse and basically said he'd do it again. Further, I had told her how Clinton had stood in the way by never volunteering any incriminating information until he was confronted with the facts. I further noted how, on occasions through my career, I felt sorry for the convicted because they were so remorseful. Not so with Clinton, I went so far as to tell her that in my many years in law enforcement this is one guy I had no compassion for at all. He did everything he could to circumvent the system by simply not cooperating until confronted directly with the evidence.

She then asked me if Clinton had "impeded justice." My response was he had not. My thoughts on impeding justice is someone who destroys evidence, pays people off or any litany of other actions to throw investigators off. I said no he didn't. Little did I realize at the time that she had played me like a yo-yo. In her report she had said that I said Clinton offered nothing until I confronted him with evidence. At no point did she stress how frustrated I was with this investigation due to his lack of cooperation but she stressed me saying he had not "impeded justice."

Mr. Zuba was livid as he felt my interpretation of impeding justice was not correct. His opinion, when Clinton wasn't forthright, he impeded justice. Mr. Zuba and I often disagreed, but I always respected his opinion. My frustration here was how the probation officer used my comment out of context on Clinton's behalf.

I do not identify her here because I had always respected her and held her in high esteem. What she did to me on this interview took all that respect away. She surely knew my true feelings and deep conviction that this guy deserved significant time. The sheer magnitude of this investigation and the in-depth work to bring it to a logical conclusion had been significant. Furthermore, his constant gamesmanship and attempts to con the system had really gotten to me.

In fairness, and going back to "impeding justice," he didn't. To AUSA Zuba he did. He and I agreed to disagree. It was now water over the dam. Reality—for whatever reason, she played me like a yo-yo, and that stings. I did the investigation and not her. My feeling—he conned her as well.

CORRUPTION

A shuddering experience for any FBI agent is to hear that their honesty and integrity is being questioned.

It happened to me in the early '80s and I will never forget it. It happened once again in my years as an Illinois state representative that will be addressed elsewhere.

One night while working surveillance in Rockford, Detective Charlie Jackson confided in me that he had heard from a Priest in Dixon, Illinois, that I could be bought. Needless to say, I was outraged but had no idea what I could do. In its proper context, Charlie had just heard that I was crooked from the Priest who was a friend of Charlie's and though he didn't know my name, had told Charlie that the FBI agent who lived in Pecatonica was "on the take." Still not knowing where to turn, I called my good friend, Ed Seyller, a State Police Detective from Sterling, Illinois, to see if he had heard anything about my integrity. Ed actually began to laugh and told me that he and his partner Bob Bales had been interviewing a person, Dave Johanson, who they believed had knowledge of stolen semitractors.

When it became apparent to Johanson that he was going to take a fall, he told Seyller and Bales that he could give them a "bigger fish." With that, he went into a story about "that FBI agent up by Pecatonica that fools with them old tractors" is taking $1,000 payoff for every stolen semi brought into Illinois.

Seyller had found it highly amusing and decided it wasn't even worth telling me about. He did say that the next time he ran into me he planned to "jack me up."

To say I was tear ass would have been an understatement. I barely knew Johanson; I had interviewed him about his boss Fred Irving. Any law enforcement officers with two weeks interview time knows one of the most elementary procedures is to put a subject at ease when an interview is conducted. I had told Johanson about my interest in old farm tractors, how I enjoyed buying them, fixing them up and reselling them. We visited for maybe a half hour before we got into the meat of the interview and I felt I had established rapport. Irving was a used heavy truck dealer and the commonality between heavy trucks and farm equipment was a given.

Somehow that had translated into taking payoffs from thieves.

Recognizing that this viscous rumor would not go away by itself, especially with a Catholic Priest believing I was crooked, I immediately got ahold of Jan, told him what I knew and asked for an immediate investigation to clear my name.

The next day Jan and ASAC Tom Duhadway traveled to Amboy, Illinois, to interview Johanson, who admitted he had no clue who I was, but had been interviewed by me so when he was pressured by Seyller and Bales he believed they would find his story plausible. He could offer no explanation.

Many outstanding law enforcement officers had had their good names ruined in similar situations and once that shadow of doubt is established about an officer's honor and credibility it's very had to retrieve.

I was put under oath by Jan and Tom and gave a signed statement. I thought in my memoirs I had retained it, somehow it got away.

Several months later, after sufficiently cooling off and remembering an old Dan Ryan saying, "Revenge is a dish that is best tasted cold," I walked into Johanson's place of business. He didn't remember me, so I asked him if he knew me as he gave me a blank stare. I reminded him that he should know me well as I was that "FBI agent from Pecatonica who fools with them old tractors," and with that, I left. I doubt if it made the impression I wanted it to, but I had the satisfaction of doing it.

Detective Ed Seyller recalls that I did chew him out, I have no such recollection. It's one of those times in my life that is simply best forgotten.

JASON DAVIS

Jason Davis (fictitious name), Trooper Illinois State Police Detective Division was assigned to District 1 in Sterling, Illinois.

At least every other week, I was at district 1 to discuss my investigations in that area and share FBI assistance wherever I could.

It was a beautiful fall afternoon as I pulled up to the back door of District 1, the investigator entrance, to be greeted by Trooper Paula Viscero also one of the detectives. "Sacia, you've got to help us," she mused. Of course, my question was "what's up."

The entire detective bureau had lost its focus, and it was time for some cop humor, which can be bizarre. Jason got a vasectomy yesterday, will you call him and pretend you are his doctor? Oh my god, a chance to truly be in my element. "Why, of course, I will."

Jim Birch, Jim Kerns, Paula, and Commander Dave Reed are summoned as we are going to set up Jason. The four of them gather around me and give the facts that his surgery was yesterday, and they would like me just to pretend I am the doctor, put it on speakerphone, and see what I can get out of him

For this, I am truly in my element.

"Jason, this is Dr. Blake, how are you feeling today?"

"Well, I'm sore, but I'm okay. Have you been icing it?" I ask.

Jason advises to the affirmative, and I assure him that is very important. I ask him if he has showered today and he states not yet. I suggest that a good hot shower would be good to alternate with the ice pack. Jason assures me he will comply. The humor on every face in the place only reinforces me to continue the charade. I ask him if he's eaten yet today and he states very little as he simply isn't hungry. I stress the importance of rest and keeping his strength up. The attempts at concealed laughter only goad me to keep it up.

Finally, with a straight face, I ask, "Have you masturbated yet?"

There is a long pause on Jason's end, and Paula is nearly hysteri-cal, and the muffled laughs almost get to me, but I can't quit just yet.

Jason says, "I didn't know I was supposed to."

I can control myself no longer. "Well, you're not but we all just wondered if you did. Now everyone is joining in. Jason recognizes my voice and responds with words to the affect "You a——, Sacia." Safe to say, the laugh was on Jason.

I don't think he ever got me back, and though I haven't seen him in years, I remember him as an excellent investigator, but most of all, I remember the details of his vasectomy.

THE NEVER-ENDING SCAMS

There is little doubt that a free society will never have a shortage of someone trying to get your money from you, no matter how you protect yourself. If it sounds too good to be true, it always is.

In law enforcement there is always job security as those unscrupulous individuals will always commit crime. A famous bank robber, Willie Sutton, is credited with replying to the question of "Why do you rob banks?" he allegedly responded with "Because that's where the money is." In his autobiography, *I, Willie Sutton*, 1953, he disavows ever having said it. He did not deny being a prolific bank robber stating that he felt fully alive while robbing banks. Some reporter along the way simply attached the oft quoted line, but Willie never said it.

He was on the FBI's ten most wanted list as the eleventh man in 1953, again because he robbed banks perpetually and in the 1950s he was sentenced to life in prison plus 135 years but was paroled in 1969 and lived until 1980. Job security in law enforcement comes from the Willy Suttons of the world.

Criminals come from all walks of life and some that I've known over the years were the kind of people who would have been great friends under different circumstances. The ones who really got under my skin were the scam artists. To many it's hard to imagine that someone could stoop so low as to take a person's last dime in a scam. With a degree in psychology I get it, but I despise those who engage in it.

Many come to mind over my years as an agent. One in particular comes to mind involving Joe Close, who had a scam set up headquartered in Rockford. You received a post card telling you that you have already won one of five valuable prizes. All that is required is that you purchase a bottle of life-enhancing vitamins for $9.95 and you will receive your valuable prize plus your bottle of vitamins. The cheapest prize was a diamond bracelet appraised at $1,500.

Of course you received your two dollars' worth of vitamins and your two-dollar bracelet, but now you are hooked. Joe's folks worked from what we called boiler rooms where scam artists, who now have your phone number, go to work on you promising "pie in the sky" and the number of people who fall for it, never ceased to amaze me. "Now that you have already won you are automatically entered as a winner for a much bigger prize." A follow up call nets more money sent for another "bite at the apple."

SA Brian Barthelmew and I worked the case against Joe, which was most difficult to get an indictment as the "victim" did receive something for their exorbitant expense. The only way it finally got together is, Joe and his henchmen allowed greed to stop sending the valuable prize.

The Nigerian scam letters are ongoing to this day. You receive a typewritten letter or email explaining that you have been chosen to hold several hundred thousands of dollars because you have been determined to be so honorable. You will be allowed to keep X percentage and all you have to do is send a copy of your deposit slip and money will be deposited into your account. Just to ensure that you will in fact comply, just send a money order for (a small amount compared with what will be deposited to your account) to ensure that we can trust each other. I've never believed it either, but I was always amazed at the number who fall for classic old "pigeon drop" schemes.

One that I must single out involved a lady from Freeport that I held in high esteem. She was well educated, very articulate but, I guess in hindsight, simply very gullible. Toward the end of my FBI career, she had contacted me about a promise from a phone call promising her "pie in the sky." I assured her it was a scam. She told me that she had already sent $1,000 to ensure that she would receive the money. After considerable effort with my most convincing lines, I believe that I had helped her to believe that it was a rip-off.

I heard no more from or of her for many years. Several years after being elected a state representative, I was contacted by Freeport Deputy Chief of Police Bob Smith telling me that the lady, who we'll call Beth, had surrendered her and her husband's entire retirement fund to "Bill" who she talked with regularly on the phone. Bill had convinced her that she had won the Irish lottery of millions of dollars. Of course Bill was getting her to forward more and more money in order for him to "pay off" the officials so it could be forwarded to her. No, I don't believe it either, but the kicker was her proclamation, she just knew Bill was a good Christian man because he even prayed with her on the phone. We will always need law enforcement but cases such as these are the most frustrating, as our bad guys are no more culpable than our gullible and greedy victims.

Sadly more often than not, they are never prosecuted. The bad guys, being exceptionally clever, are constantly moving. About the time that law enforcement locates their operation center, their method of operation and the necessary "hoops and hurdles" are overcome to obtain a search warrant, they are gone. A new state, a new town, and in many cases a new gimmick and they are back in operation again.

Greed is a powerful motivator, and if a person lacks morals, values, conscience, and the desire to make an honest living, they are "naturals" to get involved in these unbelievable moneymaking schemes.

Throughout my entire law enforcement career, and to this day, I marvel at the number of people who call me or run into me by chance and share a scam and ask my opinion if it could be the "real thing." I invariably tell them don't send any money, give them any information or if you have, don't send any more or give any more information.

Of course, they assure me that they were sure it was a scam anyway. What is tragically sad and I do mean tragically, is more often than not they'll have "just one more conversation" and set them in their place. Guess what? Yes, the good ones are just that, good at convincing you that yes, there are many scams but this one is the "real deal" and after that convincing speech, they'll send that $1,000 or however much because Jim Sacia or this or that law enforcement couldn't begin to question this deal. God help us all. The millions—no, correction—billions of dollars that citizens send in would be staggering.

How do I know this? Simple, the same way that neither I nor anyone else will know the number of crimes prevented by the presence of the marked squad car or uniformed officer. None of us will ever know the number of people who have sent the money. Would you admit it if you were that stupid? Of course not! That's the tragedy—the very number that never get reported. I get angry even writing about it. Remember my comment: "Greed is a powerful motivator." That doesn't only apply to the bad guys. We all have a bit of it in us.

I had asked Beth if she had, in fact, purchased an Irish lottery ticket. She had told me "no." Then how on God's green earth could you have won? That question seemed to go over her head.

Yes, it can be that easy by the gifted scam artist.

Our elderly are the most vulnerable. They would just love to leave a little more money to the kids. Guess what? They are about to lose what little they had.

96-12

I know it wasn't only me, I heard it many times in my senior years as an FBI agent. Comments like "These new guys and ladies just aren't the caliber of those of us who have been around a while." I will confess that weighed on me. I was (still am) extremely proud of the FBI. I just didn't want to believe that this great agency was anything less than the finest law enforcement agency in the nation.

In 1996, knowing that I'd be mandatorily retired in a few short years, I talked with Jen about the possibility of taking a new agents class through, as a field counselor, attached to the class. Jenny was always great about supporting my dreams and schemes. With her support I approached Jan (Supervisory Special Agent Jan Wilhelm) the Rockford RA boss and asked for his sanction. He wholeheartedly supported it and he contacted the special agent in charge (SAC) of Chicago and got the ball rolling.

I left Pecatonica in our "Grocery Getter"; Jenny's 1976 Oldsmobile Vista Cruiser Station Wagon and headed for Quantico, Virginia in early April. I had purchased the car from a fellow agent as he and his wife had gotten a new car. The 120,000 miles on the odometer did not bother me at all. It just picked 'em up and laid them down all the eight-hundred-plus miles to Quantico.

I would be one of three counselors assigned to Class 96-12 made up of fifty-two young men and women. For the next sixteen weeks, they would be "my kids." Special Agent Gene Klopf was the staff Counselor. The staff position was held by an agent either assigned full-time to Quantico or WFO (Washington Field Office). Typically, they were agents who were awaiting an assignment as a supervisor and certainly that position gave them additional upward mobility.

There were two of us who were "field counselors," Steve Lucchesi and me. Our job was to live in the dorm with the new agents, be their mentors and coordinate any and all issues not already specifically defined in their training manual and schedule. In other words, Steve and I were at their beck and call for any and all issues. It was an assignment I absolutely loved. Fifty two young people from all over the country gather at Quantico and become 96-12. We will be beside each other until their training is completed.

There are very few minorities in the class. When I became an agent in 1969, minorities were nearly non-existent. As of May 3, 1996, there were 576 black agents, ninety-seven of them being female; fifty American Indians with eight being female; 197 Asians with twenty-two being female; 690 Hispanics with seventy-five being female; 3864 white agents with 1,257 being female. What always amazed me was the small number of qualified blacks who apply to become special agents for the FBI. Class 96-12 has one black agent, two Asian Americans, several Hispanics, and twelve women.

I feel good to learn that most applied to become agents to hopefully better serve their country and to be a part of such an Agency as the FBI. The reality check sets in as each of the young men and women sits at a table with a firearm in front of them. Each of these weapons was in the hands of a fellow agent as they were felled in a gun battle. The names are indelibly carved in the hearts and minds of their families, friends, fellow agents and now this new breed has a new focus on how this or that agent lost their life. Each incident is thoroughly shared by a seasoned Firearms instructor as he methodically relates the terrible tragedy of each agent's tragic loss of life.

Some of the new agents look a little squeamish but no one resigns. In some previous classes it has happened where someone will ask to be excused and simply resign. There is always an effort to talk them out of it but there is never ill will. Frustrated, firearms Instructor Mike Perry says it sarcastically: Not everyone is cut out to be an FBI special agent. The world is filled with other professions.

The Academy is filled to overflowing. I marvel at the large number of law enforcement officers in training along with the in service agents (those back for refresher training) in a wide variety of subjects.

There are over three hundred agents receiving training as well as 250 National Academy students. These are select law enforcement officers from all over the world who are attending the FBI's sixteen week course on all aspects of effective law enforcement.

Police officers compete in their respective departments to earn the opportunity to attend the National Academy. It is a "feather in the cap" of any and all attendees and many who are not Chiefs of Police do go on in their careers to either become a Chief or certainly high official in their respective agency.

Their PT Instructor is Special Agent George Runkle, from the moment I met him I liked him, a no nonsense West Point graduate who has no more body fat than a survivor of Auschwitz. Runkle puts 96-12 through their paces and Steve, Gene, and I evaluate the physical condition of our kids with some puzzling results. Why anyone would come here without being in excellent physical condition is absolutely beyond me. They are run through pull-ups, push-ups, shuttle run, and of course, a two-mile run.

One young lady achieves a score of -12. A minus score is given when that person cannot do the absolute minimum number of repetitions in any of the events. For them it will be a long sixteen weeks. Those with very poor scores must participate in power PT. At the end of each day's classes and before dinner, these marginal physical specimens will be required to go to the gym and participate in the activities designed to improve their fitness.

I mentioned earlier that Steve and I live with them and are there for any needs that they should have. We are always available for any issue or call in any and all ways.

It's enjoyable going through the training experience as a counselor. Either Steve or I are nearly always with them so we get a great feel for the abilities and levels of competence of each of them. I pride myself on being able to call each of them by name by the end of their second day of training. My name is important to me, and I feel they deserve the same courtesy.

I like how the days are broken up. I give credit to the bureau for the way the training is handled, classroom, practical problems, firearms training, and physical fitness. It changes daily and no one ever gets too much of anything and it's on to something else.

Each new agent will fire over four thousand rounds from their newly issued Sig Sauer 9 mm pistol. If they have issues they will fire an additional five hundred rounds. If they don't qualify, they will not graduate. The new agents are trained on any and all weapons, not only those they will use, but those they may encounter "on the street." The H&K MP 5, 9 mm shoulder weapon is fired extensively, and the agents must qualify on it as well.

The Remington 870 twelve-gauge pump shotgun, which has been around for years, is still a big part of the Bureau Arsenal. The agents shoot trap at length to learn how to lead a target and knock it down.

A side touch of humor: One of our lady agents was having trouble racking a round into the chamber of her 870. The instructor dislodged her tube of lipstick. Then trying to help her, he realized that she had taped Kotex to her shoulder to avoid the recoil, her face was redder than her lipstick. She took the razzing in stride.

We settled in to a great routine.

One of the instructors that I greatly admired is Special Agent Sue Adams. Not only does she instruct interview and interrogation but she does a beautiful job in pointing out the importance of interacting with the DEA agents as well as the National Academy Men and Women. She actually gives assignments to 96-12 agents to interview National Academy students from the state they are being assigned to. The interaction is great and certainly appreciated by the National Academy Students as well as the counselors.

There is more and more comradery throughout the academy setting as these agents and police officers become acquainted. Behavioral science is a course that all the agents seem to appreciate. In Sue Adams's classes, it was great to see that over 95 percent of the agents are outgoing, methodical team players, and the role-playing expected and taught by Sue truly brings that out. Behavioral science gives them all some experience in not only how their minds tick but the differences in those involved in the vast number of crimes they will be investigating.

Each of the agents has filled out their "dream sheets" of where they hope to be assigned. There are fifty-six offices of the FBI, and the bureau does a much better job getting agents close to where they hope to be assigned as compared to when I came in in 1969. We have already heard that ten of the fifty two will be assigned to New York City, the bureau's largest field office. We have also heard that Honolulu has an acute need for agents which has much more appeal than New York City.

I am exceptionally impressed with the instructors in all the different facets from firearms to legal training. Each and every one is the consummate professional. Their ability to convey the knowledge that they have acquired over the years is exceptional.

One of the training aspects they received is TEVOC. I've lost what the acronym stands for but it boils down to pursuit driving. Each of the students drive specially equipped cars through a series of mazes and performs dangerous maneuvers under the careful scrutiny of an instructor and become highly proficient in pursuit driving. It was not offered when I was newly trained but I believe that the skills learned will bode well for each new agent, no matter where they end up.

I love observing the contrast between the agent instructors. Certainly the classroom guys, the legal instructors, behavioral science folks and the rest wearing suits and ties contrast significantly with those fondly referred to as "the knuckle draggers," the hands on guys teaching firearms, rough and tumble apprehension instructors. They do a great job in getting the point across on staying alive in the real world. These guys and ladies use "Hogan's Alley" to run through numerous scenarios from bank robbery issues to any number of tactical situations. Hogan's Alley even existed when I was trained in 1969, but along the way, the improvements have made it a functioning village.

Playing at the theater is "Manhattan Melodrama: the movie showing when John Dillinger was shot in front of the Biograph Theatre back in the 1930s. The Bank of Hogan remains the most robbed bank in the world and the Dogwood Café doubles as a classroom following the bank robbery. The loading dock, the motel, the pool hall tavern and laundromat all are used to give agents valuable hands on training. I smile as there is even "Jim's Used Cars."

Class 96-12's makeup is similar to the other new agent training classes. Their average age is thirty-one. Our class has fourteen former military officers, eight of them pilots; twelve females from numerous professions including police work, the military and one who was a manager of a large department store. Many possess multi lingual talents in both written and spoken language and some possess skills in languages that are only spoken. One of our females was a spokesman for the Governor of her home state and another was a news anchor. A thirty-six-year-old mother of three and devoted wife, was a coal miner, a Marine officer, and a lady who can outrun, outshoot, and physically outperform the majority of the males in the class.

This class has melded like a chunk of coal turned to a diamond.

As I spend day after day with these young men and women, what becomes more and more apparent is not only do these young agents measure up to my wishes for the future of the FBI, they far surpass them. When I leave the FBI it will certainly be in good hands. No longer will I say "the new guys just aren't the caliber of my era."

FBI director Louis Freeh ran with 96-12 at 6:00 a.m. on two separate occasions. I prided myself, as a guy over fifty able to keep up with him. Our run was typically five miles. Over an extended amount of miles, I doubt I could have kept up. Director Freeh is a class act. I'm as honored for having served with him at the end of my watch, as I was with Director Hoover at the beginning.

RETIRING

It was such a simple thing—just fill out four impersonal questions—length of service, beneficiaries, military time, "Do you want your credentials mounted on a plaque?" Not even a call from the SAC. Put the questionnaire in an envelope to the SAC secretary and it's official, you will retire after nearly twenty-eight years, such a big decision, such a simple process.

My going-away party is being planned by Karen and Jenny. I know it will be nice. The reality is I am now persona non grata.

As I travel the territory, all my policeman friends are now aware that I am leaving. The feeling is strange, no longer asked for advice, just "hope you enjoy your retirement." My friend Dave Krishovitch said it best—a doctor can retire, but he is still a doctor. A lawyer is still a lawyer, when an FBI agent leaves, he is "just another guy with his hat in his hand."

The letter to the director is a matter of choice; it is not required. I felt compelled to write him for two reasons. I wanted him to know how much this career meant to me, and he deserves to know what an inspiration he is.

My inbox suddenly starts filling with applicant cases, kind of the nemesis of FBI investigations. I ask my supervisor to let me keep my dignity; don't reduce me to an applicant agent. He graciously complied.

The process of deciding to retire is a gradual one. You start thinking about going, and you know you must as the mandatory date is a short four years away. You gradually come to terms with knowing it's time to go.

Attempting to recall when I first decided to retire is somewhat difficult. I do vividly remember what cemented it. A call to the RA at about 10:00 a.m. advises us that a bank in rural Boone County has just been robbed. Jan comes into the bull pen and alerts us of the situation, and looking straight at me states, "Jim, you take Susan with you." Of course, I'll be happy to.

Susan Hansen has just arrived from Chicago, where she just spent several weeks, following her graduation at Quantico, as a new agent. Susan is a former Army captain and a savvy lady. I had actually become acquainted with her while she was in Training School and I was assigned to Quantico as a counselor.

Susan's class graduated several weeks ahead of my "kids" in 96-12. I had received a call from the SAC (special agent in charge) of Chicago while I was in Quantico, asking my opinion if she'd "fit in" with the Rockford RA. I think Susan was known by everyone at the Academy. She was a very outgoing, well-liked agent. I assured the SAC that she'd do fine.

As Susan and I are traveling 10-39 (red light and siren) to Hebron, I am marveling at her excitement, her first bank robbery. I do remember my own exhilaration responding to my first. Now to me it's just another shithead with a gun. Maybe I'm getting jaded.

I do know I would not have been considering retirement, had I not been facing mandatory retirement in the near future. The difference in the reaction of Susan and me was evident to me, and I think it was a wake-up call. Maybe it's time to hang it up, Jimmy.

308 West State Street
Suite 350
Rockford, Illinois   61101
January 21, 1997

Honorable Louis H. Freeh
Director
Federal Bureau of Investigation
Washington, D. C.   20535

Dear Sir:

        After 30 years in law enforcement and nearly 28 of
those as an FBI Agent, I request to retire from the FBI on
February 28, 1997.

        This decision does not come lightly, but I make it with
great faith in the future of the FBI.   In view of our mandatory
retirement which I would face in a short four years, I find I
must take advantage of an opportunity which timing dictates.

        Mr. Freeh, I cannot begin to put into words what a
great experience this career has been.   I have never awakened in
the morning without looking forward to going to work.   I have had
the great honor of working with some of the finest law enforcement officers anywhere in the world in my 23-year assignment to
the northwest counties of Illinois.

        The absolute highlight to this career was serving as a
field counselor to NAC 96-12.   Although I know this was an
exceptional class, they are indicative of all of those entering
the FBI today, and I find great consolation in that.   The FBI is
in excellent hands for the next 25 years.

        Mr. Freeh, you are an inspiration to young and senior
agents alike.   To think you would find time to run, not only with
96-12, but with all of the new agent classes to this day, I find
amazing.   To see you up extremely late when the Freemen
surrendered, to running at 5:15 a.m. the next morning with a new
agent class, to a 7:00 a.m. press conference in the Hall of Honor
at Quantico, to graduating over 200 National Academy students at
9:00 a.m. and a new agent class at 2:00 p.m. the same day is
something I will not soon forget.

Ray Jones tells me you have a higher calling. I am inclined to agree. Your inspiration is only equaled by seeing the outstanding caliber of young people becoming FBI Agents today. It all makes me so proud to have been a part of it.

I leave with great pride and extend a profound thank you for all you have done for this great organization.

Sincerely yours,

JAMES G. SACIA
Special Agent
Chicago Division
(Rockford RA)

THE REASON FOR IT ALL

Kids—what would we do without them? They truly are what life is all about. It's great that somewhere along the way others put that concept together or I wouldn't be here to writing this, nor would you be reading it. At least for my part, thanks, Mom and Dad.

Sometimes when I allow my mind to wander (and sometimes when it does it on its own), I absolutely marvel at this thing we call life.

Elsewhere I've written of Jenny's and my desire for children and becoming an FBI agent gave us a better opportunity for a stable family life as opposed to a life in the Army, which initially was my first choice.

The greatest mystery to me and most who might read this, is how can we raise more than one child together and they turn out so completely different. Our son Jerry probably articulates that better than a PhD psychiatrist, "Dad, don't you get it? I tick different than you and Mom." Every parent experiences that if they create siblings.

As I reach the twilight of life (yes, I know I'm deeply into it), I reflect more on the beauty of children. Jerry, John, and Jesse—God, I couldn't be more thankful.

Someone once said, "Little kids, little problems. Big kids, big problems." I guess that's true, but in my wildest dreams, I couldn't imagine life without them, and I thank God for them. No matter how old they get, they'll always be our children.

I understand, I think, the mind-set of not having children. I just know, that for the way I tick, I thank God I have them. Life, at this age especially, would be so empty without them.

This is starting with so much pontification, but I'm reminded of a story of identical twin boys whose father was a hopeless alcoholic and an embarrassment to his family. One of the boys grew to be a renowned and successful businessman; the other, a hopeless alcoholic. When individually asked why they became what they did, they both answered very similarly, "If you see my father, you understand why." Perhaps that is way too simplistic, but I think it probably expands on "the way we tick."

Jen and I raised Jerry, John, and Jess very similarly. They are as close as any three siblings could possibly be. They are as different as Antarctica and the Sahara Desert. We love them each more than life itself.

Jerry is our first, certainly Jenny's hardest birth with a twenty-three-hour labor. Of course I'm in and out of her hospital area drinking coffee, eating donuts and though concerned for Jenny, enjoying the concern from the nurses for the "soon to be father."

As a new mom with a very colic prone baby, it was hard (mainly on Jenny), and thank God for Jen's mom, Lucille, and my mom, Katherine. I will give special kudos to my mom as Jen was breast feeding and Jerry was starving to death or so it sounded like. Mom got us fixed up with an "infafeeder" which certainly preserved both our sanity. It was a plunger device with a nipple that was filled with cereal and a baby could suck and you could help it along by plunging the cereal into the nipple area. You notice I said was, as they no longer seem to be available. I'm sure the fear was improper pressure on the plunger could cause the baby to choke. At the point in life when we were raising our three, they were a godsend.

Jerry attacked the world head-on. One of our favorite stories to this day, probably to Jerry's embarrassment, was him as a one-plus-year-old pushing a toy truck in our yard into a tree and throwing a fit because the tree was in the way.

Jerry was an excellent student and he loved sports. He excelled in all sports that he played through high school and college. When Jerry graduated from college, with a degree in business his evolution took him to a career with one of the passions that he and I shared through the years, working with Farm equipment. To this day, he manages the farm equipment purchases and sales of our family business.

John, just two years behind Jerry in age always identified with his dad's love for the military. He pursued ROTC in college and became an Apache helicopter pilot. He served three combat tours, two of them in Iraq but decided to leave the Army after nine years.

John told Jenny and I that he hoped to fly fighter jets in the Air Force. His dad, that would be me, assured him that that possibility wasn't realistic. (Oh how wrong dads can be).

Jess came along six years after John. His brothers love him dearly and during those growing-up years he had them to look up to as his heroes. One of his high school teachers probably summed Jesse up the best as she talked with Jenny. "It took you and Jim three times but you finally got it right."

Everybody loves Jesse. He has a wonderful wife and three great kids, which, of course, Grandma and Grandpa adore. Jess is always, I do mean always, sensitive that he is hurting feelings.

Jess and Jerry work together at our farm equipment business. One of our former employees, Stacy, created a "Wilbur Jar" (have no clue what that means), but Jesse had to put a quarter in every time he said, "I'm sorry." We've all had much fun with him at his expense. He takes it so well. A great young man!

During his high school days and I will always be disappointed in our school district for not giving us a "heads up," Jen, Jerry, Jess, and I traveled to Fort Rucker, Alabama, to attend John's graduation as a pilot from Army Helicopter Training and Jess was receiving numerous and I do mean numerous awards on awards night. We had no clue. We learned of it only after we got back. Jess, of course, took it in stride.

All three boys are now young men. All have college degrees. Each is successful in his own way. They love getting together. They remain as different as different can be. We certainly love them deeply, and they love each other as well.

Jer and Jes we work with daily at NITE Equipment. They both are great contributors to the business success. John left the Army after nine years and is now a lieutenant colonel in the US Air Force and an F-16 fighter pilot. Jenny and I are truly blessed. Not in my wildest dreams could I have been so fortunate in this life.

FEBRUARY 11, 1997

Sitting at my desk, just got off the phone with my good friend Bill Hoyt. We reminisce a bit, and I explained that I had come to terms with my retirement and I had crossed the threshold of that mental process. Bill commented it would be like getting out of the Army. As I hung up, Roy Orbison's "Only the Lonely" came on the radio. Talk about déjà vu—in 1965 I remember sitting at my desk at Selfridge, my last few days in the Army and Roy Orbison, one of my favorites, was singing to me.

February 28 was my last day as an FBI agent. I started to dress down and wear a sweatshirt that Tom Kellen, postal inspector from Indianapolis, had given me at my retirement party. It says, "I'm retired. This is as dressed up as I get." I couldn't bring myself to do it.

The retirement thing is not programming, I should feel something different shouldn't I?

I had the oil changed in CG438 a 90 burgundy Chevrolet Caprice. The odometer read 108,872 miles most of them put on by me.

I turned my credentials, badge and gas card over to my supervisor. I think he was more nostalgic than I. We both came to Rockford in 1972. Though I arrived first on a recruiting trip, he got orders in April due to his father being very ill. I was officially transferred in September of 1972.

Earl Nightingale says we become what we think about. For years throughout my FBI career, I looked forward to the day when I could buy and sell tractors. Well, here I am—chasing my tail.

Do I have regrets—I think everyone who leaves a profession they loved has some, but I know I left at the right time. My mind was going more and more to Northern Illinois Tractor and Equipment and less to the FBI.

Do I miss the job and the people; of course, I do, much like graduates miss their classmates. The security is gone, but we must move on and light other candles, being careful not to light them at each end.

I've got fire at each end and I'm getting a good spark in the middle.

I sent the following handwritten letter to my Rockford FBI colleagues the day after I retired from the FBI. It truly was an amazing ride, and beyond my wildest dreams.

stolen Stationary

U.S. Department of Justice

Federal Bureau of Investigation   3/1/97

Dear Jerry and FBI Associates

What can I say. Its been a hell of a ride.

I obviously will miss seeing & working with all of you. You've made a great career even better.

Though it hasn't sunk in yet. I know I will miss it all.

The plaque is beautiful, the picture is overwhelming. and Miller, you even embelish Fidelity, Bravery, and Integrity, — but I was ham enough to love it.

Its going to be an adjustment but I look forward to a continued close association, which I know every retired agent before me has experienced.

I hope NITE equipment becomes a regular stop off for all of you.

Warmest Regards

Jim

294

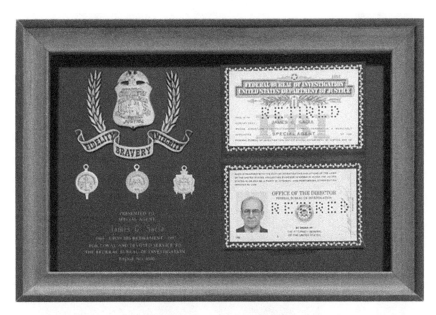

About the Author

Jim Sacia grew up one of ten children on a thirty cow dairy farm north of LaCrosse, Wisconsin.

Jim joined the Army following graduation from Melrose High School in 1962. After a three-year stint, with the Vietnam War heating up, he attended college at the University of Wisconsin in River Falls, where he also served as a police officer. He planned to return to active duty as a commissioned officer upon obtaining his degree.

He graduated from US Army Ranger School and obtained a commission while serving in the Wisconsin Army National Guard. Fate intervened when he learned that the FBI needed agents. With degree in hand, the FBI, not the Army, became his next step.

Jim and his wife of forty-eight years, Jenny, have three grown sons and reside on their farm in Pecatonica, Illinois.